DON'T FLY TODAY

When God Speaks- <u>LISTEN!</u>

COL. DAVID O. SCHEIDING, USAF (RET.)

Warning to Atheist -
<u>GOD DOES EXIST!</u>

978-1-965552-28-5 (Paperback)

BOOKWRIGHTS
HOUSE

admin@bookwrightshouse.com
☎ (213) 286 6700

TABLE OF CONTENTS

David O. Scheiding is also the author of
Hank: An Angel Dog
and
The Long Return

To the unfailing grace of God. I have written this book for the sole purpose to honor God and to provide the empirical evidence that God really does exist. It is also, hopefully, a warning to atheists, who will definitely find this truth out during the final judgment of man by God. It is my humble way of thanking God for all the blessings that he has bestowed upon my family and me throughout my entire life.

PREFACE

WHENEVER THERE IS A discussion of God, Jesus Christ, and/or the Holy Spirit, it must include discussion of God's Word, the Holy Bible. Since the original books of the Bible were not written in English, we must depend on translations of the books of the Bible out of the original tongues and previous translations that have been diligently compared and revised. I prefer the King James Version (KJV) of the Bible that was originally published in 1611. The version of the KJV Bible that I prefer is the Authorized King James version published by Thomas Nelson Publishers in 1976. My wife did give me a copy of the New International Version (NIV) of the Holy Bible published in 1984 for my second baptism as a Baptist on January 24, 1993. Most of the Bible references in this book are from the King James Version (KJV), with the exception of those from the New International Version (NIV) when I felt that version contained the clarification needed for emphasis.

When I was in Vietnam as an Air Force pilot and forward air controller (FAC) during the 1972 spring offensive, I experienced what I now know and believe was God speaking to me. It occurred on a clear day with no problem with weather or the aircraft.

I was scheduled for a day reconnaissance mission, and as I was taxing out to the end of the runway for takeoff, I felt a very strong, overwhelming feeling come over me that something was wrong. There also was a distinct voice in my head saying, *Don't fly today.* I taxied a little further and the voice got a little louder and more stern and said *Don't Fly Today*, I continued to taxi and as I approached the runway, the voice said again but this time in a very loud and stern voice *DON'T FLY TODAY*. I have never experienced that type of feeling before on any other of my combat missions nor before or after on any of my flights during my twenty-five years in the Air Force. I aborted the takeoff and taxied back to the parking area. I know that God had spoken to me, and he did not want me to fly that day. When God spoke to me, I listened!

I have heard people ask, "Does God really exist?" How many times have you heard someone ask this question? You may have even asked it yourself, especially when something bad has happened to you, your family, or your friends. You may even ask it when you see something terrible on the news. We ask ourselves, "If God exists, why does he let bad things like that happen?"

I am now eighty-two years old, retired, and I now have a lot of time to reflect back over the path that I have traveled throughout the course of my life. As I look back over my life, and from all of the empirical evidence available, I can only conclude that *yes*, God does exist, and he does have a plan for each and every one of us as part of his overall plan for his creation.

I reached this conclusion based on all of the empirical evidence present over the past eighty-two years of my life. I realized that a higher power had to have been guiding me in order to explain everything that has happened to me over the course of my life. It just could not have been just coincidence or random events that occurred which resulted in the obviously defined path on which I have traveled.

A person cannot just look at individual events, decisions, and actions or singular random events that occur in the course of one's life. We have to take into account the totality of the sum of all these events, decisions, and actions in order to see just how they all fit together over the entire span of one's life. When we do, we can see that God has a specific plan and purpose for each of us. The following pages document the empirical evidence of all those individual events, decisions, and actions that have occurred in my life, which produced the plan that God had for me.

ACKNOWLEDGMENTS

I WOULD LIKE TO THANK the following people for all of their help with this book. Without their help, this book would not have been possible.

I want to thank my wife of sixty-two years for putting up with me and helping me, her dumb fighter pilot and engineer husband, to not only write one book but three. I am also truly indebted to Melissa Supak, who word-processed the manuscript on her own time. I also need to thank my son, Doug Scheiding, for helping me with all things computer. Even though I flew the F-111D for seven years (the first digital Air Force fighter), I do not like computers and try to avoid them as much as possible. Last but not least, I especially appreciate the staff at Bookwrights House for giving me the opportunity to tell my story.

INTRODUCTION

To assist in answering the age-old question of "does God really exist?" we, of course, have to consider the Bible. The Bible is known as the *Word of God* and is also referred to as *Scripture*. So what is the Bible?

The Bible is a collection of a total of sixty-six different books written by different people at different times and places. It is divided into the Old Testament and the New Testament. The Old Testament contains thirty-nine books while the New Testament contains twenty-seven books. The Bible is essentially a history book of our creation and existence. Both the Jewish and Christian people accept the Old Testament as Scripture. The Bible is God's Word to his creation that provides insight into God himself. It also provides his guidance, guidelines about what he expects from us as his creation.

There is, however, a significant difference between how the Jewish people view the New Testament and how we Christians view it. The Jewish people believe in God as outlined in the Old Testament, but as of today, they have not yet accepted Jesus as the "Son of God" and the Messiah that was prophesized in the Old Testament. On the other hand, we as Christians have accepted Jesus as the "Son of God" and believe in the New Testament's teachings of the Christian faith. We Christians do believe that Jesus was the Messiah that was prophesized in the Old Testament, who was provided by God as the path for salvation and forgiveness of our sins.

This explains why our Christian calendar has the current year as AD 2025 (which stands for after the death of Jesus) while the Jewish calendar has the current year as 5786. Jesus was born to Jewish parents, and God chose the Jewish people to be his chosen people as documented in the Old Testament. The Jewish people only consider that Jesus was a very good man, but was not the Messiah that was prophesized in the Old Testament.

The New Testament documents Jesus's life and teaching as the Messiah, the Son of God. Jesus's teaching established the Christian faith and Church. Jesus's death is the path that God has provided to eternal life and salvation from evil. Christians believe that both the Old and New Testaments provide God's Word to his total creation. It is his plan for believers when God is forced to defeat Satan at the end of the world, as we know it. We must, therefore, first address the question—is the Bible fiction or nonfiction?

CHAPTER 1

The Bible—Fiction or Nonfiction

To decide if the Bible is fiction or nonfiction, we first must consider some basic facts about the Bible. My research into the Bible indicated that it took approximately 1,500 years for all the books of the Bible to be written. This includes the time from the first book of the Old Testament, Genesis, to the last book of the New Testament, Revelation. The apostle John wrote Revelation approximately sixty-five years after the death of Jesus Christ. This means that the writing of the Bible was initiated approximately 3,400 years ago based on our calendar year of AD 2025. This means that the book of Genesis had to have been started in the year approximately 2,380 BC (before Christ). Since the Jewish people have not accepted Jesus as the Messiah and the Son of God, their current calendar year is 5786. This indicates that humans had been in existence for at least 2,300 years before the first book of the Bible was written. The book of Genesis essentially provides the history of the creation of our world and humans and the history of the first 2,300 years. This would indicate that the Bible was started after Noah's time and the flood when God destroyed all the earth and his creation. This is confirmed in Genesis 6:5-7(KJV).

> And God saw that the wickedness of man was great in the earth, and that every imagination of the thoughts of his heart was only evil continually. And it repented the Lord that he had made man on the earth, and it grieved him at his heart. And the Lord said, I will destroy man whom I have created from the face of the earth; both man, and beast, and the creeping thing, and the fowls of the air; for it repented me that I have made them.

Noah, who was alive at the time, found grace in the eyes of the Lord. God decided to give his creation a second chance by sparing Noah and his family. God directed Noah to build an ark in order for his creation to survive. When God does speak to you—listen!

With his decision to allow a second chance for humans, God needed a way to communicate with his creation and to document what had happened and why. This to me is the most likely reason that the writing of the Bible was initiated after the flood. God led the authors of the Bible to write the books of the Bible in order to provide his creation with his word and just what he expected of his creation.

The Old Testament of the Bible provides us with God's laws and how he expects us to live our lives in order for us to find grace in his eyes. The Old Testament also documents what will happen in the future as part of God's plan for his creation through prophecies.

It should be noted that the first humans had a much longer life span than we humans do now. The first man Adam is documented to have lived a total of 930 years. Even Noah lived for a total of 950 years and was six hundred years old when God caused the flood that destroyed the earth and his creation. This early time length of human lifespan to me does not seem to be unreasonable. It would require a significant period of time for humans to be fruitful, multiply, and replenish the earth as commanded by God. Now when you consider the fact that there were many different authors who lived during different time periods and in different locations, not one of these authors had contradicted any other author or any other book of the Bible. This fact alone is truly remarkable and would lead one to conclude that only a single higher power could have guided all these authors to write what God wanted his creation to know. This to me is how God was able to communicate to his creation after the first 2,300 years of human existence. To further understand why a single higher power had to be guiding these authors over the 1,500-year time period it took to write the books of the Bible, we must also consider the level of human knowledge during the time period that the Bible was written. It then is not hard to understand why many of the events described in the Bible have been written in a manner that humans at that time would be able to understand what God wanted us to know and still be applicable today. The Bible has been around for a very, very long time, and it is still just as relevant today as it was back in the day when it was written.

The first of the thirty-nine books of the Old Testament describe the creation of the heavens and the earth. This is documented in Genesis 1:1–31 as being accomplished in six days. This is where atheists start trying to justify their nonbelief in God. They attempt to use current science as their justification that God does not exist by saying that we now have scientific evidence that the earth is millions of year old. Many also like to claim that the earth was formed by the big bang theory, not by God in six days.

My educational background is in science and engineering. I also was raised by a strong religious family that lived in the Midwest part of our country. I also know that, as humans, we have gained knowledge through science over the years. This to me only verifies that a higher power had to have been at work in order for humans and our world to even exist.

Science has proven that our earth is millions of years old; however, we really only have the Bible as documented history for approximately the last 5,800 years to consider. This is like a grain of sand on a very large beach, which represents our existence when compared to the totality of just our earth. Even our earth only represents nothing more than a grain of sand on a beach when it is compared to the totality of all the heavens and the millions of additional solar systems throughout the heavens that we now know exist.

I think one of the most important concepts to consider when discussing the Bible and God is the concept of time. When atheists justify their nonbelief in God based on their own concept and knowledge of time, they do not consider what the concept of time is to God. God's concept of time, I am sure, is totally different from our concept. In fact, time to God may not have any meaning at all. I think that this is evidenced in the book of John in the New Testament. In John 1:1–3 (KJV), John writes:

> In the beginning was the Word, and the Word was with God, and the word was God. The same was in the beginning with God. All things were made by him; and without him was not anything made that was made.

Since God has always been in existence, he would have no need for a concept of time to apply to him. God did, however, create us in his image, but he created us as mortals. This means that we all do have a definite period of time on this earth. Time, therefore, is important to us, but not to God. We need to remember that Adam, the first man, lived 930 years while our current lifespan is somewhere between seventy-five and eighty years on the average. Some atheists use the age of Noah and others as their proof that the Bible is fiction. However, in Genesis 6:3 (KJV) it states: And the Lord said, "My spirit shall not always strive with man,for that he is also is flesh: yet his days shall be an hundred and twenty years."

The Bible does, however, give us some insight into God's concept of time. In 2 Peter 3:8 (KJV), the apostle Peter writes, "But beloved, be not ignorant of this one thing, that one day is with the Lord as a thousand years, and a thousand years as one day."

In addition to the concept of time, I feel another important fact that atheists do not consider is the available body of human knowledge when the Bible was being written approximately 3,400 years ago. This would apply to both the authors of the Bible as well as those reading it. Can you imagine God trying to convey the big bang theory to the authors? It is obvious to me that God was inspiring the Bible's authors to document his message in terms of their knowledge level at that time so that they could understand. This would also apply to the readers of the Bible. Even with my educational background, I have no problem accepting the big bang theory as the method that God may have used to create the heavens and the earth.

In addition, God does give us another indication about his concept of time in Genesis 2:4 (KJV). This verse states, "These are generations of the heavens and of the earth when they were created in the day that the Lord God made the earth and the heavens."

This would suggest that many of our years might have been involved in the creation of the heavens and the earth. We still do not know if the big bang theory was the method that God used to create the heavens and the earth as it is still just a theory.

It is not until Genesis 2:7 (KJV) when God actually created man. This verse states, "And the Lord God formed man of the dust of the ground, and breathed into his nostrils the breath of life; and man became a living soul." Atheists and other nonbelievers do not accept this as how mankind came into existence. Many believe that man actually evolved as described by Darwin's theory of evolution. This too, however, is still just a theory, which has not been scientifically proven. We must remember that there is still a missing link in this theory.

This may well have been how God did create man, but again, can you imagine how God would convey such a theory to the authors of the Bible 3,400 years ago? God knew what was required as well as how he was going to tell man about his creation and man's existence in a manner that they could understand. One has to remember that is was not too long ago that we humans thought our world was flat.

Our body of knowledge has grown significantly over the years since the Bible was written. We are continually learning new things every day about our world and our universe that the early humans would not have been able to even comprehend, let alone believe. In fact, it recently has been discovered that our universe is still expanding. The universe is so large it is even difficult for us to comprehend just how large it is with our current level of knowledge.

The Old Testament also gives us some insight into the heavenly realm. This indicates that there are other hosts that reside in heaven with God. As an example, Genesis 1:26 (KJV) states:

> And God said, "Let us make man in our image, after our likeness: and let them have dominion over the fish of the sea, and over the fowl of the air, and over the cattle, and over all of the earth, and over every creeping thing that creepeth upon the earth."

The use of the words "let us" and "in our image" indicates that there are other spiritual beings in heaven.

From the Bible, we also learn that some of these heavenly hosts are at work against God in the form of evil. This is evidenced at the time of Adam and Eve when they were in the Garden of Eden. This is when a serpent tempted Eve to eat of the tree of knowledge after God had instructed both Adam and Even not to eat the fruit from this tree. This is considered to be the first sin by mankind and is evidence that the devil (Satan) is present and is working against God. Satan is the devil and is the leader of the fallen spirits from the grace of God. Satan is the most powerful enemy of God and humans as he wages his constant battle against God.

The Bible clearly documents that the evil caused by Satan is the reason why God had to destroy Sodom and Gomorrah and finally all of his creation with the flood. Satan is the reason why bad things happen to us in this world and why God had to provide a path for mankind to be forgiven of our sins in order for us to achieve salvation and eternal life after we die.

The Old Testament also has many prophets that predicted upcoming events about God's plan to save the human race from sin. These prophets foretold of a Messiah that would come to save mankind and provide the path to salvation. In Isaiah 9:6 (KJV), the author prophesized that a Messiah will be born. It states, "For unto us a child is born, unto us a son is given: and the government shall be upon his shoulder: and his name shall be called Wonderful, Counselor, the mighty God, the everlasting Father, the Prince of Peace." This is the prophecy of the birth of Jesus, the Son of God, as documented in the Old Testament. This is the prophecy that the Jewish are still waiting to be fulfilled.

The New Testament is made up of twenty-seven books that are accepted by Christians as being the Scripture. The New Testament describes the arrival of the Messiah (Jesus Christ) and the beginning of the Christian faith and church. It describes the life, death, and resurrection of Jesus. It explains why he died, and it teaches us that because of his death, we can be saved and forgiven of all of our sins.

The New Testament also warns us about Satan and his efforts in this world. In Ephesians 6:11–12 (KJV), the apostle Paul writes:

Put on the whole armour of God that ye may be able to stand against the wiles of the devil. For we wrestle not against flesh and blood, but against principalities, against powers, against the rulers of the darkness of this world, against spiritual wickedness in high places.

The New Testament is where the Christian faith differs from the Jewish religion. Both the Jewish people and Christians believe in God; however, the Jewish people have not yet accepted Jesus Christ as the Son of God. They believe that Jesus was a good man but that he was not the Son of God or the Messiah that was prophesized in the Old Testament. This is why the Jewish calendar is not the same calendar that we use.

Our Christian calendar starts with the death of Christ and why our calendar year is AD 2025 (after death). The Jewish calendar year is 5786 since they have not accepted Jesus as the Son of God, and they are still waiting for the Messiah. This, I think, unfortunately is a concern for God since the Jewish people are his chosen people.

Jesus was born of Jewish parents. The Jewish people, however, did not accept him as their Messiah. In the Gospel according to John 1:10–11 (KJV), John writes, "He was in the world, and the world was made by him, and the world knew him not. He came unto his own, and his own received him not."

The Jewish people do have a very strong belief in God and do believe in the Old Testament teachings. They do not, however, seem to accept the New Testament as their Scripture because they believe the Messiah has not yet arrived. If they had accepted Jesus as their Messiah, they would have known that he is indeed the Son of God. Matthew 3:16–17 (KJV) is the documentation of Jesus's baptism by John the Baptist. Matthew writes:

> And Jesus, when he was baptized, went up straightway out of the water: and, lo, the heavens were opened unto him, and he saw the Spirit of God descending like a dove, and lighting upon him: And lo a voice from heaven, saying, "This is my beloved Son, in whom I am well pleased."

After his baptism, Jesus began his three years of teaching, which resulted in the creation of the Christian church.

When I consider all the facts about the Bible, I can only conclude that the Bible is indeed the Word of God. It took 1,500 years to write the Bible by many different authors, not one of whom contradict themselves or one another. This to me is extremely strong evidence that God had to be the one guiding power behind the writing of the Bible. As such, I have no problem believing that the Bible is the Word of God, and as such, it is indeed nonfiction.

Atheists, on the other hand, believe that the Bible is fiction. To me, this is Satan using his power to deceive people into believing that the Bible is not God's Word. This is just part of Satan's battle against God as he wages war against God in order to claim as many souls as he can. This is why the apostle Paul cautioned us to put on the armor of God in order to stand against the wiles of the devil. If the devil can convince people that God's Word is fiction, then those people's names will not be listed in the book of life, which will be opened on judgment day. On judgment day, what these people will earn is a place with Satan in the eternal lake of fire. To me, there is no doubt: God does exist!

CHAPTER 2

God, Mom, and Dad

M Y LIFE BEGAN AS a blessing from God. We do not get to choose our parents, but God does. I do firmly believe that God chooses our parents as part of his overall plan for each member of his creation. As part of his plan for each of us, I believe that he guides each individual to meet others that he has chosen, who then fall in love and get married. This creates a family of a mother and father, which fulfills his guidance in the Bible to go forth, be fruitful, and multiply. This was evidenced when God directed both Adam and Eve in the beginning and then Noah and his family after the flood, to be fruitful and multiply. This was required to first populate the earth and then to replenish it after God destroyed it. This tells me that the sanctity of marriage, as being one man and one woman, is very important to God. He destroyed the earth and all of his creation due to wickedness of mankind during Noah's time. I was blessed and very fortunate in that God chose my mother and father to be my parents. One's birth is when God's plan begins for each of us.

I learned a lot from my mother's extremely cruel experiences in her life. She was born to parents that were not religious and did not follow God's teaching. My mother's father and her three brothers were all alcoholics. In addition, one of the worst aspects of my mother's life occurred when she was nine or ten years old. Her mother abandoned her and one of her brothers on the steps of Marshalltown, Iowa's courthouse in the town where they lived. It was extremely hard for me to imagine how any parent could do such a thing. This had to have had a significant impact on my mother.

She and her brother were finally rescued by an aunt who lived in another small town north of Marshalltown. Her brother was later reunited with their father, but my mother stayed with her aunt. Her father did finally divorce her mother after she abandoned the entire family.

After her father remarried, my mother rejoined her father and her new stepmother, but only for a short time. This new family environment was not a pleasant environment in which to raise children. Her father and stepmother seemed to fight continuously. This toxic environment contributed to her father and three brothers all becoming alcoholics. My mother decided she did not want to live this type of life and went back to live with her aunt.

My mother had to quit school after the seventh grade and work in order to support herself. She also went to church and accepted God as her Savior. I firmly believe that God was definitely guiding my mother through the early portion of her life as part of his plan for her.

This is one of those situations where it is easy to ask, "If God exists, why does he let things like this happen?" To me, this is just evidence that Satan is always at work in his constant battle against God. God was, however, in the case of my mother, guiding her through this period of her life. God does not challenge us beyond what we can handle as long as we believe in him and trust that his will, will be done.

There is evidence of God challenging his believers throughout the Bible. An excellent case in point was when he challenged Abraham to sacrifice his son Isaac in order to determine if Abraham's heart was true and if he feared God. God does guide his believers on the path that he has planned for each of us, but he may challenge us along the way.

My dad, on the other hand, was born into a family that was more like a normal family. He had two sisters and a brother, with my dad being the youngest of the children. His mother did adopt another child much later in life who became a third sister to dad. This sister, however, was only five years older than me. Dad's adopted sister came from a family that lived just up the street from my grandmother's house when her parents could no longer take care of her.

My dad's mother, my grandmother, was the kindest, sweetest, and gentlest person I have ever known. In fact, she helped raise me because both of my parents worked. I would spend all weekdays at my grandmother's house growing up while my parents worked.

Dad's family was religious and did follow God's teaching, especially his mother. This is why she adopted his third sister so late in life. I did, therefore, learn some very important lessons from dad's side of the family as far as seeing how the devil works and how God helps individuals when evil is at work.

My mother and father actually met at church. God had to be the one who led them to meet as part of his plan for each of them. They began to date and fell in love. Dad wanted to get married, but my mother was very reluctant to do so. I am sure that this was due to her experience growing up and having been abandoned by her mother. This was also reinforced later on when she witnessed her father and stepmother fighting and arguing all the time. She thought that was what married couples did. She did not want to get married because she actually thought that she and my dad would begin to fight and argue if they got married. It took my dad three years to convince her that all marriages were not like her father's two marriages.

I truly believe that God had led her to my dad, who was a kind, hardworking, honest, and just man that believed in God. God knew that my dad would treat her well. God was guiding my mother's life to help make up for her rough childhood experiences. My mom and dad had a long and happy married life together for fifty-two years before my dad passed away.

I learned two very important lessons from my parents' families growing up as a youth. The first lesson was on my dad's side of the family when I learned just how the devil uses greed to impact a family as he works his evil. When my dad's father, my grandfather, passed away, one of his birth sisters and her husband were tempted by the devil with greed. Their greed manifested itself when they were able to take control over a major portion of my grandmother's inheritance after the death of her husband.

My grandfather owned a large farm, on which dad's other birth sister and her husband were living. They were paying rent to my grandfather and grandmother until his death. The rent from this farm would have taken very good care of my grandmother's needs as far as income after my grandfather's death. Because of the greed of this sister and her husband, they were causing significant disruption in the family as they pursued their goal to gain control of the farm. This disruption was pitting brothers against sisters and literally tearing the family apart. This was hurting my grandmother so much that she finally asked my dad, his brother, and the other two sisters to just sign the farm over to the greedy sister and her husband. She just did not want to fight the legal battle due to the discord that it was causing within the family. My dad, his brother, and the two sisters agreed to do so in order to keep the family together and to honor their mother's wishes. This showed me just how kind and gentle my grandmother was and why she would adopt another child so late in life.

The loss of the farm income to my grandmother caused her to have to take in the laundry of others in order to make ends meet. She also had to plant a garden on a piece of land that was part of her home to help with food. In addition, she kept and raised chickens for additional food such as eggs and meat. I do not know how anyone could treat their mother that way, especially when they claimed to be very religious members of a church. This had to be Satan at work as he battled God.

The church that my dad's family was members of was the First Evangelical United Brethren Church (EUB) and was located near my grandmother's house. The greedy sister was the pianist for the church, and her husband was the church secretary. Each Sunday, she played the piano, and he would take the attendance and count the offering for the church. He would then post the results on the church wall as part of his duties. The lesson that I learned firsthand was just how Satan uses greed to impact families and that evil is constantly at work in our lives. I also learned just how God wants us to respond by watching just how my grandmother responded to the greed of her daughter and her husband.

The greed of this sister and her husband was again on display when my grandmother passed away. She lived to be ninety-two years old, but when she did pass away, the sister and her husband rushed to my grandmother's house the very next day and removed all of her furniture. They took the furniture to their house and stored it in their basement. Needless to say, the furniture was old and not really of much value; but because of their greed, they did not even want to share any of the furniture with the other members of the family. Once again, the rest of the family did not protest, out of respect for their mother. This was a powerful lesson for me on how greed can destroy a family, if allowed to do so.

As I was reflecting back over this experience for this book, I have to note two observations that come to mind. The first one was that the sister and her husband did not seem to have a very happy relationship in their marriage. Their greed did not bring them happiness.

The second was the fact that both the sister and her husband passed away at a rather young age. In fact, the greedy sister passed away a number of years before her husband. This reminded me of Exodus 21:12 (KJV), which states, "Honour thy father and thy mother: that thy days may be long upon the land which the Lord thy God giveth thee." I have to say Dad's sister's actions certainly did not honor their mother after the death of their father.

God, however, did take care of my grandmother after her husband's passing. While all of this was going on, God was guiding my father to get out of the foundry where he had been working and start a new occupation. I know that God was guiding him because the career he decided to get into was that of becoming a butcher and then acquiring a small neighborhood grocery store and meat market. This had to be God's hand guiding my father because that grocery store and meat market had an immediate impact on my grandmother's life and a significant impact on Jan, my future wife, and my life later. Dad was able to help his mother with food and groceries from the store, which allowed her to not have to worry about food. The Bible teaches us that God knows what we need even before we ask him in our prayers. This is documented in Matthew 6:8 (KJV), where Matthew writes, "Be not ye therefore like unto them: for your Father knoweth what things ye have need of before ye ask him." The groceries really helped my grandmother because she always wanted to cook Sunday dinner for her entire family after church.

Each Sunday, the entire family would gather at her home where she would prepare a tremendous meal for all of us. The greedy sister and her husband were always there, but they never contributed anything to help with the meal. This Sunday meal was extremely important to my grandmother, and it made her very happy to prepare it. With my dad's help, she never had to worry about having enough food to prepare the meal. I firmly believe that God made sure that my grandmother's food needs were met by guiding my dad to change careers and acquire the grocery store as part of his plan for our family.

If one just considers the change in my dad's occupation as an isolated decision and event, one would not think too much about it. But the actual timing of this change was crucial for my grandmother and then later for my wife and me. I firmly believe that this was not just a random decision and event but the work of God as part of his plan for our family.

My mother, however, never really liked the grocery store business. After I graduated from college, my dad did finally sell the store and meat market, which made my mother happy. He wanted to keep it long enough to put me through college, which he did. This I know was all part of God's plan for our family.

After my dad sold the store, he was offered a job back at the foundry where he had worked before he changed his career. He was offered the job of superintendent of the foundry, which was a significant promotion for him. His boss was the general manager of the foundry. The foundry itself was just one of many locations of a large corporation that had its headquarters in Oklahoma. My mother was very happy about being out of the grocery-store business and went back to work herself.

Everything seemed to be going along well for my parents when Satan reared his evil head and began to work his evil against my dad. At the foundry where my dad was working, quantities of raw materials began to disappear. The home office in Oklahoma detected the loss of these materials. The home office discovered that a significant amount of raw materials was being purchased but did not equal the amount of product being produced. When personnel from the headquarters came to Marshalltown to investigate the discrepancies, the general manager, my dad's boss, tried to blame the loss of material on my dad.

My dad was extremely honest and would never steal anything from anyone, let alone from his place of employment. This accusation of theft hurt my dad tremendously. It was even more hurtful in that his boss was the one making the accusation. My dad thought his boss was his friend. His boss and his wife had even had my mom and dad over to their house for meals. They seemed to have a friendly relationship outside of work.

My dad took after his mother in temperament, kindness, and honesty. He also did not like discord in his life. This was evidenced when Dad decided to sell the store and go back to the foundry. He knew that Mom did not like the store, so he decided to sell it and go back to a job that was difficult, dangerous, and not necessarily a comfortable working environment. He had been burned several times by molten metal when a mold that he was working on would explode and spray molten metal all over. In spite of these negatives, in order to please his wife, Dad elected to return to the foundry.

During this time period is when I firmly believe that God once again interceded into my dad's life. He led my dad to install a camera in the area where the raw materials were being stored. It was not long until dad captured his boss, the general manager, on camera as the culprit who was stealing from the company. His boss went to jail, and the company's head office had an immediate opening for a general manager. They offered the position to my dad, who accepted. God's intervention was all part of his plan for my dad and further evidence of Satan's evil efforts in his battle against God.

My dad was a very kind and gentle person. I can only remember one incident when I actually saw him lose his temper. Usually when he was hurt or did not agree with what was happening, he would become very quiet and just go about his normal activities. This incident that I remember when he lost his temper occurred when I was with him in our car.

My dad and I were going on an errand, and as we were entering the major street that ran in front of our store, he did not see another car, and my dad ran into him. My dad pulled over to the curb and got out of the car and was walking over to the car he had struck, when the driver rolled his window down and began to curse at my dad. This was a very bad mistake by this individual.

My dad was a very stout, husky man and weighed around 230 pounds. He had the build of a football linebacker. Having been a foundry molder and a butcher, he had no problems lifting heavy objects.

During this man's tirade, he made a crucial mistake of calling my dad an SOB. I watched as my dad's pace to the man's car increased. When my dad arrived at the man's car, my dad reached into the man's open window, grabbed the man by the front of his coat and shirt, and literally pulled him over to the window. We did not have seat belts in cars back in those days. My dad then, in a very stern and forceful voice, said, "Don't you ever speak about my mother in that way again! This accident was my fault, and I was coming over to tell you that."

That man had a very startled and surprised look on his face and seemed to know that my dad meant business. I do not think he wanted to test my dad any further. He even apologized to my dad. The situation then calmed down, and the accident paperwork was handled in a very calm manner. That was the only time I ever saw my dad angry and actually act in an aggressive manner. He was a kind, gentle teddy bear of a man that would give you the shirt off his back if you were in need.

The second lesson I learned from my parents' families was on my mother's side of the family. After many years, my mother's mother came to regret that she had abandoned my mother and her brother on the courthouse steps so many years before. She asked my mother if there was any way that my mother could forgive her. My mother never hesitated and forgave her immediately. They were able to have somewhat of a mother-daughter relationship during the remainder of her mother's life.

In addition, when my mother's father ran into financial trouble after all the effects of being an alcoholic took its toll, the court asked my mother to be the executive of his few remaining assets in order to pay off all of his debt. Her three brothers had all killed themselves as a result of alcohol mishaps, and she was the only one left in the family besides her father. My mother did not hesitate and took over his financial obligations and established ways to pay off his debts. She set up payment schedules to each debtor for as little as $1 or $2 a month out of his social security check. She did this until his death when he died in a fire at his house after falling asleep while smoking in bed.

I never really knew the members of my mother's side of the family. Their lives were so much different from my mother's life. They really never came around. In addition, I do not think my mother was very excited about introducing them to me. I do remember, however, one day when I was working at the grocery store with my dad when Mom's dad came into the store. I was probably fourteen or fifteen years old, and my dad had taught me how to butcher meat. Mom's dad came back to where I was cutting meat and asked me if I knew who he was. I said, "Yes, I know who you are," but I really did not know him. I just kept on cutting meat since I did not know him well enough to ever start a conversation with him.

My mother and father both set good examples for me and taught me the ways of God. They established a firm religious foundation for me in my life. Anytime that I did ask my mother about her family, she never spoke in a derogatory manner about them. My dad was the same way about his wayward sister and her husband. My parents were following God's teaching, which set a good example for me as to what God expects his followers to do.

In addition, anytime that I would bring up the actions of my mother's mother or her father, she would always quote Exodus 20:12 (KJV), which I previously noted. She would always say,

"Honour thy father and mother, that thy days may be long upon the earth." The truth of this commandment is evidenced by the fact that my mother lived to be ninety-two years old before she passed away. God definitely rewarded my mother for her actions toward her mother and father even after the terrible treatment they had dispensed upon her. My mother had followed God's commandment.

My dad's wayward and greedy sister was not rewarded with a long life. I think that this was a result of her not honoring her mother. I do think that God did reward my grandmother with a long life because of the way she responded to the actions of her greedy daughter and her husband. My grandmother lived to be ninety-two years old when she passed away.

My parents raised me to believe in God as well as set a good example for me. This is why I feel that I was truly blessed to have them as my parents. All the empirical evidence supports the fact that God had to be guiding my life from birth. This to me also supports the fact that life is not just a series of random events or incidents that happen but are all pieces of God's plan for each of us. When all these events are placed together, they form the path that he has chosen for each of us. It also reflects how God's plans for all of us mesh together for his overall plan for his total creation.

CHAPTER 3

My Youth Years

As I continue to reflect back over my life, there is just so much empirical evidence that only a higher power could have guided me on the path of life that I have traveled. It was not until many years later that I came to the realization that God had definitely been guiding me as I grew up. I now know that God had to be watching over me and protecting me when an incident occurred when I was six or seven years old. I have never told anyone about this incident, but I do know now, without a doubt, that it was God who protected me the day I met evil face-to-face.

The incident occurred during the time period when my grandmother was taking care of me during the day while my parents were working.

We did not have a car, so my parents would walk me or pull me in my wagon down to my grandmother's house each day on their way to work. My grandmother's house was about a half mile from where we lived, and I would stay there during the day while they worked. Then they would come by after work to get me, and we would walk back to our house. My parents also had to walk to their work locations after they dropped me off at my grandmother's house. My mother worked for a company that made and packaged pickles, and my dad worked for a foundry as a molder.

On this particular day, I was playing outside in front of my grandmother's house by myself. It was about 3:00 p.m. when a man in a car was driving by my grandmother's house saw me and stopped. My grandmother's house was not a very busy street, and there was not ever much traffic on it. In fact, the street she lived on was a dead-end street, so there had to be a reason for anyone to be driving by.

It was summertime when he stopped and motioned for me to come over to his car. When I got to the side of his car, he asked me if I knew where the new drive-in theater was located. A new drive-in theater had just opened up south of town. I did happen to know where it was located because it was on the way to the farm that my grandfather owned. My dad's other sister and her husband lived on this farm. This was the farm that Dad's greedy sister and her husband cheated their mother out of after my grandfather's death.

I gave him directions on how to get to the drive-in theater. This is when I met evil face-to-face. He said that he was new in town and asked me if I could show him how to get there so that he would not get lost. Being just six or seven years old and very naive and innocent, I was not thinking badly of people. I agreed to show him where it was located, and I got into his car. I was not thinking about how wrong this was or even thinking that I should let my grandmother know what this individual wanted me to do. I now know that God was definitely watching over me that afternoon as I, not knowingly, was facing evil in the face.

I got into the car, and we started south of town to where the drive-in theater was located. He seemed very nice at first and was talking to me about how he wanted to take his girlfriend to the drive-in that night. The theater was about five miles south of town. When we got to the drive-in, he turned around, and we started back into town. This is when his conversation and actions changed.

His conversation changed to the topic of what he was planning on doing to his girlfriend while at the movie. He also began to fondle himself as we were driving back to town. He was talking about sexual activities about which I had no idea. Neither my parents nor anyone else in our family had ever talked about the things he was saying. I did not say anything, but I think the expression on my face told him that I was very uncomfortable with his comments and his actions.

He continued to fondle himself, and it became very apparent that he was becoming sexually aroused. He then unzipped his slacks and exposed his private part to me. He then asked me if I wanted to touch it. This is when I became quite upset and said that I wanted to go home. This is when I know that God interceded on my behalf in this incident.

This was evidenced because the man seemed to become worried about my reaction, and he stopped fondling himself. In addition, he slowed the car and turned off the highway onto the first gravel road that we came to. He traveled on this road for a short time, which was in an area with only cornfields on both sides of the road. There were no farmhouses, only cornfields as far as one could see. There also was no traffic on this road. When we went over a small hill and descended to the bottom of the hill, he stopped the car and told me to get out. I did not hesitate. I immediately got out of the car, and he immediately sped off.

What this man did not know—but God did know—was that God had caused him to turn onto a very familiar gravel road to me. I knew exactly where I was. The road he had turned on was about half a mile south of the street where my parents and I lived. On the other side of the cornfields was the street that ran by our house. I essentially was one cornfield away from my home.

I walked across the cornfield and went into our house. It was about 4:00 p.m., and this was the usual time that my parents picked me up from my grandmother's house. When I got into the house, the phone rang. It was my parents, and they were wondering if I had decided to walk home before they arrived at my grandmother's house to get me. Since I was so ashamed and embarrassed about what a stupid thing I had done, I just agreed that was what I had done.

When they got home, I was in trouble for not letting my grandmother know what I was going to do. I never told them what actually did happen. I was just happy that I was home when they called. This was just more empirical evidence that God had made it all right.

They did send me to my room as punishment for not telling my grandmother that I was going home, but that was just fine with me. God had protected me from a pedophile and had also provided me the opportunity where I did not have to lie or tell anyone what actually had happened. It became a secret between God and me. I did, however, learn a significant lesson about evil being present in our world.

The rest of my youth was pretty much uneventful. My parents took very good care of me and were very good parents. My dad taught me how to hunt and fish. They allowed me to make as many decisions as I could, which helped me grow and develop into manhood.

At nine years of age, they let me have a paper route so that I could earn my own money. I was eleven years old when my parents acquired the grocery store, and Dad taught me how to butcher meat. By age twelve, I could butcher and run the store on my own. We had one employee who worked at the checkout, but they did teach me how to run the store for them. I did this when they would go on vacation a number of times.

My dad also essentially let me start my own business as a butcher. I began cutting and wrapping sides of beef for customers who wanted to buy a side of beef, cut and wrapped. I would do this after we closed the store for the day. We were open from 6:00 a.m. to 8:00 p.m., six days a week. We were closed on Sunday as this was our day to go to my grandmother's house for a Sunday meal. My dad was essentially at the store fourteen hours a day, six days a week. Because of this, he did not mind if I worked on the sides of beef after we closed. It would take me about two hours to cut and wrap a side of beef. This helped my dad since he was tired at the end of each day, and it was a very good deal for me. He also let me keep the profit from the sale of each side of beef. I learned a lot from this endeavor.

This too is additional empirical evidence that this was all part of God's plan for me. The money I earned allowed me to buy a 1955 red Ford convertible that was a major factor later on in attracting my future wife.

As far as sports go as a youth, I did play basketball and tennis while in school. God gave me the talent to play tennis, and I essentially taught myself how to play. Again as I reflect back over my life, this too is further empirical evidence that God was guiding my life, and this was part of his plan for me. Tennis was an important factor during my college years. This was just another piece of my life's puzzle on my path through life. God and my parents prepared me well for my life after high school.

CHAPTER 4

The College Years

After graduating from high school in 1960, God guided me to go to college. The only school that I ever considered was Iowa State University (ISU) in Ames, Iowa. I always had an interest in flying and airplanes, which instilled an interest in engineering.

At that time, ISU was in the top ten engineering universities in the nation. The decision to go to ISU had to have been guided by God as part of his plan for me since I had no interest in any other school. This decision essentially shaped the remainder of my life. This decision resulted in me meeting my wife, joining the Air Force, and preparing me for my occupation after the Air Force.

I was accepted by ISU and enrolled in the aerospace engineering program. In 1960, all state-funded universities required that all male students enroll in the Reserve Officers' Training Corps (ROTC) during their first two years. At ISU, ROTC had three branches of service available. These were the Army, Navy, and the Air Force. With my interest in flying and aerospace engineering, it was only natural for me to select the Air Force ROTC program. The majority of the male students signed up for the Army ROTC, figuring they would complete the first two years of Army ROTC and then get on with their plan for life. As I look back, it had to be God's plan for me to choose Air Force ROTC because the Air Force turned out to be a very large part of my life.

After the first two required years of ROTC, each male student had to decide if he wanted to sign up for advanced ROTC. Advanced ROTC meant that if you completed all four years of ROTC, you would be commissioned as a second lieutenant in the branch of service you had selected.

When it came time for me to decide if I was going to sign up for Advanced ROTC, I now know that God was guiding me. I thought that if I could pass the pilot flight physical, I would sign up for Advanced ROTC. I figured if I was studying to learn how to design airplanes, I also would like to fly them for the Air Force, at least for a while.

I did pass the pilot flight physical, and I was now on the path to spend at least four years in the Air Force after graduation from college. The ROTC decision was obviously God's plan for me as was the decision to attend ISU in the first place.

We all think that we are in control of our lives, but are we really? My choice of colleges, initial branch of ROTC selected, and then the selection of Advanced ROTC decisions all turned out to be very significant decisions in my life. I now know that these decisions were all part of God's plan for me. In addition to getting a degree in aerospace engineering and being commissioned as a second lieutenant in the Air Force, the choice of ISU was also a very significant choice for me because it was at ISU that I met my wife, Jan. We have now been married for over sixty-two years.

At ISU, the Greek fraternity system was very strong for both male and female students. At that time, ISU's enrollment was around seven thousand students. Being an engineering and agricultural state school, ISU enrollment was heavy on the male side. There were approximately four thousand male students and three thousand female students. ISU was not a good place for a shy male to find a wife. I was very shy around females in high school and really did not date very much. Finding a wife, therefore, was not my motivation for choosing ISU.

With the Greek fraternity system being so strong, I did decide to participate in the fraternity rush program during my freshman year. I did not know much about the Greek system before my arrival at ISU. Here again is where I now know that God was guiding me on the path that he had planned for me.

I received an invitation to pledge the Delta Tau Delta fraternity, which I did. Out of all the fraternities that I rushed, this was the only one where I felt comfortable and the one I wanted to become a member. This ordinary decision at the time did not seem to be that significant, but it turned out to be very important decision in my life. This decision led me to meet my future wife, Jan.

Jan was also a freshman and had pledged the Kappa Delta sorority. The Delta Tau Delta fraternity and the Kappa Delta sorority houses were located relatively near each other and also held social functions together as part of the Greek system. I first saw Jan at one of these social functions.

At that time, Jan was dating one of my sophomore fraternity brothers. They were both from the same small town in Southwest Iowa. My fraternity brother was a year older than Jan, and this was his second year at ISU. It was not too long after this social function that Jan and my fraternity brother broke up. This is when that red 1955 Ford convertible came into play. This was the car I had been able to purchase while in high school because my dad let me cut and wrap sides of beef—just pieces of the puzzle beginning to fit together.

When I first saw Jan with my fraternity brother, she really caught my eye. I had not officially met her or talked to her, but I know now that I wanted to. I also knew that she had broken up with my fraternity brother. Being very shy and after much consternation, God finally gave me enough courage to call Jan and ask her for a coffee date at the Student Union. Of course, she did not know me; but when I told her I was a Delt and that I drove the red 1955 Ford convertible (which she had seen), she accepted. She later told me that she accepted the coffee date only because she liked my car.

As I reflect back over all the circumstances that had to align for us to meet, it became obvious to me that these factors were all just part of the empirical evidence that God was guiding my life. Let's review some of those factors:

1. ISU was the only college I considered attending.

2. I pledged Delta Tau Delta fraternity, and Jan had been dating my fraternity brother when I first saw her.

3. I had a red 1955 Ford convertible.

When I consider all the intricate interactions that had to occur for all the above to work out, only a higher power could be responsible for all these things to occur. This to me is also further evidence that God does exist, and he has a plan for all of us. For example, as I previously mentioned, ISU was the only college that I even considered attending. Before I left Marshalltown to attend ISU, I did not have any intention of joining a fraternity. I did not even have enough information about the Greek system and fraternities to even have an opinion about them. God, however, did have a plan for me.

As far as getting my red 1955 Ford convertible, God had a hand in this also. I had always wanted one as a kid, but I never thought I would have enough money to purchase one. God's plan for my dad when he changed careers and bought the grocery store and meat market gave me the opportunity to learn how to butcher meat. This resulted in me being able to buy that red convertible during my junior year in high school. There is even a story behind acquiring this car that had to be part of God's plan.

It was the middle of winter when I convinced my dad to go to Des Moines, which was about fifty miles southwest of Marshalltown, to look for a convertible. Winter in Iowa is not the time to look for a convertible. We began our search by stopping at a number of used-car lots. As we asked the salesmen about convertibles, we got some very strange looks at our request. Finally, however, we did find one salesman who indicated that he did have a 1955 Ford convertible; but being winter, it was being stored in a warehouse at a different location. He did indicate that he would be happy to take us over to the warehouse to see it. It was red and exactly what I was looking for. We bought the car and drove it back to Marshalltown. Since it was winter and the heater in 1955 Ford convertibles did not work very well, we nearly froze to death. God, however, had seen to it that I got the red convertible that would catch my future wife's eye enough for her to accept a coffee date with me two years later.

After our coffee date, our first real date was to a Kingston Trio music concert at ISU. I was very shy in high school around girls, but I was never shy around Jan. From that date on, we would go to the library each night to study, and we dated each weekend thereafter. God had made it possible for us to meet as part of his plan for both of us.

I later found out as additional empirical evidence that God had to have been guiding us to meet because Jan had wanted to go to college at the University of Iowa and not ISU. The University of Iowa is located in Iowa City, which is approximately one hundred miles to the east of Ames, Iowa, where ISU is located. Jan's home was on a farm near the small town of Underwood, Iowa. Underwood is located on the western border of the state of Iowa. Jan's parents thought that the University of Iowa, being an additional one hundred miles farther away, was just too far away from home for their daughter to go to school. Jan's parents convinced her to go to ISU instead of the University of Iowa. There is no doubt in my mind that God had to be at work in the decision as to where Jan was going to school. God was guiding her path in order for us to meet as part of his plan for me.

During the summer between our freshman and sophomore years, we dated. Each weekend I would drive from Marshalltown to her parents' farm that was located near Underwood, Iowa. Underwood was approximately 180 miles from Marshalltown. We did not let that stop us from seeing each other. I put a lot of miles on that 1955 Ford convertible that summer.

This was the time when my parents owned the neighborhood grocery store and meat market.

During the week, I would butcher and help run the store; however, on the weekends, I had to go see Jan. My parents were very good about me going to see Jan on the weekends. In fact, my mom told my dad that she thought that Jan was the one. My mom and God did know that Jan was the one for me. At the end of that summer, I proposed to Jan. Fortunately for me, she said yes!—which I know now was all part of God's plan.

I had done well in the fraternity and had been elected as vice president at the end of our freshman year. As I mentioned earlier, I had taught myself how to play tennis while growing up and had played in high school. I decided to try out for the ISU tennis team and fortunately was successful there too. Here again is where I know that this was all part of God's plan for me. I never had a tennis lesson in my life, but by my senior year at ISU, I was the number one player on the ISU tennis team. This too became a significant factor in Jan's and my life that helped us when we needed it.

Since I had proposed to Jan during the summer between our freshman and sophomore years, I was more interested in Jan, school, and tennis as opposed to the fraternity. Jan seemed to feel the same way, so we decided to get married between the fall and winter quarter break of our sophomore year. This was quite a surprise to both of our parents, as well as to my fraternity and Jan's sorority. My fraternity housemother did not approve and told me that I was way too young to get married. I did not really care what she thought as long as Jan and my parents approved.

I told my mom first about our plan. She said, "Go tell your dad." My dad did not say much but did ask me if we planned to finish school. Both Jan and I had every intention of finishing our degrees. Neither of us had any plans to quit school. With this understanding, Dad agreed to continue to pay for my college tuition.

After getting my parents' approval, the next step was to determine how Jan's parents felt about her getting married. I felt I had a good chance with her parents since I knew they had gotten married when her mother was very young. I first asked her dad if I could marry his daughter. Herman (Jan's dad) was a farmer and also worked for the Union Pacific Railroad. Herman was a very wise man who, like my mother, had to quit school when he was young in order to help support his family. Herman was one of twelve children in his family. He was a quiet and gentle man. When I asked him if I could marry his daughter, he just listened politely in his quiet manner. After I told him how I felt about his daughter, I finished up with my promise to him that I would take very good care of her. He just smiled at me and shook his head in an affirmative manner.

When we told Jan's mother about our plans, her only concern was that Jan would finish school and get her degree. When we both confirmed that we were determined to finish college, she also agreed to our request for her approval. In addition, Jan's parents also agreed to continue paying for Jan's college tuition, which was great news to me.

With our parents agreeing to continue to pay for our college tuition, we next had to figure out how to support ourselves. This is where I know that God's plan for my parents to go into the grocery-store business entered in as help for Jan and me. In addition to continue paying for my college tuition, they also volunteered to allow us to get our food from the store. Since ISU was located only thirty miles from Marshalltown, it was no problem for us to drive to Marshalltown every couple of weeks to get food. My parents also agreed to pay our rent since it was about the same as my monthly fraternity dues. I know that God had laid all the groundwork for us to get married as part of his plan for us.

With the approval of both our parents, Jan and I were married on November 25, 1962, between fall and winter quarters of our sophomore year. At that time, ISU was on a quarter system and not a semester system. Each college year consisted of three quarters instead of two semesters.

As I now think back about how our parents must have thought about us getting married so young, it could only have been God's guiding hand making everything possible. Growing up, both of our parents believed in God and raised both Jan and me to also believe in God. I will say that at that age, I was not thinking about all that was happening in my life, that it was actually all part of God's plan for me. I think that people at that age are more concerned with living their lives as opposed to thinking about God even having a plan for each of us.

Now, after sixty-two years plus of marriage, it is much easier to reflect back over the years to see how God had to have been guiding our lives for all of it to happen. We just had to listen to him and trust him. I also now wonder what my fraternity housemother would now think about Jan and me getting married at such a young age.

After we got married, Jan moved out of her sorority house, and I moved out of my fraternity. We rented an apartment and began our lives together. We were very happy as we continued on with our education. God blessed us during this time by having our parents pay our tuition and my parents providing our food and paying our rent. God also provided us with other opportunities that helped us support ourselves. I was selected to become a student manager for the ISU basketball team. My tennis coach, who was also an assistant basketball coach, helped me get this position. As payment, I was given student food vouchers to eat at the Student Union. This helped us significantly during basketball season with our food supplies. I also was given free basketball tickets for my parents to come over to ISU for the home basketball games. They really enjoyed the basketball games. It was also a small way for me to pay back my parents for all of their help.

I also got a job during the summers between our sophomore, junior, and senior years to work for the university's Landscape Department. This allowed us to go to the Dairy Queen once a week to get some ice cream as a treat for ourselves. It was great, and we were extremely happy. This helped us a lot financially during this time period. There were two other financial factors that also helped us, which I have to attribute back to God's plan for us. This first was the decision for me to apply for Advanced ROTC. The Air Force paid a small stipend to each Advanced ROTC student each quarter. We would get a check each quarter from the Air Force. This really helped us during our junior and senior years at ISU. It always seemed to arrive just at the time when we really needed it. I remember one time when we did not have $0.19 to buy a loaf of bread. The next day, the Air Force check arrived. God knew our needs and took care of us.

Another financial factor that God provided us occurred during our senior year. My tennis coach put me on a tennis scholarship for that year. I know that it had to be God's work because ISU did not offer tennis scholarships. This is just more empirical evidence that God does exist and that he has a plan for all of us.

Another piece of empirical evidence that God was guiding me became apparent while playing tennis during my senior year. Since God had led my tennis coach to provide me with a tennis scholarship at a school that did not previously have tennis scholarships, it was very important for me to remain the number one player on the team at ISU. It was during my senior year that a very good tennis player was also attending ISU. He had played number one for the freshman team during his freshman year as I had done. At that time, freshmen athletes were not allowed to play on the varsity teams, and we had to wait until our sophomore year to play varsity sports. I had played number one during my freshman year, and then I was able to play at the number three position during my sophomore and junior years. I was number three behind the number one player who had been the Nebraska state champ while he was in high school. Our number two player had been the South Dakota state champ while he was in high school. I was not the Iowa state champ, but I was part of the Iowa State High School District doubles team champions.

As a senior on the tennis team, I was now playing the number one position as the previous number one and two players had graduated. I had to earn that position at the start of the fall tennis season when the tennis coach held a challenge tournament to determine what position each of the members of the team would play before the start of the season. During this tournament I was able to defeat the now sophomore tennis player that had played number one as a freshman. He did, however, obtain the number two position on the team.

This individual's name was Bill O'Brian, and I remember him well because he was a very good tennis player. I did not, however, remember the names of any of the other members of our team my senior year, but I do remember him. I know that God had helped me defeat him and secure the number one position, which led the coach to put me on scholarship.

Once the spring tennis season started, however, other team members could challenge for a higher position on the team. Bill O'Brian was a baseline tennis player and was extremely adept at keeping the ball in play, which would allow opponents to make mistakes and essentially beat themselves. My game was more of a serve-and-volley game, which meant that I would attempt to overpower my opponent. I would serve and then make my way up to the net in order to put away the opponent's return. To defeat a baseline player, a serve-and-volley player really has to be on his game in order to defeat someone who is doing everything he can to keep the ball in play until a mistake is made. Approximately midway through the season, Bill challenged me for my position. I knew that it was going to be very difficult for me to defeat him again. He had been playing very well.

This is when I now know that God stepped in to help me maintain my number one position and be able to retain my scholarship. If I had lost, it would have been difficult for my coach to defend me having a scholarship while Bill O'Brian did not. This would have been especially true since ISU supposedly did not offer tennis scholarships. On the day that the challenge match was scheduled to be played, it was raining. The outdoor courts at ISU had lay-cold surfaces. This is a green coating that is placed over a hard surface such as concrete and provides an excellent surface to play on. It plays faster than a clay court surface but slower than a concrete surface. If a serve-and-volley player is any way off of his game on a fast surface, baseline players can be very effective. Since it was raining, the coach had to move the match to our indoor court, which was in the armory building at ISU. The armory is where ISU played basketball. The basketball court was placed on the concrete floor of the armory. During the spring quarter, the basketball floor is removed, and this then became our indoor tennis court.

The floor of the armory consisted of a polished concrete surface slab. This type of surface is a much better surface for a serve-and-volley game because it plays so fast. Slower surfaces give the advantage to a baseline player. Having watched Bill play during the first half of the season, I was not sure that I could beat him again. He had really improved from our first match in the fall to the now spring quarter. This is where I feel that God intervened with the rain because it forced us to play indoors on a surface that was more suitable to my type of game. The polished concrete floor of the armory was much faster than the lay-cold surfaces on the outdoor courts. I again was able to defeat Bill relatively convincingly enough that he never challenged me again. I kept my number one position and did not put my coach in a position of having to defend my scholarship at a school that did not previously have tennis scholarships. This had to be God's plan for me.

It is so true what the Bible says. If you put your faith and trust in God, he will provide you with what you need. I had seen him do that for my grandmother after the death of her husband, and now I was seeing it in my life.

The engineering curriculum at ISU during the 1960s was very intensive and required 219 quarter hours to graduate. This required a student to carry an average of 18.25 quarter hours of credit each quarter to graduate on time. This did not include any quarter hours for Advanced ROTC. In fact, because of Advanced ROTC, I could not complete two of the required engineering courses and had to substitute Writing Military Staff Reports and Military Briefings for the engineering required courses of Writing Scientific Papers and Speech class.

Engineering at ISU was very rigorous and required significant effort in order to complete any of ISU's engineering disciplines. ISU used physics as the yardstick to determine if a student was capable of becoming an ISU-trained engineer. Physics was required during the sophomore year for all engineers and was required for all three quarters of the sophomore year.

We had approximately 900 total engineering students begin physics in the fall quarter of my sophomore year. We lost 300 engineering students by the end of the fall quarter. With 600 students starting the winter quarter, only 300 finished the quarter. Of the 300 that started the spring quarter, only approximately 150 students finished the complete physics course. Physics was very tough at ISU.

With the class of potential aerospace engineers that I enrolled with my freshman year, we had a similar loss rate. My class started out with approximately 250 freshmen, and we graduated approximately 35 aerospace engineers in 1964.

It also was very difficult for engineering students to complete all the required courses to obtain an engineering degree in four years. I was no exception, especially with Advanced ROTC and being on the tennis team all four years. This resulted in my being six hours short for graduation at the end of my senior year. I had to go the fall quarter of my fifth year. Jan did graduate at the end of her fourth year and was able to get a job as a secretary at the agriculture engineering office while I finished my studies.

Another piece of empirical evidence that God was guiding my life was revealed by how my ROTC summer camp requirement worked out. This, along with the fact that it took me an extra quarter to graduate, all worked out better for me than if I have been on time. Advanced ROTC had a requirement that everyone had to attend a summer training camp at an active Air Force base (AFB) during the summer between his junior and senior years. This training camp was essentially basic boot camp for all future Air Force officers.

I was scheduled to go to Schilling Air Force Base (AFB) in Salina, Kansas, during the summer between my junior and senior years. The week before I was scheduled to leave, however, I was playing in a tennis tournament on the ISU campus. I was fortunate to have made it to the tournament finals. I wanted to practice for the finals, so I had asked my ISU tennis coach to practice with me. We were playing a match when I stepped on a tennis ball and severely sprained my ankle. I spent the night in the ISU hospital with a cast on my ankle. Naturally, I had to forfeit the finals of the tennis tournament, but the worst thing was that I was not going to be able to go to the ROTC summer camp. This would have been a real problem if I had graduated in the normal four years.

God's plan, however, was evident in that since I had not completed all of my engineering requirements in four years, I had to go during the fall quarter of my fifth year. This provided me with an extra summer between my senior and fifth year. This allowed me to go to ROTC summer camp during this extra summer and put me back on schedule for commissioning as a second lieutenant in the Air Force upon graduation. Once again, God had to be in control to make this all work out with no problems.

Another significant piece of empirical evidence that God was guiding both Jan and my life was revealed by the following: When Jan first started at ISU, she was majoring in psychology. After we got married, she changed her major to English. This helped her get the secretary job at the agriculture engineering office when she graduated while I still had a quarter to go. In addition, the fact that she changed her major to English played a large factor for me.

At ISU, there was a requirement that all students had to pass what was known as a senior English exam. Each student had three opportunities to pass this exam. I can honestly say that I was not very proficient in grammar and with writing the English language while in high school or college. This exam was a timed exam that all students were required to pass in order to graduate. It was a pass-or-fail type of exam.

I took the exam my first quarter of my senior year. Needless to say, I did not do very well. Students were allowed only three grammatical errors on the entire exam. My expertise was in math and science, not English. After I failed the exam, I went in to review my exam in hopes of doing better on my second try. I reviewed my exam, but I can honestly say I did not have a clue as to what I had done wrong on any of the grammatical errors that I had made. Since I had three attempts at passing the exam, I signed up again to take it during the winter quarter.

At ISU, English courses were required during all three quarters of the freshman year. Grammar, however, was not part of the instruction in any of these three quarters. The course content consisted of reading books and then discussing them in class. This was not really my cup of tea. My wife, on the other hand, had changed her major to English, but my pride kept me from asking her for help. I took the English exam again during the winter quarter with the same disastrous results. I knew then that I was in deep trouble. I had failed the senior English exam twice, and now I had only one more opportunity to pass it. I know that it was God who helped me overcome my pride and ask my wife for help.

Since I had gotten absolutely nothing out of reviewing my first failed exam, I asked my wife is she would go in to review my second failed exam. Here is where God's guiding hand was again evident in my life. He helped me overcome my pride and ask the one individual that he had provided me two years earlier. He also had to be the one guiding Jan to change her major because that became a significant factor during this situation. Only God could have orchestrated all these events that helped me pass this written requirement for graduation.

While Jan was sitting at a desk reviewing my masterpiece, her current English advisor happened to walk by the room and saw her sitting at the desk reviewing my failed exam. Since she was an English major and he was her advisor, he was very concerned about the possibility that she may have failed the senior English exam. Of course, he had to come into the room and research this possibility. He asked her if she had failed the exam. He was greatly relieved when she said no, that she was reviewing her husband's failed exam. She informed him that I had asked her to review my exam since my review of my first failed exam had not produced positive results.

Her advisor, who also was the head of the English Department, sat down and began to ask her questions about me. He asked what my major was and if I had a job lined up after graduation. My wife informed him that I was in aerospace engineering and that I was also in Air Force ROTC. She also informed him I already had an Air Force pilot training slot after graduation. I will never know, but I strongly suspect that this chance event was just all part of God's plan to get me through the senior English exam. I really do not think that I did it all on my own.

What I feel happened was that God had led Jan to change her major to English and then provided the head of the English Department to be her advisor. He then set up this chance meeting in order to allow my wife's advisor to intervene on my behalf. Being the head of the English Department, I am sure he would have had no problem reviewing my third attempt. Jan was an excellent student and her advisor liked her. All I know is that I did pass the senior English exam on my third attempt.

I think what really happened was that as head of the English Department, he decided to grade my third exam attempt. I also think that he took into account that I must not be too dumb if I was able to complete the ISU's aerospace engineering degree curriculum. I also feel that since he knew that I already had an Air Force pilot training slot, I would not necessarily need a high level of English grammatical skills for a while. Even though this senior English exam was supposedly a requirement for graduation, I never heard of anyone not graduating for not passing this exam. There may have been some, but I never heard of anyone not graduating because of this exam. I feel that Jan's advisor just passed me as I do know that I had not improved between my second and third attempts. What I also know is that if Jan's advisor were alive today, I think he would feel that he made the correct decision. This book is my third book that I have written—one book for each failed English exam.

I am just an old dumb fighter pilot and engineer, but I do consider myself a logical person. As a logical man, as I look back over my college years, I know that with all the empirical evidence that is available, only a higher power had to be at work in order for all the events to have occurred. There is no way I would believe that these events were just random. God gave me the talent to play tennis. He led me to attend ISU and study engineering. He led Jan to attend ISU when she really wanted to attend the University of Iowa. God led me to pledge the Delta Tau Delta fraternity through which I met Jan. He guided my decision about selecting advance ROTC and then helped me pass the pilot physical. He led Jan to change her major to English, with her advisor being the head of the English Department. He knew I would need help getting through the senior English exam. He had led my parents to buy the grocery store at the time that they did because he knew my grandmother needed help then, and Jan and I would need the help while we were in college. He provided all the financial help that we needed while we were in college.

There is one additional event that I should point out as further evidence of God guiding my life. As part of the Advanced Air Force ROTC program, pilot candidates got the opportunity to enroll in what was known as the Flight Instruction Program (FIP). This was a program where the Air Force would pay for thirty-six hours of civilian flight instruction toward a private pilot license at the local airport. There were four of us pilots in my ROTC class that were eligible for this program. To get a private pilot's license, it required forty hours of instruction. However, for the FIP, if the instructor thought that you could pass the flight check given by an FAA flight examiner, he could put you up for the flight check after thirty-five hours of instruction. If you were able to pass this flight exam, you received your private pilot civilian license.

My instructor thought I could pass the flight check and put me up for the ride. I did pass, and I received my civilian private pilot's license. Out of the four pilot ROTC students, I was the only one put up for the private pilot check ride. This is just more evidence that God was with me, and he was guiding my life.

I graduated from ISU on November 25, 1964, with a bachelor of science (BS) degree in aerospace engineering and was commissioned as a second lieutenant reserve officer in the United States Air Force. This was exactly two years to the date after Jan and my wedding date of November 25, 1962. We were now ready to begin the next portion of the journey on the path of life that God had planned for us. We were on our way to Reese Air Force Base (AFB) in Lubbock, Texas, for Air Force Undergraduate Pilot Training (UPT).

CHAPTER 5

The Military Years

As I continued to look back over my life, there was further empirical evidence that God was indeed guiding our lives. The next phase of our lives began in February of 1965 when we reported for Air Force Undergraduate Pilot Training (UPT) at Reese Air Force Base in Lubbock, Texas. Air Force UPT was a yearlong course at that time.

The UPT class that I was in was Class 66E. I do not remember how many students actually started out in our class, but we graduated thirty-seven pilots at the end. We had a number of students that washed out. They were eliminated due to a lack of flying proficiency. Having earned my private pilot license in college was a great advantage for me.

We had two captains: one first lieutenant, and the rest of us were second lieutenants. We also had a foreign exchange student from Morocco. He had been washed back from earlier classes to due to his flying proficiency. The Air Force was not allowed to wash him out of training no matter how long it took for him to complete the training.

One of the captains became our class commander as he was the ranking officer in our class. His name was Ray Leach and had previously been a navigator in B-47s before applying for pilot training. God had to have been guiding my life in order for our paths to cross. Ray Leach later played a major role in my military career as well as he and his wife have been great friends of ours for the last sixty years.

At that time, aircraft pilot assignments after graduating from training were based on each person's class standing. Class standings were determined on our academic test scores and our flying proficiency scores received on flight check rides for each phase of training. We were essentially competing against one another in our class for choice of aircraft assignments.

At graduation time, the Air Force Assignments Division at Randolph Air Force Base in San Antonio, Texas, would send the training base a list of pilot assignment slots by aircraft types based on Air Force pilot requirements at that time. These lists would include pilot assignments for fighters, bombers, airlift, and instructor pilot slots for each class graduating. Each class member was asked to write down their top three choices for assignments. The higher one's class standing, the higher probability you had to get your first choice of assignment from the list.

I know that God was guiding me through training because I was able to stay in Class 66E through graduation. I had incurred a severe knee injury during physical training the day before our Christmas break. If this injury had occurred before or after the Christmas break, I most likely would have been washed back or even out of pilot training altogether. If I have been washed back, I would not have been able to stay in contact with Ray Leach and may not have received the assignment that I did get upon UPT graduation. Some lists of assignments that came down did not have any instructor pilot slots.

The injury that I suffered occurred on the day before our Christmas break was to start. I had already flown my last flight the morning of the day before the break. We were playing basketball in the afternoon as part of our physical conditioning when I dislocated my knee. In today's vernacular, it was a very hard foul. I was going in for a layup and while in the air, an opposing team member tried to block my shot. Since he fouled me so hard while in the air, my body's direction of movement was changed by ninety degrees. When my leg landed on the floor, my knee dislocated due to the change in path of motion as I landed. When I fell to the floor, I felt my knee pop back into place. I knew it was bad based on my experience as a student basketball manager at ISU. I had seen a number of injuries just like the one I had just experienced. I was immediately taken to the flight surgeon for evaluation. I tried to act like it was not too bad so that he would not ground me from flying. I knew that I had two weeks to recuperate if I could just get out of the flight surgeon's office.

The flight surgeon examined my knee, and since it was back in place, he decided that it was not too severe of an injury. My knee had not swollen yet, and it was still numb. I also think since it was Friday afternoon just before Christmas break, he wanted to get out of the office and go home. Since he did not seem to be too concerned, I asked him for a couple of tenure bandages and indicated that would be all I needed and left his office. From my previous injuries playing tennis and basketball, I knew it was a bad injury. I went home and immediately lay down on the couch and essentially remained there for the entire two weeks of Christmas break. That knee, to this day, still bothers me. I also knew that the knee would probably not withstand a parachute-landing fall if I ever had to eject out of an aircraft.

When training began again after the Christmas break, I was only able to get around on crutches in order to walk. I still had my crutches from when I sprained my ankle at ISU while playing in that tennis tournament. No one questioned me since they all knew that I had been to the flight surgeon, and he had not grounded me. It was very humorous, and I would get strange looks from the crew chiefs when I would arrive at the aircraft on crutches. I could not do the aircraft preflight, so my instructor would do it for me. The crew chief would take my crutches as I struggled up the ladder to get into the cockpit. We were training in the T-38 at that time, so I did not have to use the rudder very much during the flight. My only real problem was that I could not hold the breaks for takeoff while doing the engine run-up check while the throttles were being advanced to 100 percent. My instructor pilot (IP) would hold the brakes while I completed the engine checklist, and then he would release the brakes for takeoff. I did not have any other problems during flight. If it had not been for the Christmas break, I know that I would have been washed back a class or even totally out of UPT. Our class was close to graduation, which was scheduled for February 7, 1966.

The rest of pilot training was pretty much uneventful. I did well enough to finish number five in my class. Having been able to get my private pilot's license in college really helped me to do well in flying proficiency during training. Since God had provided me with that opportunity in college, I know it was all part of his plan for me.

Finishing fifth in my class of thirty-seven resulted in me being able to get my first choice of assignments upon graduation. I chose to become an instructor pilot (IP) after graduation. My thought was that I would really learn how to fly if I became an instructor. It was a good choice because the flying experience I gained as an IP helped me tremendously throughout my military career. This choice had to be part of God's plan because I passed up a fighter assignment after graduation.

There were a number of F-4 fighter slots available to our class. However, at that time, F-4 assignments for new pilots were to the back seat and not to the front seat as pilot in command. As an IP, I knew that I would be the pilot in command. This to me was far better that flying fighters in the back seat of an F-4 as a copilot. Later on, the Air Force stopped putting pilots in the back seat and assigned navigators or weapons systems operators (WSOs) to the back seats of the F-4.

At that time in my life, I still thought that I was in charge of my life. I now know that it was God guiding my life in order for me to be and remain in Class 66E, which allowed me to meet Ray Leach and then be able to become an IP after graduation. Both of these factors played a large part during my military career. Furthermore, at that time, I had not even decided if I was going to stay in the Air Force after I completed my four-year commitment to the Air Force due to ROTC.

The instructor pilot assignment that I received was for the T-37 aircraft at Laughlin AFB in Del Rio, Texas. My pride again raised its head in that I was a little disappointed that the assignment was for the T-37 aircraft and not the T-38. The T-38 aircraft was a lot more fun to fly as compared to the T-37. However, it worked out that the T-37 assignment was a great assignment for me. God knew what I needed as opposed to what I wanted. In addition, God blessed Jan and me with a tremendous blessing while we were in Lubbock. Doug, our oldest son, was born on February 15, 1966, just after I had graduated from UPT.

After graduation from UPT, we were assigned to Randolph AFB in San Antonio, Texas, to attend T-37 pilot instructor training (PIT) before going to Laughlin AFB. With our family now being three, we arrived at Randolph AFB in March of 1966 for PIT. This training lasted for two months, and then we were on our way to Laughlin AFB in Del Rio, Texas.

We arrived at Laughlin AFB in May 1966, where I began my IP duties. I instructed a total of five classes before God provided me with an opportunity that allowed me to advance as an IP. In each class, I was responsible for four or five students. The opportunity that God provided me was a significant challenge, but it turned out to be very helpful in my career.

The opportunity and challenge that God provided me was being assigned a foreign student named Ammand, who was from Iran to train how to fly. At that time, our country still had good relations with Iran and the shah of Iran. My student Ammand was also royalty and was number three in line to the shah. When he was assigned to me, the squadron commander called me to his office and told me that I had to get him through the T-37 program. He said that if I did not, Ammand would be put to death on his return to Iran. He had to finish the T-37 program. He indicated that if I could get him through the T-37 program and he washed out of the T-38 program, he would become a C-130 copilot in Iran as he completed his time in the military. No pressure here!

Ammand was a very nice individual, but he had zero—and I mean zero—flying abilities. He was a real challenge for me due to his total lack of flying capabilities. I knew that I was in deep trouble with him as a student after our first flight. I had never before or since flown with someone who lacked totally on coordination and did not have any natural instincts for flying. I knew that it was going to be a real challenge to teach him how to land the T-37.

It normally only required ten to twelve flying hours to teach a new student without any flying experience to fly solo. When we reached twenty hours of flying time, Ammand was nowhere near being able to solo. I informed my squadron commander about his total lack of aptitude for flying. He said he understood, but we did not have a choice. The squadron commander said, "Let's give him thirty hours and then see where he is, and then we will talk again."

When we soloed students in the T-37, we would start out as a dual ride with student and instructor. The student was required to complete three satisfactory landings and a go-around. We would then complete a full-stop landing and then taxi back to the takeoff end of the runway. Next, we would shut down the right engine, and the instructor would get out of the aircraft. The instructor would then monitor the restart of the right engine. After the restarting of the engine, the instructor would then walk over to the runway supervisor unit (RSU) and monitor the student as he performed three more landings solo. An experienced instructor pilot always manned the RSU and had the responsibility to control the traffic pattern for that runway. It was his responsibility to verify that each aircraft was properly configured for landing and to direct aircraft to go-around if any safety condition was in question. The RSU duty was assigned to different flights of the squadron each day, so you only knew who was the RSU supervisor on the days that your flight had the duty. On the day Ammand was going to reach thirty hours, my flight did have the RSU duty, and everyone in my flight knew about him as a student. On this day, my assistant flight commander was the one assigned RSU duty for the day. His name was Bill Russell, and he was highly experienced. Before Bill left the squadron for the RSU, I informed him that I was going to try to solo Ammand. He looked at me, raised his eyebrows, and said, "Okay, I guess we both will be playing 'you bet your wing' today." He was right!

Ammand and I took off, and we stayed in the traffic pattern in order for me to monitor his three landings and a go-around. On his first landing, I had to assist him. It was not looking good for him. On his second landing, he improved and was able to land the aircraft on his own. It was not a good landing, but I did not have to help him. His third landing was again a little better, but still not a good landing. I decided that we would complete two more landings before I would decide if I was going to solo him. The fourth and fifth landings were marginally acceptable. On the fifth landing, Ammand had called for a full-stop landing. He knew that we were getting low on fuel, and if he was going to be able to complete his three landings, we would have to full stop on this landing. However, I still had not made up my mind if I was going to solo him. My decision was made for me when we taxied past our parking row, and we were now headed back to the takeoff end of the runway.

At the end of the runway, I had him shut down the right engine, and I got out of the aircraft. Ammand restarted the engine and was now going to solo. I walked over to the RSU where Bill was performing RSU duties for the day. As I entered the RSU, we both just looked at each other, and neither of us said a word. As he took off, all we could now do was sit, wait, and hope for the best.

As we watched Ammand begin his first attempt at landing solo, we could tell that he was fighting the aircraft as he began the final turn. We both watched him very closely as he struggled around the final turn. He did at least have the aircraft properly configured for landing with the gear and flaps extended. As he arrived over the threshold of the runway, he was higher than he should have been, but he did not elect to go-around. Instead, he pulled power, and both Bill and myself came out of our chairs. Bill had raised the radio that was in his hand to direct him to go-around. However, with a T-37 once you pull power it takes approximately twelve to thirteen seconds for the engines to advance to 100 percent. Bill did not say anything on the radio as we watched the aircraft drop out of the sky, hit the runway, and bounce back into the air. We could hear the engines begin to spool up. The aircraft was now beginning to drift off the runway centerline over to the grass and weeds that were along the sides of the runway as Ammand struggled to keep the aircraft airborne. As the aircraft was descending lower and lower to the ground, grass, and weeds, dust began to fly up from the engines exhaust. When the aircraft was approximately a foot or so above the ground, the engines reached 100 percent, and the aircraft slowly began to climb. Ammand had managed to keep from crashing. Bill and I were both standing now and just looked at each other with neither or us saying a word.

Then just as luck would have it, we noticed a blue Air Force car approaching the RSU. It was our squadron commander's car. This was the last person in the world that I wanted to see come out to the RSU for this event. He parked his car, got out, and entered the RSU. He said, "Dave, I heard that you were soloing Ammand today, so I thought I would come out and see how it goes." Bill and I did not say a thing as the squadron commander took a seat. Bill and I again could only hope for the best. This was especially true now after his first almost disastrous attempt at landing.

As Ammand came around for his second landing, I think both Bill and I really were playing "you bet your wings." As Ammand turned final for his second landing, he did not seem to be fighting the aircraft as much. In fact, as he arrived over the threshold of the runway, he was in pretty good position. He actually touched down normally and advanced the power to take off again for his third landing. Bill and I just looked at each other and did not say a word. The squadron commander also did not say anything.

As we waited for Ammand to come around again for his final landing, I think both Bill and I had our fingers crossed, hoping Ammand could do it again. Thankfully, his last landing was very similar to his second landing. After Ammand's full stop landing, the squadron commander got up and said, "Good job, Dave," and left. Both Bill and I breathed a tremendous sigh of relief because we were going to be able to keep our wings.

I think because Ammand scared himself so bad on the first landing, he really was concentrating on the last two. Those last two landing were the best landings I ever saw him make.

As a further example of just how bad of a pilot Ammand was, he actually got me into an inadvertent spin on one of our missions. He was the only student that ever did that to me as an instructor pilot. In fact, he was the only student that I ever heard of that got anyone into an inadvertent spin.

The T-37 aircraft was the only Air Force aircraft that would spin and the pilot could recover it if he recognized the spin. This was the reason we taught spins in the T-37 in order for the pilot to recognize a spin if they happen to get into one. In all other Air Force aircrafts, if you get into a spin, the normal course of action is to eject. You really have to be a bad pilot if you did get into a spin.

On the particular day that Ammand got us into the inadvertent spin, we were practicing aerobatics. He was attempting to do an Immelmann maneuver. This aerobatic maneuver is when you dive the aircraft to get sufficient airspeed to pull up like you are doing a loop. Only at the top of the loop when you are inverted, you roll the aircraft to the upright position. A spin consists of stalling the aircraft and then introducing yaw, which causes the aircraft to snap into an accelerated spin. At this point, the aircraft is no longer flying and is spinning and falling vertically like a spinning rock. The problem that Ammand had was that he misread his airspeed indicator and entered the maneuver one hundred knots low on airspeed. As he pulled up to the inverted position, the aircraft ran out of airspeed and stalled. When he tried to roll the aircraft, yaw was introduced, and the aircraft immediately snapped into an accelerated spin. This now was a significant problem for us.

The altitude loss during a spin is approximately ten thousand feet per minute. Because of this, when we practiced spins, we had to be above eighteen thousand feet to enter the spin. If you are not out of the spin by ten thousand feet, you are supposed to eject.

Our problem began with our entry into the spin. We were only approximately at fifteen thousand feet when we entered the spin. I had to allow Ammand time to see if he was going to recognize that we had entered a spin and to see if he could recover the aircraft. As we were passing nine thousand feet, it became totally obvious that Ammand did not have a clue as to what was happening. I calmly told Ammand to give me the aircraft so that I could save our lives. He did let go of the stick and held his hands up above his head and said, "Ammand make mistake." This was his normal response anytime that he would dazzle me with his lack of flying abilities.

I took control of the aircraft. Since we were in an accelerated spin, I had to get the aircraft back into a normal spin before I could affect a recovery. I completed the spin recovery at about two thousand feet directly above the small Texas town of Spofford, Texas. God was definitely with us that day. If we had ejected, the aircraft would have crashed into Spofford with a high probability of catastrophic results on the ground.

Needless to say, that was the end of that mission on that day. My only concern now was that someone from Spofford would call the base and complain about someone buzzing his or her town. No one did, so I escaped any serious problems after that.

With God's help, I did get Ammand through the T-37 program. I knew, however, that he would never be able to complete the T-38 program. The T-38 aircraft is a high-performance aircraft, and I knew it was well beyond Ammand's flying capabilities.

I was correct. After just seven flights in the T-38, including his elimination flight, he was washed out of the training program. It was very obvious to everyone that he would certainly kill himself and maybe others if he were allowed to continue.

Ammand returned to Iran and was assigned to fly the C-130 aircraft. Since he was royalty, I am sure he flew as a copilot in the C-130 aircraft for a minimum respectable period of time and then assumed his place as third in line to the Shah.

I think my success with Ammand impressed my Squadron Commander. It was not long after Ammand washed out of the T-38 program that I was selected to become a Squadron Check Pilot. We had four check pilots for the entire squadron and we administered check rides to all of the students as they completed each phase of training.

I was in check section for about a year when God provided me with another opportunity. The Vietnam War was building up and a number of pilots were getting assignments to go to Vietnam. When an opening occurred in the wing standardization/evaluation (stan/eval) section after one of the T-37 pilots left for Vietnam, I was selected to be his replacement. There were only three T-37 slots in the wing stan/eval section. The function of the wing stan/eval section was to administer check rides to all the instructor pilots on a yearly basis to ensure their proficiency. In addition, wing stan/eval pilots checked out all newly assigned instructors before they were assigned to the training squadrons.

Of the three T-37 stan/eval pilots, one was also the wing's T-37 spin pilot. The T-37 had seven different spin modes, which also included an inverted spin. The wing's spin pilot's job was to train all T-37 instructor pilots on all seven of the spin modes. Only the normal spin mode was instructed and practiced with the students. I do not know if it was because of Ammand getting me into that inadvertent spin or not, but I was selected to be the wing's spin pilot. I would instruct all newly assigned T-37 pilots on the seven different spin modes of the T-37, including the inverted spin. The inverted spin was very uncomfortable because the aircraft would spin in the inverted position with negative g-forces (gravity forces) being felt by the pilot until recovery. Squadron instructor pilots only taught the normal spin mode but needed to be at least familiar with the other six modes that could occur.

As I mentioned earlier, I had not yet decided if I was going to stay in the Air Force beyond my initial commitment that I had incurred by choosing advanced ROTC in college. Here again, I now know that God's plan for me was to stay in the Air Force. Another example of empirical evidence that God was at work in my life is when he provided the opportunity to become a regular officer in the Air Force.

Upon graduation from college, I had been commissioned as a second lieutenant as a reserve officer in the United States Air Force. As a reserve officer, if a reduction in force (RIF) was to occur, the reserve officers are forced out of the Air Force first. At that time, with the Vietnam War going on, a RIF was not very likely. However, after the war and depending on the need of the Air Force, an RIF was not out of the question. This is when God led me to make my decision on an Air Force career.

In late 1967, I was offered a commission in the Regular Air Force. As a regular officer, I knew that I would not be subject to any RIF actions if one were to occur. With the offer of the regular commission, I knew that I could not turn it down even if I did decide later to separate from the Air Force. God led me to accept the regular commission. On January 15, 1968, I was commissioned as a first lieutenant in the Regular Air Force. I now know that this was just part of God's overall plan for me.

As an instructor pilot, I knew if I stayed in the Air Force, my next assignment would be to Vietnam. The only assignments that instructor pilots at Laughlin AFB were getting were to Vietnam. The year 1968 was the year of the largest buildup of American forces in Vietnam. At that time, instructor pilots were either deciding to separate from the Air Force or go to Vietnam. Approximately half of the pilots were choosing to separate from the Air Force in lieu of going to Vietnam.

It was now time for me to make my decision as to whether I stayed in the Air Force or separate to civilian life. This was the empirical evidence that God was leading me because he had provided the opportunity for me to become a regular officer in the Air Force. This factor, along with a second consideration, led me to make the decision to stay in the Air Force.

The second consideration had to do with what would I do if I did separate from the Air Force. My commitment to the Air Force was going to be up in 1969. With my degree in aerospace engineering, I had to consider what would be my opportunities to get a job in engineering in the civilian world. I also knew that the economy was starting to enter a downturn. I had heard that engineering job opportunities were few and far between, even for experienced engineers. I knew that if I got out of the Air Force, I would be a person who had graduated four years earlier in engineering and had never worked a day as an engineer. That future did not look too bright to me. I now know why God had led me to accept the regular commission and now to stay in the Air Force.

In 1968, as the buildup of forces was occurring, the Air Force instituted a policy that pilots could volunteer for the type of aircraft they wanted to fly if they volunteered for Vietnam. When I decided to stay in the Air Force, I volunteered to go to Vietnam in July 1968. I volunteered for fighters and then just waited for my turn to go.

Even though I had volunteered for Vietnam, Laughlin did have a say as to when they would release me to go. Since I was the wing's only T-37 spin pilot and one of only three T-37 stan/eval flight examiners, they were not too excited to release me. I remained on the Vietnam volunteer list until December 1970, when Laughlin did finally release me. This was two and a half years after I had volunteered.

Here again is where I now know that God was guiding my life on the path that he had chosen for me. The first nineteen pilots that received assignments off the volunteer list from Laughlin AFB did not return from Vietnam. They were either killed in action (KIA) or were shot down over North Vietnam and became prisoners of war (POWs). These pilots had all volunteered for fighters or as forward air controllers (FACs). It was not looking very good for pilot volunteers from Laughlin AFB.

Forward Air Controlling (FAC) duties were part of the fighter category of aircraft assignments when volunteering for fighters. The Army had a requirement that any FAC that supported the Army for close air support had to be fighter qualified. It made sense that if you were going to control close air support, you should know how to deliver ordinance from fighter aircraft. Assignments in the fighter category ran about 80 percent fighters and 20 percent forward air controllers, with not all FACs requiring fighter qualification.

This is more evidence that God had to be guiding my life. If Laughlin had released me in 1968 when I volunteered, I would have been part of those first nineteen pilots that did not return from Vietnam. However, when Laughlin released me in December 1970, we finally got three pilots back from Vietnam. We got two F-105 pilots and a F-4 pilot back that had completed their one hundred missions over North Vietnam. At that time, if a pilot completed one hundred missions over North Vietnam, he was sent home.

In January 1970, I received an assignment to Vietnam as an O-2A Forward Air Controller (FAC) with fighter qualification. With the fighter qualification, I knew that I would be supporting the Army while in Vietnam. The O-2A aircraft is a civilian Cessna Skymaster aircraft that was converted to military use. It was essentially a slow-speed light aircraft that was being used for combat. It was a far cry from a fighter. This was even more of a difference than between a T-37 and a T-38.

Just like my first assignment, I wanted a T-38 instructor slot, but God knew better and provided me with a T-37 instructor slot. The opportunities that he provided me while flying the T-37 as far as experience were invaluable throughout my entire career. I do not think that I would have gained as much experience if I had been a T-38 instructor. Now, once again, I wanted a fighter, but God had planned for me to become a FAC. I still had not put everything together on how he was in control and was guiding my life.

I departed Laughlin AFB in Del Rio, Texas, in January 1971 to begin my training to become a FAC. Since I was required to be fighter qualified, I first had to go to Cannon AFB in Clovis, New Mexico, to get trained. This was a two-month long training course where I became qualified as a fighter pilot on guns, bombs, and rockets. After fighter qualification, I went to Homestead AFB in Florida where I received water survival training. From water survival training, I was sent to Fairchild AFB in Washington State for basic survival training. After this training, I was headed to Hurlburt Field in Fort Walton Beach, Florida, for O-2A FAC training. This training also lasted for two months. I was now almost ready to go to Vietnam except for jungle-survival school training held in the Philippines.

I left the States in late June 1971 for jungle survival training at Clark Air Base in the Philippines. I arrived in Vietnam in July 1971 for my year tour of duty as an O-2A Forward Air Controller (FAC). My departure and arrival in Vietnam had lasted from mid-1968 when I volunteered to my arrival in Vietnam in July 1971, three years later.

This is the major reason that there are seven years between our first son, Doug, who was born in 1966, and our second son, Randall, who was born in 1973. After I volunteered for Vietnam in mid-1968, I did not want to leave my wife, Jan, with two children if I did not make it back. Our second son was born on August 11, 1973. Families also serve while the member is in the military.

I should note that in the ten years of the Vietnam War, a total of 238 forward air controllers were lost. This averages out to be almost the loss of two FACs every month of the war. I do not know how many fighter pilots were lost, but I do know that it was also a significant number. I lost to the Vietnam War many friends from my pilot training class, fellow instructor pilots from Laughlin, and a number of students that I had trained while at Laughlin.

It was in Vietnam that I finally became aware of the fact that I was not the one in control of my life and that God was. With my selection as a T-37 instructor pilot instead of a T-38, God provided me with tremendous opportunities. He guided me to be selected as a squadron check pilot and then to become just one of three T-37 Wing stan/eval pilots and the only T-37 spin pilot at Laughlin AFB. I feel that the experience I gained at Laughlin in T-37s far exceeded the experience I would have gained flying the T-38. As it worked out, the same thing happened as a result of being an O-2A FAC in Vietnam instead of flying fighters.

In Vietnam, the Air Force close air support was the responsibility of the 504th Tactical Air Support Group (TASG). The group was composed of four Tactical Air Support Squadrons (TASSs) that provided close air-support duties for most of Vietnam. Vietnam had been divided into four military regions (MRs) for tactical air support. These military regions were called MRI, MRII, MRIII, and MRIV. The Air Force and the 504th TASG had responsibility for combat tactical air support for MRI, MRII, MRIII, and Laos and Cambodia. The Navy had responsibility for MRIV. To handle the tactical air-support duties, the four TASSs of the 504th TASG were located at different bases throughout Vietnam and Thailand.

The 504th TASG was located at Cam Ranh Bay along with the 19th TASS. The 19th TASS had responsibility to provide close air-support duties for MRII. The 20th TASS was located at Da Nang and had close air-support responsibilities for MRI. The 21st TASS was located at Tan Son Nhut and had close air-support responsibilities for MRIII and one-half of Cambodia. The 23rd TASS was located at Nakhon Phanom in Thailand and had close air-support responsibilities for the Ho Chi Minh Trails in Laos and the other half of Cambodia. In addition, each of the tactical air-support squadrons in Vietnam also operated out of forward operating locations (FOLs) throughout South Vietnam in order to provide all the close air support that was required.

The 504th Group was different from the normal configuration of a standard Air Force wing. In a normal Air Force wing that has three or four squadrons assigned to it, they all operate out of a single location. Each squadron controls flight operations of these squadrons with close oversight by the wing. With tactical close air-support duties and flight operations being conducted out of forward operating locations (FOLs), each FOL essentially operated as minisquadrons with a major or senior captain in charge. There was little control by the squadron and essentially none by the 504th Group. At each FOL location, there were five or six aircraft, ten to twelve pilots, and thirty to thirty-five maintenance personnel assigned to support the aircraft. Each FOL location operated independently of the main location of the TASS. This is why the 504th Group was called a group and not a wing.

Since I was fighter qualified, I was assigned to the 20th TASS at Da Nang where the 20th TASS was supporting the Army's 101st Airborne Division. The 101st Airborne Division had the combat responsibilities for MRI. I was then assigned to Hue Phu Bai FOL to support the 2nd Brigade of the 101st Airborne Division.

As I mentioned earlier, the O-2A is a light civilian Cessna Skymaster aircraft that had been converted to military use. To be an effective FAC, the aircraft needs to be able to fly low and slow in order to be able to provide the type of close air support needed by Army troops on the ground. The Air Force had tried to use fighters as "fast" FACs, but they just were not very effective.

The O-2A is a light aircraft that does have two engines. One engine is located on the front of the aircraft and operates in a pull thrust mode of operation. The second engine is located behind the cockpit and operates in a push-thrust operation. This engine configuration dictates the aircraft to have two tail sections. The two engines will provide sufficient thrust to get the aircraft up to approximately ten thousand feet of altitude if required. Single-engine operation, however, is significantly limited, depending on just which engine fails. The rear engine is much more efficient that the front engine due to all the aircraft accessories being operated off the front engine. In addition, the rear engine runs approximately three hundred degrees hotter than the front engine due to less airflow. The primary purpose of the rear engine is to provide sufficient thrust for flight. Loss of the front engine is not as much of a problem for flight as compared to the loss of the rear engine. If you lose the rear engine, the best altitude that you can maintain and sustain level flight with only the front engine is approximately 1,000 to 1,100 feet of altitude.

During my time in Vietnam, I lost the rear engine on three occasions. Failure of the rear engine occurred most often due to the fact that the rear engine ran three hundred degrees hotter than the front engine. In all three cases, engine failure was due to oil pump failure. On two of these three occasions, altitude available became a major factor for me due to the mountains that are present in MRI and MRII. The third incident occurred in MRIII, where the terrain is very flat. Most of the rice grown in Vietnam is produced in MRIII.

In Vietnam, I had a number of close calls that I know about, and I am sure that there were close calls that I did not know about. Two of the close calls that I know about had to do with two of the engine losses that I experienced. A third incident was when I experienced God talking to me and telling me not to fly that day. I now know that was God letting me know that he was in control of my life, not me.

The first rear engine loss that I experienced was when I was supporting the Army in MRI. This military region (MR) is the farthest northern portion of South Vietnam. It is located next to the demilitarized zone (DMZ) with North Vietnam. The terrain in MRI is primarily mountains and triple canopy jungle. The mountains in MRI range from 3,000 feet to 5,000 feet. I had only been in country for less than two weeks when I was on one of my first FAC-support missions in support of the Army. I was on a reconnaissance mission in the A Shau Valley. This valley is located on the western border of Vietnam with Laos. Mountains that ranged from 3,000 to 5,000 feet in altitude surround this valley. There was only one pass into or out of this valley where the ground level was below 1,000 feet.

On this mission, I was down in the valley at approximately 1,500 feet above the ground when my rear engine failed. We normally flew our FAC missions at 1,500 feet above the ground in order to be able to see targets and still be mostly out of the small-arms envelope. With the loss of the rear engine, this of course became a significant problem for me. With only the front engine operating, the best that I could hope for was to try and maintain 1,000 to 1,100 feet of altitude. With mountains ranging from 3,000 to 5,000 feet between Phu Bai, my base of operations, and me—I had a problem. My only chance to get back to Phu Bai was to get back to the northern end of the valley where the only pass into or out of the valley was low enough for me to fly out of the valley. This pass had a road as the only ground access into and out of the valley.

I turned around and headed back north to this pass. I was originally at 1,500 feet, but with the loss of the rear engine, I knew that I was going to have to descend in order to keep from stalling the aircraft. I slowly descended down to one thousand feet where I determined I could maintain level flight and headed north. When I got to the pass, I turned east to exit the valley. The pass was very narrow, and when I was going through this pass, I began to see tracers passing my aircraft. The only problem was that the tracers were coming down from above me as I was attempting to exit the valley. When you see tracers, you are only seeing every fifth round that is being fired. The other four rounds are regular rounds of lead. The bad guys were on top of the mountain ridge near the pass, firing a .50 caliber machine gun down at me.

It had to be the hand of God protecting me for me to have made it through that pass that day and make it back to Phu Bai in one piece and no hits. At that time, I did not attribute this event to God's hand protecting me but more to luck than anything else. I still thought I was in charge of my life.

It was not long after I was assigned to Phu Bai that my previous experience as a T-37 instructor pilot, squadron check pilot, and wing flight examiner began to manifest as evidence of what God had planned for me in Vietnam. I was soon designated as the FOL flight-scheduling officer for all flight operations out of Phu Bai. It became my job to schedule all of our support missions for the Army and our assigned missions by the Air Force on each day's selected targets.

The next opportunity that God provided me occurred when the O-2A Training Squadron at Hurlburt Field in Florida sent a message to the 504th Group asking them what they thought about the quality of the O-2A training that was being displayed by the newly assigned FACs. The 504th Group knew about my previous experience as a T-37 UPT instructor pilot prior to my arrival. In addition, the FAC pilots during this time period were very young and inexperienced pilots. Many of the newly arriving FACs were recent UPT graduates, and this was their first assignment after graduating from UPT.

The 504th Group asked me for my opinion about the O-2A training that I had received. This was unfortunate for the Hurlburt Field training people. I was very dissatisfied with the quality of training that I had received at Hurlburt Field.

My instructor at Hurlburt Field was a very senior major who had been passed over for lieutenant colonel and was just waiting to retire. On many of my training missions, we would take off, fly down to the coast, and fly along the coast between Fort Walton Beach and Pensacola looking for fish. At the end of his day, he would go fishing in the gulf. My instructor would then have me take him back to Hurlburt Field where he would get out. I would then go solo to complete the mission. Having been an IP myself, this did not impress me. I was doing a lot of self-instructing during my O-2A training in Florida. This was okay for me because of my experience, but I knew it would not be satisfactory for a new pilot right out of UPT. I also knew that I was not his first student, and I knew that I was not his last. This type of training in my opinion was totally inadequate to prepare a new young pilot to be a FAC in Vietnam.

My second concern was with the fact that Hurlburt Field was located on the Gulf Coast on the Florida panhandle. This area is extremely flat and fully developed with man-made features. The map-reading skills that they were teaching just were not adequate for a recent UPT graduate that was flying in MRI or MRII in Vietnam. These two military regions were primarily mountains and triple canopy jungle with very few man-made features. I also knew that map-reading skills were not a major focus in UPT. Because most Air Force aircrafts are flown under instrument flight rules (IFR) at high altitudes, pilots do not have much need for map-reading skills using only topographic relief to locate target locations. This probably was not completely Hurlburt Field's fault since the Air Force chose this location to do the O-2A training. It was chosen by the Air Force because of all the fighter bases in this area. This allowed for great training in actual control of fighter aircraft in the close air-support role because of all the ranges available. The 504th Group agreed with me and asked me to prepare a response, which they sent on to Hurlburt Field.

This is when God provided me with the next opportunity as he was guiding my life. The 504th Group agreed with me about the quality of O-2A training and asked if I would go to Nha Trang and set up an in-country training program for all newly arriving FACs. My mission would be to provide the necessary training that I felt was required for all young FACs to be better equipped to be able to successfully do their jobs. I agreed, and after just two months at Phu Bai, I left for Nha Trang to set up a new in-country FAC training program.

At Nha Trang, I was provided with four aircraft and the maintenance personnel to do the training. Additionally, a 504th Group lieutenant colonel, who also had previously been a UPT instructor pilot, volunteered to help me train the new FACs. With his arrival, I knew that I had the full support of the 504th Group. The lieutenant colonel let me design the training syllabus, and then we started the in-country FAC training program out of Nha Trang. I now feel that this new training program was part of God's plan for other pilots whose lives he was guiding. God was leading me to provide the training that these young pilots were not receiving prior to coming to Vietnam. This to me is evidence of how God's plans for all of us are intermingled as we all live our lives. God had seen to it that I was prepared for this important task, which may have saved some of these young pilots' lives in Vietnam.

It was December 1971, and President Nixon was beginning to accelerate the "Vietnamization" of the war. Vietnamization was the US policy to shift the responsibility of the war effort from US troops to the government of South Vietnam. Nixon's goal was to reduce our combat troop strength to 140,000 by January 1972. As part of this reduction of forces, the 504th Group and the 19th TASS were deactivated. All members of the 504th Group and the 19th TASS that had less than four months to go on their one-year tour were going home. I still had seven months to go; therefore, I was going to stay in Vietnam. This was the next opportunity that God provided for me and for which he had prepared me with all the experience I had gained from my T-37 instructor pilot assignment.

Even though the Nineteenth TASS was deactivated on paper, all the aircraft assets were just combined with the Twenty-First TASS located at Tan Son Nhut Air Base at Saigon. The Twenty-First TASS was now a very large squadron with 40 aircraft, 80 pilots, and 230 maintenance personnel. The Twenty-First TASS's area of responsibility for close air-support activities now included MRII, MRIII, and half of Cambodia. I was now on my way to Tan Son Nhut and the Twenty-First TASS. I had never been that far south in Vietnam, and I was not sure what was in store for me.

The squadron commander of the Twenty-First TASS was a lieutenant colonel who had flown B-52s his entire career. He was not very enthused about being a FAC and was going to retire as soon as he returned to the States. The maintenance officer was also a pilot and a major, and he too was not excited about being a FAC. In addition, he too was going to retire upon return to the States. The next opportunity that God provided me with my arrival at the Twenty-First TASS was when I found out that I was the next ranking officer in the squadron. At that time, I was only a midrange captain. This was a total surprise to me, but it did indicate just how young and inexperienced the FACs were in January 1972 in Vietnam.

After I reported in to the Twenty-First TASS, the squadron commander told me that I was going to be the squadron operations officer. This was a job normally filled by a lieutenant colonel. He told me that I would be responsible for all the flying operations of the squadron and that he would take care of all the paperwork. I did not see much of the commander nor of the major maintenance officer as neither of them wanted to fly FAC combat missions. Here I was, a captain, filling a lieutenant colonel's position of a very large combat close air-support squadron with the responsibility for support of half of Vietnam and Cambodia. This kind of reminded me about my Iranian student at Laughlin. I had to get him through the T-37 just to save his life. There was no pressure there, and now I was an operations officer as a captain in Vietnam. Again, no pressure here! We pilots used to have a joke we used when things did not seem to be going well in our careers. We would say, "What are they going to do to me, send me to Vietnam in a O-2A?" Well, they did, but it was all part of God's plan for me.

On March 30, 1972, North Vietnam initiated the 1972 Spring Offensive in an attempt to take over South Vietnam and embarrass the United States as we were drawing down our troops. Our troop levels were scheduled to be down to seventy thousand combat troops by April 1972 when the offensive started. Needless to say, the war was now a very active and "hot" war. I saw even less of the squadron commander and the major during this time period. I will say that the major did a super job keeping our aircraft flying. We were flying twenty-four hours a day every day. The squadron commander did take care of all the paperwork, which allowed me to fly two combat sorties at night and then run the squadron during the day. At times, it was necessary for me to fly the two sorties at night and then two sorties during the day. I was working twenty hours out of every twenty-four-hour day, with four hours of sleep. Our normal requirement for crew rest was not a consideration. In combat, you do what you have to do to save lives and win.

It was during this Spring Offensive when I suffered the second loss of the rear engine during flight. This incident occurred in MRII at night, when I was on my forth mission for that day. MRII was also known as the Central Highlands because the highest peak in South Vietnam, which is 8,524 feet, is located just north of Pleiku. I was checking out a new young FAC. We were returning to Tan Son Nhut from Pleiku after having flown three combat air-support missions in the area around Pleiku.

It was approximately 10:00 p.m., and we had taken off from Pleiku and had climbed up to 9,500 feet of altitude since we were in the mountains of the Central Highlands. This was approximately 3,000 to 4,000 feet above the mountains in the area we were flying over. We had just leveled off, and we were above an overcast in the clear when we lost the rear engine. Of course, it had to be the rear engine that we lost. This was now a situation similar to the first time I lost the rear engine when I was in MRI supporting the army, only worse. We were at night, above an overcast, over mountains in the Central Highlands—where the enemy was known not to take prisoners. As with the first situation, when I lost the rear engine, we were only going to be able to maintain 1,000 to 1,100 feet of altitude for sustain level flight. This meant that we were going to have to descend down to at least that altitude in order to maintain level flight in an area where the terrain was higher than that all the way to the east coast of South Vietnam.

Our choices were very limited. We were too far south of Pleiku to return to Pleiku because of its location in the Central Highlands. Pleiku's elevation was higher than what we were going to need before we would be able to stop our descent. Bailing out at night over an overcast and in the mountains would not be fun. The enemy in MRII did not take prisoners even if we survived the bailout; the one FAC that had bailed out in MRII was found with his Geneva Convention card nailed to his forehead.

The other option we had was to try to make it to the coast where Nha Trang was located, hoping that the decrease in terrain altitude loss going east would be greater that the rate of altitude loss that we were going to be making. The only problem with this option was that Nha Trang is surrounded by mountains on three sides, and we were going to have to make it to the water on the east side of Nha Trang before we arrived at one thousand feet of altitude. Based on my experience, I did feel that we possibly could make it to the east coast and the South China Sea before we got to one thousand feet of altitude. This would place us over water at one thousand feet above the water if all went well.

Since I had this young lieutenant with me, I felt that he should have a say in what we should do. I explained to him our options since we could not make it back to Pleiku. I told him about our bailout option and how the "bad guys" treated prisoners in MRII. I then explained to him that I thought we could make it to the coast before we arrived at one thousand feet. Being young, he deferred the decision to me as to what I thought we should do. I turned east as we began the slow descent heading for Nha Trang. Nha Trang is located on the coast in a valley surrounded by mountains up to 1,500 feet on all sides except the east coast side.

It was going to take us approximately thirty minutes to get to Nha Trang on one engine. I also knew that the next thirty minutes were going to be intense as we began our descent down toward the cloud deck below us. I was hoping that I was correct and that we could make it to the east coast side of Nha Trang before we entered the cloud deck. If we did not make it, I knew the cloud deck would be full of granite.

God had to be watching over us that night because after entering the cloud deck, we broke out over the Bay of Nha Trang about two miles east of the runway. We leveled off at 1,100 feet under the clouds, turned around, and landed uneventfully at Nha Trang.

It took two days to get another engine from Tan Son Nhut to fix our aircraft; after which we returned to Saigon. It was during these two days that I began to really consider that God must have been watching over me. This was totally confirmed on a scheduled mission about a week later after we got back to Tan Son Nhut. This was the mission that I described in the preface of this book, where I knew that God spoke to me, telling me not to fly that day. The important thing about this was that I listened to him. That is when I became a firm believer that when God speaks to us, we need to listen and obey!

I did lose one more engine before I left Vietnam. It was again the rear engine that I lost, but this time, I was in MRIII, which is very flat. The area consists mostly of rice patties with very few mountains in the entire MRIII region. I lost the engine on a mission two days before I was scheduled to return to the States. After I landed at Tan Son Nhut, I decided that I did not really need to fly anymore in Vietnam. The Spring Offensive had pretty much been stopped, and the enemy was retreating back into Cambodia and Laos. Since I was the operations officer, no one was going to direct me to fly anymore.

I finished my tour in Vietnam after completing 317 combat missions and 630 hours of combat time during the 334 days that I was there. I left thirty-one days short of a year due to my follow-on assignment from Vietnam.

The experience I gained in Vietnam as an FAC would never have occurred flying fighters. As a captain, I would never have been an operations officer of a fighter squadron. The Air Force had many lieutenant colonels available to fill fighter squadron slots as operations officer. They certainly would not need a captain to fill one of these positions, even in Vietnam. God made sure that I received an O-2A assignment instead of a fighter to go to Vietnam, just like he made sure I received a T-37 instead of a T-38 for my instructor pilot assignment. Being an operations officer in Vietnam provided me with tremendous experience that helped me throughout the rest of my Air Force career. Once again, God knew what I needed, which was not necessarily what I wanted.

My follow-on assignment was to the Air Force Institute of Technology (AFIT) to obtain a master's degree in engineering. It was during April of 1972, and we were deep into the Spring Offensive, when Air Force Personnel headquarters at Randolph AFB in San Antonio sent a message to me in Vietnam. This message asked me if I would like an AFIT slot after Vietnam to get a master's degree in engineering. Being a pilot, my first instinct was to say no. I wanted to continue flying. In addition, going back to school in engineering was the furthest thing from my mind. I had not thought about engineering since I had graduated from ISU approximately six and a half years earlier. However, I did know that with the war winding down, the Air Force had too many pilots and were looking for ways to get pilots out of the cockpit and into other duties. Besides, with the offensive going on "hot" and "heavy," I was not even sure I was going to make it out of Vietnam. I had lost three of my FACs during April. I needed to think about my follow-on assignment for a day or two.

Here again is more empirical evidence that God was guiding my life. I wanted to continue flying, but God had a different plan for me. As I thought about this opportunity, by the second day, I began to think that getting a master's degree in engineering would not be so bad. By the third day, God had convinced me to accept the assignment. Once again, God knew what I needed, which was different from what I wanted.

My next problem arose when the Air Force Personnel Center said that I needed to take the Scholastic Aptitude Test (SAT) for college admission. So here I was, in Vietnam, fighting a very "hot" war, and going back to school was definitely not my primary focus. In fact, the war was so "hot," and being the operations officer, I was flying two combat sorties each night and was then running the squadron during the day. I was getting four hours of sleep each day between 6:00–8:00 a.m. and 6:00–8:00 p.m. I also wondered where I could even take such a test in Vietnam.

I went over to my local base personnel office and asked them if they could help me. They said that they could not, but they thought that the Military Assistance Command, Vietnam (MACV) could help me out. I went over to their headquarters to see if indeed they could possibly provide me with the assistance that I needed. They indicated that they could not provide me with the SAT test, but they could give me the Advanced Test for Graduate Studies for Business (ATGSB) test. I let personnel know that I could only get the ATGSB test and not the SAT test. They said take the ATGSB test as soon as possible, which I did.

I scheduled the ATGSB test with MACV as soon as they could give it to me. It was during the time that I was flying two night sorties and then running the squadron during the day. I did take the test, but I really do not remember much about it. My mind was definitely elsewhere during that time period. I guess I passed it because I never heard another word about the test. God had to be the one helping me with that test.

The AFIT assignment I received was to the University of Denver (DU) in Colorado to get a master's degree in civil engineering. I needed to be in Denver by June 6, 1972, to start school. This is why I left Vietnam thirty-one days before the end of my scheduled one-year tour.

When my wife and I arrived in Denver with our son to go back to school, reality began to settle in. I had not cracked a college book since 1964, and I became very concerned about being able to compete with these young college students in engineering. I remembered just how difficult the engineering program was at ISU, and I was not sure that I could compete.

It was during my first semester at DU that God provided me with a sign that this was all part of his plan for me, and I should not worry. I was sitting in one of my first engineering classes the day before the midterm exam was scheduled when I felt a tap on my shoulder. I turned around to see the individual that had tapped me was a longhaired hippy type individual who always brought his dog to class with him each day. The dog, a German shepherd, would lie down at the back of the classroom and chew on a beer can. The instructor did not seem to mind, so who was I to say anything. After I turned around, this individual asked me what the textbook for this class looked like. God had just given me the answer to my concern about if I could compete with this younger generation.

I know now that I should not have been worrying about whether I could compete or not since it was God's plan for me to go back to school. The Bible teaches us in Matthew 6:34 (NIV), when Jesus was teaching his followers about worrying, "Therefore do not worry about tomorrow, for tomorrow will worry about itself. Each day has enough trouble of its own." I should not have been worried or concerned since God was guiding my life and knew exactly what I could do even if I did not.

In addition to being able to get my master's degree in engineering, God also provided me with an additional opportunity while at the University of Denver. The Air Force had given me a year and a half to get the engineering master's degree. However, since my undergraduate degree was in aerospace engineering, I only needed one year to complete the requirements for the master's degree in engineering. This left me with a half of a year for me to take other courses. With this extra time, I was able to complete the first year of the master's degree in business administration (MBA), which is a two-year program. I essentially left the University of Denver with one and a half master's degree. What I did not realize then, but God was preparing me for the remainder of my Air Force career and for my life after the Air Force. In addition to the above blessing, God bestowed a second major blessing on Jan and me. Our second son, Randall, was born on August 11, 1973.

I graduated from the University of Denver on December 7, 1973. My next assignment was to Kelly AFB in San Antonio, Texas. I was assigned to the San Antonio Air Logistics Center (ALC) of the Air Force Logistics Command (AFLC) as an engineer. I was assigned to the C-5A Aircraft System Program manager as a structural engineer for the C-5A fleet. Vietnam was now the furthest thing from my mind, but this assignment is what precipitated my return to Vietnam in April 1975. I did not know it yet, but I am sure God did as part of his plan for me.

It was during my first two years at Kelly AFB that God provided me with four opportunities and/or blessings that were all pieces of the puzzle of his plan for me. These four opportunities and/or blessings are also additional empirical evidence of how God works his plan for each of us.

The first blessing that I received was that AFLC had submitted my name to the Air Force promotion board for consideration for promotion to major early. This had to be God's hand at work because I was not yet eligible for promotion to major yet, and AFLC did not even know me as I had never been assigned to AFLC. However, each major command does have the opportunity to submit a very limited number of names for consideration for promotion to the next rank early. The only reason I can think of why AFLC submitted my name had to be due to God's plan for me.

I feel that AFLC submitted my name after reviewing my experience and job levels while being assigned as a T-37 instructor pilot at Laughlin and my efforts in Vietnam. My experience as an O-2A FAC and as a captain filling a lieutenant colonel's position as the operations officer for the Twenty-First TASS had to have impressed them. I would have never been able to gain the level of experience that I did if God had allowed me to do what I wanted instead of what he knew I needed. God knew what he had planned for me, even if I did not know. I was promoted to major a year early by what is known as a "below the zone" promotion.

The second opportunity that God provided me was that I was selected to become the lead structural engineer for the C-5A fleet. I never thought that I would become the lead structural engineer, just like I never thought that I would end up as an operations officer while in Vietnam. This position did, however, precipitate my return to Vietnam in April 1975.

The third opportunity that God provided me was the opportunity to complete my MBA degree. The University of Utah was offering a MBA program at Kelly AFB. They would fly their instructors down to Kelly AFB from Salt Lake City on weekends to provide their courses in order to complete their MBA program. Since I had already completed the first year of the MBA program at the University of Denver, God provided me with the opportunity to be able to complete the last year. This worked out well, and I obtained my MBA degree from the University of Utah. This is just more empirical evidence of how God works his plans for us.

The fourth opportunity that God provided me while at Kelly AFB was that I was able to become a Texas licensed professional engineer (PE). This along with the MBA degree all played a very large part in my life after I retired from the Air Force. God was preparing me for life after the Air Force, and I did not even know it.

It was April 4, 1975, when Vietnam came back into focus as part of my life. When I had left Vietnam in late May 1972, we had been able to stop North Vietnam's attempt to take over South Vietnam during the 1972 Spring Offensive. The United States government had signed the Vietnam Peace Accord with North Vietnam on January 27, 1973. The cease-fire went into effect on January 28, 1973, and we began to pull out the remainder of our combat force. In February 1975, our government cut off all funding for South Vietnam, which left them now on their own. This to me was a signal to North Vietnam that the United States did not care what would happen to South Vietnam.

It was not long after our government cut off the funding to the South when North Vietnam saw an opportunity to once again attempt to take over South Vietnam. In March 1975, North Vietnam once again began another offensive to take over the South. They used the same battle plan to attack the South that they had used in the 1972 Spring Offensive.

In 1972, our airpower and advisors were enough to stop the North, but it was very close. They essentially took over MRI and most of MRII. We were just able to stop them fifty miles north of Saigon in MRIII in 1972. In 1975, without our help, South Vietnam did not have a chance.

When the 1975 Offensive was initiated, President Ford requested $750 million as emergency aid for South Vietnam. Our Congress, however, turned down President Ford's request, which meant that the United States had just turned its back on South Vietnam. To us military types, this felt as if we had sacrificed the loss of over fifty-eight thousand American soldiers for nothing. What it also said was that the military win the battles, but the politicians lose the war. The outcome of the 1975 Offensive was never in doubt: South Vietnam was going to fall.

It was April 4, 1975, when God began to reveal his plan for me. This is the day that a C-5A aircraft crashed in Vietnam after takeoff. This aircraft had just delivered the last of the 105 Howitzers (artillery weapon) from the last approved aid to South Vietnam. Since the war was going very badly for the South, the United States had agreed to airlift a number of orphan children out of the country. The mission was known as "Operation Babylift." These orphans were children who had been fathered by American soldiers whose mothers had abandoned them after the soldiers had left.

It was 5:00 a.m. on April 4, 1975, when I received a phone call from the Kelly AFB command post informing me that a C-5A aircraft had crashed near Tan Son Nhut AB in Vietnam. Being the lead C-5A structural engineer, I was on the list to be notified if any C-5A aircraft had a serious problem. Even with this call, I still was not thinking that this might have a significant impact on me. That all changed when the command post called me again at 8:00 a.m. They informed me that the four-star commander of the Military Airlift Command (MAC) had requested two C-5A engineers from Kelly AFB be assigned to the aircraft accident board that he had just formed. The command post also informed me that our two-star Logistics Center commander had chosen our lead mechanical engineer and me, the lead structural engineer, as the two engineers. They also informed me that the MAC commander was sending his C-135 aircraft to Kelly AFB to pick us up at noon that day to go to Vietnam. I was now on my way back to Vietnam.

It was not until I started to reflect back over my life that I began to understand that all of this was part of God's plan for me. He had provided me the opportunity to go to AFIT after my O-2A FAC assignment to get my master's degree (MS) in engineering. He then provided me the opportunity to be assigned to Kelly AFB where the C-5A aircraft was being managed by the Air Force. He then saw that I was selected to be the lead structural engineer, which I know now was all part of his plan for me.

The accident board arrived in Vietnam on April 5, 1975. There were thirty-four members assigned to the board with a two-star general as the accident board president. The Air Force does not assign many two-star generals as accident board presidents. This indicated just how important this accident was to the Air Force and why the cause of the accident had to be determined.

As far as the number of people on board this aircraft, we knew that there were 145 orphan babies and 102 older children. There also were 50 secretaries from the US Embassy who were being evacuated out of South Vietnam. Because the conditions of the war were getting very serious, an additional unknown number of US personnel had also been loaded on the aircraft just before takeoff that had not been included on the manifest for flight. They had been added at the last minute just before takeoff. All we knew was that 175 people had survived, but more than 150 had been lost. This was a very serious accident investigation, and it was very critical that the cause be determined.

The accident investigation was conducted under very difficult conditions. The aircraft accident site could not be secured, and hundreds of local South Vietnamese were picking up parts of the aircraft on a daily basis to sell to junkyards. In addition, the war was going on all around the accident site. It was becoming very obvious that the South was not going to be able to stop the North from taking over the country this time. In fact, while we were there, two South Vietnamese F-5 pilots defected and tried to bomb the South Vietnamese president's palace. Soon after that, the South Vietnamese president resigned and left the country. It was not looking good for South Vietnam.

We did what we could, and then on April 27, 1975, the team had to leave Vietnam. We departed Vietnam on two C-141 aircraft filled with recovered accident aircraft parts. These two C-141 aircraft were the last fixed wing aircraft to leave Tan Son Nhut AB. The next day, the North cratered the runway, which closed the base for fixed wing aircraft operations. On April 30, 1975, three days after we had departed, South Vietnam fell to the North. God had to be watching over us and got us out just before the country fell.

There were two reasons we were able to determine the cause of this accident in the limited amount of time that we had in Vietnam. The first was due to the fact that both the pilot and copilot had survived the crash. They were able to provide us with the information as to when the incident that caused the crash actually started.

The incident that started the sequence that resulted in the crash actually started after the aircraft had taken off and was climbing to altitude over the South China Sea approximately twenty-five miles southeast of Tan Son Nhut. At approximately twenty-three thousand feet, there was a very loud explosion, and a rapid depressurization of the aircraft occurred. It was soon very evident that the aft ramp of the aircraft had failed and split in half with one-half of the aft ramp and pressure door departing the aircraft. With the ramp and pressure door departure, the hydraulic lines to the flight controls were severely damaged. The ramp section and pressure door fell into the South China Sea. This information allowed us to focus on the aft ramp area and locking system of the aft ramp. With limited flight controls, the aircraft crashed as it was trying to return to Tan Son Nhut AB.

It turned out that it was very important that the accident board president was a two-star general. He had enough rank to get the Navy to search the bottom floor of the South China Sea in an attempt to recover the missing aft ramp section and pressure door. They were successful in their attempt, and the aft ramp section and pressure door were recovered two days prior to our leaving South Vietnam. This was the second reason that we were able to determine the cause of this accident.

These two facts allowed us to determine that we probably had all the information and physical evidence that we were going to get to determine the cause of this accident. This allowed us to depart on April 27, 1975, three days before the South fell to the North. God definitely had to be guiding our efforts.

The next challenge that the board faced was with the two-star general board president. When the board began analyzing all the information and physical evidence available, we had determined that the initial cause of the accident sequence started with the right side of the aft ramp locking system. The C-5A aft ramp locking system consists of seven locks on each side of the aft ramp. These locks are activated by a single hydraulic actuator, which locks and unlocks all seven locks when activated. When we inspected the aft ramp section that the Navy had recovered from the bottom of the South China Sea, we found that the first two locks had come unlocked as there was no damage on these locking mechanisms. The third lock had only minor damage. We knew that somehow these three locks had come unlocked during the climb out phase of the flight at twenty-three thousand feet. When this occurred, all the aircraft pressurization forces that these three locks were holding immediately transferred to the remaining four locks. This loading overstressed the aft ramp, causing it to split in half. Since the pressure door is connected to the aft ramp, both the aft ramp section and pressure door departed the aircraft, causing the rapid, explosive depressurization of the aircraft. The question that needed to be answered became just what caused these three locks to come unlocked in flight. A little history is now needed concerning the two-star general and the actual procurement of the C-5A weapon system.

When the two-star general board president was a colonel, he had been the System Program Office (SPO) director when the Air Force procured the C-5A aircraft. He was now the deputy director of Maintenance for all the Military Airlift Command's aircraft. There were two different theories being discussed by the board, which caused the problem.

The first theory, which was being sponsored by the two-star general, was "DESIGN DEFICIENCY." The second theory being proposed was "maintenance error." Myself and the other engineer from Kelly AFB and Lockheed were sponsoring this theory. The general was basing his theory on the fact that there was only one actuator for all seven locks. He was insisting that Lockheed should have designed the system with a separate actuator for each lock. The other engineer and I, on the other hand, believed that although not the best design, the single actuator system was adequate but did require a significant amount of maintenance activity to keep the system operating properly.

The way the seven-lock system with a single actuator works is that a system of tie rods are installed between each of the seven locks. These tie rods have to be of a precise length to ensure all seven locks reach an overcenter and locked position when the actuator is activated to lock the ramp. The overcenter and locked position is achieved when all seven locks are driven to a position that is three to seven degrees overcenter. This position is extremely critical for this type of system. When the system is properly rigged, the single actuator is adequate to do the job. The rigging of the system ensures that the tie rods establish the proper position between each lock to ensure that all seven locks are driven to the three to seven degrees overcenter position. This only becomes a problem if any of these tie rods are removed for maintenance activity and then replaced and the system is not rerigged. Even if only a single tie rod is removed and replaced, all seven locks have to be rerigged to ensure the proper distance between each lock is reestablished when the single actuator is activated.

When we reviewed the aircraft maintenance records for this aircraft, we discovered that the two tie rods between locks 1, 2, and 3 had been removed. When these two tie rods were replaced, we discovered that the right side aft ramp locking system had not been properly rerigged to ensure proper distance between these three locks. It takes a full eight-hour shift to properly rerig a locking system if any component of that system has been removed and then replaced. On this particular aircraft, these two tie rods had been replaced at the middle of an eight-hour shift. The shift ended without the rerigging of the system completed. This shift merely replaced the tie rods. When the next maintenance crew began their shift, they saw that the tie rods had been replaced and assumed that the system had been rerigged by the previous shift of maintenance personnel. The rerigging procedure had not been completed on this aircraft.

The difference in these two theories as to the cause of the accident would have a significant impact on who would be held responsible for this accident. If the cause was determined to be

DESIGN DEFICIENCY, then the aircraft manufacturer, Lockheed, would bear the responsibility. If the cause was determined to be "maintenance error," then the Air Force and the Military Airlift Command (MAC) would bear the responsibility for the accident. This put the two-star general in a no-win position.

As with most Air Force aircraft procurement programs, the weapon system program usually runs into cost and weight overruns. This results as additional requirements for the weapon system are added after the initial contract is issued. The C-5A program was no exception. In fact, the Air Force gave Lockheed an incentive of $300 for every pound that it could save. Therefore, a gang-locking ramp system for seven locks with one actuator would save the weight of six actuators on each side of the aft ramp. This would be a significant weight savings of twelve aft ramp actuators. The resulting locking system would be adequate, but not the best system. The price that is paid is that a significant amount of maintenance activity is required to keep the system operating properly.

As previously mentioned, when the two-star general was a colonel, he was in charge of the System Program Office (SPO) for the C-5A. Therefore, he had to know about the decision to allow a single actuator system to be used. In fact, as the C-5A SPO director, he most likely had to sign off on the approval for Lockheed to use this system. Now as the deputy director of Maintenance for MAC, he was responsible for any maintenance actions that had been completed on this aircraft. As a result, he was now forced to choose between "I didn't do my job as a colonel" or "I am not doing my job now as a two-star general." Since he was now in charge of the accident board to determine the cause of this accident, he obviously chose the former to be the cause of this accident.

This caused the other Kelly engineer and me a significant problem, myself in particular since I had just received my registration as a licensed professional engineer (PE) in the state of Texas. I just could not accept his version as the cause of the accident as DESIGN DEFICIENCY because I truly felt that the cause was maintenance error. My integrity as a PE just would not let me accept a cause that I truly felt was not correct.

The problem began when each day the general would hold a 9:00 a.m. meeting to discuss the progress of the investigation. Each day he would walk into the meeting room and write "DESIGN DEFICIENCY" in big bold letters on the blackboard. He was a large intimidating man standing at six feet four or six feet five with two stars on his shoulder. He was not having any problem convincing the remaining members of the accident board to agree with him as to the cause of this accident. However, each day after he wrote "DESIGN DEFICIENCY" on the blackboard, he would then turn around and either the other engineer from Kelly AFB or I would raise our hand. When the general acknowledged us, we would then say that we could not support "DESIGN DEFICIENCY" as the cause of this accident. We would then go on further to say that we strongly felt that the cause of this accident was "maintenance error." We took turns doing this for a week.

This action, of course, did not go over well with the general. He obviously was not accustomed to having two majors disagree with him, especially in front of others. Each day after we made our statement, the general would immediately go into a tirade about why the cause was "DESIGN DEFICIENCY," after which he would end the meeting. At the end of a week and his daily tirades, he said he no longer wanted us on his accident board. He essentially kicked us off the board. We indicated to him that we would have to write a dissenting report to his accident board report that was going to the Air Force Safety Office. His response was, "Do whatever you have to do."

Since I was the C-5A lead structural engineer, and Kelly AFB was the C-5A system program manager, all of the C-5A recovered aircraft accident parts belonged to Kelly AFB for disposal. So essentially, the other engineer and I took our parts and went home. We now had to inform our two-star general ALC commander that we had been kicked off the accident board and why.

When two major disagree with a two-star general, it usually does not turn out well for the two majors. Our two-star general, however, supported us and gave us an empty hangar for all the parts and said, "Go prove your theory." He also indicated that he would sign our dissenting report if we could prove our theory. Our theory became known as the *San Antonio Position*.

Our theory was based on the engineering aspects of this type of locking system. The way the engineering aspects of this system works is that there are forces generated in the tie rods as the inside cabin pressurization forces build while the aircraft climbs to altitude. If the locks are in three to seven degrees overcenter and locked position, these forces attempt to drive the locks further to an overcenter and locked position. If these locks, however, have not achieved the three to seven degrees overcenter position during the locking sequence, then the forces generated in the tie rods while the cabin pressurization forces increase during the climb to altitude will try to drive the locks to an unlocked position. This is why the rigging of the locking system is so critical.

Based on the physical evidence found on the aft ramp section that the Navy had recovered from the South China Sea, the locking mechanisms on the first two locks had no damage. In addition, the third lock mechanisms on the ramp had only very slight damage present. Our theory was that since the right side aft ramp locking system had not been rerigged when the tie rods were replaced, the evidence indicated that the first three locks on the right side had not achieved the three to seven degrees overcenter and locked position after the ramp had been closed at Tan Son Nhut prior to takeoff.

The next question we had to answer was why did this accident happen on takeoff from Tan Son Nhut and not on the first takeoff from Travis AFB when the aircraft departed for Vietnam. The answer was that the aft ramp had not been used prior to its arrival in Vietnam. When the tie rods were replaced at Travis AFB, the aft ramp had been locked, and the system had not been activated since the tie rods had been removed. This meant that the three locks were in the three to seven degrees overcenter and locked position when the tie rods were replaced, but the maintenance personnel failed to rerig the system. Therefore, on the initial takeoff and climb out from Travis AFB en route to Vietnam, the locks were still in the three to seven degrees overcenter and locked position. As the forces were generated in the tie rods as the cabin pressurization forces increased, these three locks either stayed in the locked position or at least were not being driven to an unlocked position.

The conditions to cause this accident, as a result of not rerigging the system, were put in place with the use of the aft ramp at Tan Son Nhut AB. This was the first opening of the aft ramp since the tie rods had been replaced. Our theory was that when the aft ramp was closed at Tan Son Nhut, this was the first activation of the aft ramp with the system not being properly rigged. As a result of not being properly rigged, on closure, lock number 1 did not reach the overcenter position at all due to a short tie rod distance. We also theorized that lock number 2 stopped at the top dead center location during locking. We further theorized that lock number 3 did reach an overcenter position but was short of the three to seven degrees locked overcenter position.

With the closure of the aft ramp at Tan Son Nhut, the conditions were now in place for the engineering aspects of this locking system to be in play in a negative way. As the forces in the tie rods were developed as the cabin pressurization forces increased while the aircraft was climbing to altitude, the forces being generated in the tie rods were actually working in a negative way. From the engineering perspective, since the first three locks were not in the proper three to seven degrees overcenter position, the forces being generated in the tie rods were actually trying to unlock these three locks. We theorized that at approximately twenty-three thousand feet, the developing pressurization forces in the tie rods were sufficient to cause the number 2 lock that was top dead center to move to the unlocked position. This was the loud bang that had been reported just prior to the rapid explosive decompression that was experienced. With locks 1 and 2 now unlocked, the number 3 lock was now pulled back to the unlocked position since it had not achieved the proper three to seven degrees overcenter position. With all the pressurization forces now being dumped onto the remaining four aft ramp locks, the structural limit of the aft ramp was exceeded, causing the aft ramp to split. With the pressure door being connected to the aft ramp, it too departed the aircraft when the aft ramp failed.

With our ALC commander's support, computer and metallurgical failure analysis, we were able to prove our theory. We were able to duplicate the failure pattern and sequence of our theory to within three hundred feet of the twenty-three thousand feet where this aircraft had experienced the rapid, explosive depressurization event that caused this accident. Our theory of "maintenance error" as the cause of this accident had been proven.

We wrote our dissenting report, and our two-star commander signed it. We then submitted it to the Air Force Safety Office for consideration as to the cause of this accident as opposed to "DESIGN DEFICIENCY" that had been submitted by the accident board.

It was a very difficult time for us at Kelly AFB as we waited for the Air Force Safety Office to decide which cause of the accident they were going to accept. Even our two-star general now had "skin in the game." He was essentially disagreeing with another two-star general. For me, it was very critical because if Air Force Safety did not accept our report, I knew I would no longer have a career in the Air Force. If we lost, at least our two-star commander could retire. I did not have sufficient time in to retire.

As we were waiting, the other engineer elected to retire. He had been enlisted before going to Officer Candidate School (OCS) to become an officer. He had obtained his engineering degree and now had reached twenty years of service and decided he would retire. That left my commander and me waiting to hear the result of the Air Force Safety Office since both of our careers were at stake.

After a six-month wait, the Air Force Safety Office finally released their decision. It was a very short message that was sent directly to my commander, who immediately called me at my desk. When I answered the phone, my commander said, "Dave, I want to read something to you." He read, "The Air Force Safety Office concurs with the 'San Antonio Position' as the cause of the C-5A aircraft accident on 4 April 1975 in Vietnam."

With that phone call, a tremendous weight was lifted off my shoulders. I knew that if the Air Force Safety Office had agreed with the accident board's position, I would no longer have a career in the Air Force. In fact, the two-star general accident board president was not as fortunate. He was given a week to retire, and he also lost a star. I did feel sorry for him, but on the other hand, I was now going to be able to continue with my career.

As I reflected back over this time, I feel that this period of time contains a significant amount of empirical evidence of God's work in my life. Only God could have guided all these events to happen. He guided my education decision in college, and then he guided my postgraduate studies to get a master's degree in engineering. He guided my assignment to Kelly AFB and then provided me the opportunity to become the lead C-5A structural engineer. He also provided me with the opportunity to become a licensed professional engineer (PE) in the state of Texas, which has a specific code of ethics that we are required to follow. If the accident board's report had been accepted, the true cause of the accident would not have been determined. I truly feel that God wanted me on that accident board investigation team as part of his overall plan.

As a result of this accident, a number of lawsuits were filed against the Air Force. If "DESIGN DEFICIENCY" had been determined to be the cause, all the lawsuits would have been filed against Lockheed. This would not have been a fair or just action for Lockheed. The amount of the lawsuits totaled $50 million. That was a very significant number back in 1975. With "maintenance error" being the cause of this accident, the Air Force was now being held accountable for all lawsuit settlements and correctly so. God made sure that the correct cause was determined as it had a significant impact on a large number of people.

With the Air Force Safety Office concurring with the "San Antonio Position" as to the cause of the accident, I was not finished with this event. With me being the only one left in the Air Force who had written the report, the responsibility to defend the Air Force in the legal defense of these lawsuits fell upon me. This took approximately the next ten years to settle all these lawsuits.

The lawsuits had been filed on behalf of the fifty embassy secretaries, the orphans from Vietnam, and the other service members that had perished in the accident. When one of these lawsuits would come to trial, I would be required to go to Washington, DC, to give a deposition on behalf of the Air Force. With each of these depositions, the Air Force did provide me with three lawyers to assist me.

Having been promoted to major "below the zone" automatically qualified me to attend the Air Force's Command and Staff College

(ACSC) at Maxwell AFB in Alabama. This course of study is equivalent to getting a master's degree in Air Force doctrine. Being able to go in residence is a significant honor. After completing my assignment at Kelly AFB, I was assigned to go to ACSC in 1977, which was a yearlong course.

It was at ACSC that again I realized that God was guiding my life as additional empirical evidence surfaced. This is when Ray Leach from my Undergraduate Pilot Training (UPT) class had a significant impact on my life. This is why I feel that God kept me in Class 66E when I had hurt my knee so badly. Ray and I had kept in touch periodically throughout the years. We even made contact in Vietnam. He had also chosen an instructor pilot (IP) slot out of UPT. Being number one in the class, he got his choice of assignment. He elected to stay at Reese AFB in T-38s. He chose an IP slot because, being a captain and now a newly rated pilot, he knew that he had to acquire a lot of flying time in a short period of time in order to be competitive with his peers for promotion to major. After he completed his IP assignment at Reese, he received an F-4 fighter assignment to Vietnam. He was stationed at Da Nang when I was at Hue Phu Bai flying O-2As.

We both had chosen IP slots because we both wanted to get a lot of experience and flying time in a short period of time. He wanted it to be competitive with his peers, and I wanted it because I did not want to fly as a copilot in the back seat of an F-4. It worked for me because when I left Laughlin AFB in January 1971, I had over 2,500 total flying hours with over 2,000 IP hours and zero copilot time. I am sure he did as well.

While I was at ACSC, Ray was flying F-111s at Cannon AFB in Clovis, New Mexico. Ray had been able to stay in fighters after leaving Vietnam. He did this even though the Air Force did not have enough cockpits available for all the pilots as a result of the Vietnam War. Ray, however, knew the fighter assignment representative for Air Force fighter assignments at Randolph AFB in San Antonio, Texas. They had served together, so Ray made a few calls for me and got me as assignment to F-111s at Cannon AFB. I had always wanted a fighter, and this time, it was God's plan for me to get one. Only God could have guided me in the Air Force to arrive at this point, and the empirical evidence supports this.

I received an F-111 assignment to Cannon AFB in 1978. When I arrived at Cannon AFB, I was told that I would be there for two years and then I would be going to Lakenheath AB in England. Lakenheath AB also had F-111s stationed there, and this was the normal follow-on assignment for F-111 pilots leaving Cannon AFB. However, this was not God's plan for me. He had a different plan as far as where I would be flying the F-111.

Cannon AFB was the home of the Twenty-Seventh Tactical Fighter Wing (TFW). There were four squadrons of F-111D aircraft at Cannon. The 481st Tactical Fighter Squadron (TFS) was a training squadron for the 27th TFW. There were two combat squadrons stationed at Cannon: the 522th TFS and the 524th TFS. The other squadron was the 523th TFS and was a replacement training unit (RTU). Their mission was to provide replacement training for all aircrew going to Lakenheath AB in England. Lakenheath AB had F-111F aircraft stationed there. The F-111D was the first digital aircraft for the Air Force, and the F-111F was the follow-on version of the digital aircraft. Ray Leach was the 523 TFS Squadron Commander when I received my F-111 assignment.

After completing my checkout in the 481st TFS, I was assigned to the 524th TFS. This is when God's plan for me at Cannon AFB began to be revealed. Being a major, I was assigned as an assistant operations officer for the squadron. I was very surprised as this was a high position for someone who had just become an F-111 pilot. I do not know, but I suspect that Ray Leach might have had a say as to where I was assigned.

As I was approaching the two-year point at Cannon AFB, I was expecting to receive an assignment to Lakenheath as I had been told would happen. God, however, had a different plan for me when he provided a new opportunity at Cannon AFB. The wing commander asked me if I would like to stay at Cannon AFB as the director of wing training for the Twenty-Seventh TFW. I guess they felt that because of my UPT instructor experience and the fact that I had set up an O-2A in-country training program in Vietnam, I would be a good fit for them as the director of wing training. This position also provided me with another opportunity, in that I was upgraded to an Instructor Pilot (IP) in the F-111. I know that God had to be guiding me because he had provided all the previous flying training experience in my previous assignments as he guided my life. This Wing position also froze me at Cannon AFB for another two years. In addition, I had been promoted to Lt. Colonel while I was in the 524th TFS.

After two years as director of wing training, God provided me with another opportunity at Cannon AFB, which again froze me for an additional two years. The wing commander selected me to become the operations officer of the 523rd TFS. This was the RTU squadron for the training of aircrews going to Lakenheath AB in England. Since I was already an IP, I had no problem fitting into the 523rd TFS. It is kind of ironic, but I had now gotten back to the level of responsibility that I had as a captain when I was the operations officer of the Twenty-First TASS in Vietnam. This is just more empirical evidence of God's plan for me.

When the two years as the 523rd TFS operations officer was up, God provided me with another tremendous opportunity at Cannon AFB. When the 523rd TFS squadron commander position became available, I was selected to become its squadron commander. This was also ironic because this was the same squadron that Ray Leach had been the commander of when I arrived at Cannon AFB. Being selected for this position could have only been due to God's hand in making this happen. There were many factors involved that indicated that I would not be selected to become a squadron commander.

This first major factor was that all squadron commanders had to live on base. When I was first assigned to Cannon AFB, base housing was not available, so we had purchased a house in town. To live off base as a squadron commander required the approval of the Twelfth Air Force commander, a three-star general stationed at Bergstrom AFB in Austin, Texas. This is where I know that God had to have intervened on my behalf because the three-star general approved my living off base. This was against normal Tactical Air Command (TAC) policy for their Squadron Commanders.

The second major factor for me to be approved as a squadron commander involved my wife. Jan had always worked during most of my assignments. She had her teaching degree in English and had taught English at Del Rio High School during our assignment at Laughlin AFB. Her teaching job in Del Rio was one of the reasons she stayed in Del Rio while I was in Vietnam. We had purchased a house in Del Rio again because of the lack of base housing at Laughlin AFB when we arrived.

While we were in Denver and I was going to school, she did not teach since we were only to be there for a year and a half. In addition, God blessed us with our second son while we were in Denver.

While we were stationed at Kelly AFB in San Antonio, Texas, she actually taught at two different high schools. Even when we were at ACSC College at Maxwell AFB in Montgomery, Alabama, she taught that year at a private school. When we arrived at Cannon AFB and thinking that we would only be there for two years, she decided to get her master's degree in guidance and counseling at Eastern New Mexico University. When it became apparent that we were not going to Lakenheath on the time schedule that we had been told, she got an opportunity to be the director of guidance and counseling at the local junior college in Clovis, New Mexico. This was the job she had when I was selected to be the 523rd TFS commander. To me, this is empirical evidence that God was also guiding Jan's life, as he was mine, as he was providing opportunities for her.

In the Tactical Air Command (TAC), squadron commanders' wives are considered to be a very important aspect in the life and functioning of the squadron. They essentially have to be den mothers to the wives of all members of the squadron. Normally, wives of squadron commanders do not work because it possibly would interfere with the duties that the squadron commander's wife is expected to perform.

Naturally, Jan did not like the idea that she would have to give up her job. She felt that she was not the one in the Air Force; only I was. I really could not blame her for feeling that way. She had worked very hard to get to where she was, and she had an excellent job. Being in the TAC and flying F-111s, we deployed a lot, and her job helped her while I was gone. I also was not going to ask her to give up her job. Although, I knew she would have if I had asked her. That is just the kind of wife she is.

This again is when I know that God intervened on our behalf. To become a TAC squadron commander, all candidates had to be interviewed by the three-star Twelfth Air Force commander. The subject of my wife's working came up in my interview. The wing commander had briefed the three-star general that I lived off base and that my wife was working. The general asked me if she would be able to complete her duties as the squadron commander's wife. I knew that Jan did not want to quit her job, and I also knew she would perform her duties as the squadron commander's wife in an excellent manner.

I confirmed to him that my wife could do both: work and perform her squadron commander's wife duties. The three-star paused a moment and then agreed to allow her to continue working. I think I was the first squadron commander to live off base and have a wife that worked. Only God could have made this possible. To me, this is just more empirical evidence that God does exist.

As I reflect back over this time period, I feel that God was working to keep me at Cannon AFB beyond the two years that I was initially told for a specific reason. We actually stayed at Cannon AFB for seven years.

The reason I feel that we stayed at Cannon AFB so long goes back to the C-5A accident and report. I feel that it was his plan for me to be on that accident board, and that was the reason he provided me with the opportunity to get my master's degree in engineering and then be assigned to Kelly AFB. He also guided me to obtain my professional engineer (PE) license while at Kelly AFB and become the C-5A lead structural engineer. It was his plan that I was assigned to that accident board, and then he guided me to stand up to the two-star general accident board president. This resulted in the correct cause of that accident being accepted by the Air Force.

Now I feel that God wanted me at Cannon AFB for the seven years so that I would be available to provide the depositions for the lawsuits against the Air Force as a result of that C-5A accident. If

I had been in England at Lakenheath AB, there would have been significant delays on getting me back to Washington, DC, each time a deposition was required.

During the seven years that we were at Cannon AFB, I was called to Washington, DC, a number of times. When I was needed, the wing commander would get a call from the Pentagon, and then he would call me and tell me to take an F-111 and go to Washington to give my deposition. This made it very handy and allowed me to be able to be responsive to the lawyers' requests. This saved time and did not detract much from my assigned duties at Cannon AFB. It would have been a lot more difficult if I would have to come from Lakenheath each time a deposition was needed.

During my time at Cannon AFB, I also know that God was watching over me and was guiding my life. We did not have any aircraft accidents in any of the squadrons that I was in during my time as assistant operations officer, operations officer, and as squadron commander. There were aircraft accidents in the wing, but none in any of the squadrons that I was in.

It was during the time that I was assigned as the director of wing training that a reorganization of the wing occurred. The wing decreased from four squadrons to three. This was due to the loss of a few aircraft. The 481st TFS remained as the training squadron for the Wing. The 522nd TFS remained as the primary combat squadron for the Wing. The 524th TFS, which was the second combat squadron, was disbanded as part of the reorganization. The 523rd TFS remained as the replacement training unit (RTU) for Lakenheath, but also picked up the responsibility as the second combat squadron. This meant that the 523rd TFS had instructor pilots and instructor weapons system officers (IWSOs) for the RTU responsibilities and also had combat crews assigned to fulfill the combat role that the 523rd now had for the wing.

The reorganization was also completed to better utilize the aircraft and help the wing be able to maintain the aircraft more efficiently. This allowed the wing to be able to obtain and then sustain the level of mission readiness required for tactical fighter wings in the Air Force. The F-111D fleet of aircraft had always been hindered by a lack of spare parts, and being the Air Force's first digital aircraft, we could never reach the mission-readiness level required by the Air Force. It was not until President Reagan increased the military budget that sufficient parts were procured for the F-111D that we were able to meet and sustain mission-readiness standards. During the time period that the F-111D aircraft had been assigned to Cannon AFB, the wing was never at a high enough mission-readiness level to receive an Operations Readiness Inspection (ORI) from headquarters of the Tactical Air Command (TAC).

The Operations Readiness Inspection (ORI) exercise is when a wing is tested by the Tactical Air Command (TAC) to determine if it can perform its wartime mission responsibilities. The results of these ORI exercises determine if tactical wing commanders make general and if squadron commanders make full colonel. I was the 523rd TFS commander when Cannon AFB received its first ORI exercise.

These inspections usually start at some very unusual time of the day or week. It is normal to think that an enemy is most likely not going to start a war on Monday at 8:00 a.m. Our ORI started on Sunday at 10:00 a.m. when no flying was scheduled. A team from the Tactical Air Command (TAC) landed unannounced at Cannon AFB and started our ORI inspection. Once started, the two combat squadrons had one hour to get everyone back to the base. In our case, it was the 522nd TFS and my squadron, the 523rd TFS, which were being tested. The 481st training squadron was not involved.

With the ORI starting on Sunday morning, and with no cell phones, pagers, or other modern-day communication devices available, we had to depend on our squadron alert rosters. This roster was a paper list of all member of the squadron listed by flights. Each flight commander was responsible for getting his aircrews back to the base within the one-hour period required. It was my responsibility to contact each flight commander to get the alert roster started as soon as I was notified by the command post that the ORI had started. If this one-hour time period is not met, the wing fails the ORI before it even gets fully started.

You can only imagine what it was like getting all of our aircrews back to the base with only landline phones and face-to-face contact. All four of my flight commanders and I were going around to the churches in Clovis looking for our Air Force personnel to get them back to the base before the hour was up. My living off base turned out to be an advantage for me. Both squadrons were able to get everyone back with God's help.

The next critical point was that both squadrons had to pack up all of their war reserve materials (WRM) that would be required if we were actually going to war. In fact, in a way, we actually were. We had twenty-four hours to complete this task for both of the flying squadrons. The maintenance squadrons were required to pack up all of our war reserve spare parts kits (WRSK) that would be required, as well as get all twenty-four aircraft in each squadron ready for flight. At the end of the twenty-four-hour period, both squadrons had to deploy all twenty-four of their aircraft to prove that we could actually do it and that all aircraft were actually mission-ready. Both the 522nd and the 523rd squadrons completed this requirement.

The next phase of the ORI started twenty-four hours later after we had proven that we could deploy all of our aircraft. Each of the squadrons had to be able to fly forty-five sorties a day on their twenty-four aircraft for three days and then continue operations by flying thirty sorties a day thereafter. Our normal flying schedule consisted of flying fifteen sorties a day for each squadron. The forty-five-/thirty-sortie rate for each squadron was our wartime tasking if we ever did have to go to war.

To maintain this sortie rate for the F-111D aircraft was very taxing for both maintenance and the flight crews. It meant that most crews had to fly twice a day, and the aircraft had to turn two or three times in a twenty-four-hour period in order to achieve this sortie rate. This included any aircraft repairs needed after each flight as well as the loading of the weapons on each aircraft for each mission. For the F-111D aircraft, this was a significant challenge since our mean time between failures (MTBF) was only 6.8 hours. This sortie rate was a formative tasking for the F-111D.

I know that God had to be watching over us and was guiding our efforts. I did not have to worry much about my instructor pilots and instructor WSOs, but I did have to worry about my young and inexperienced combat crews. All of my combat crews were young lieutenants on their first assignments after undergraduate pilot or navigator training. I had approximately twelve of these young lieutenant crews.

It is interesting to note just how fast experienced combat pilots were no longer present in the field. The US pulled all of its combat forces out of Vietnam in 1973. At that time, a significant number of fighter pilots had combat experience. Just ten years later in 1983, in the 523rd TFS, we had only 4 percent combat-experienced pilots present. My operations officer and I represented this 4 percent. We both had been O-2A forward air controllers (FACs) in Vietnam. There were no other combat-experienced pilots available.

With the ORI being a test of our wartime capabilities, and with only myself and my operations officer with combat experience, the remainder of my squadron did not have any idea just how taxing this exercise would be. This is where my experience as an operations officer in Vietnam during the Spring Offensive in 1972 paid off. This is another example of empirical evidence of God's plan for me. I knew exactly what it was going to take to ensure the 523rd TFS did well on the ORI.

I flew the first mission of our assigned missions because I knew I would have to work very closely with our maintenance personnel to match aircrews to aircraft. I know that many of the aircraft would not be completely mission ready for each mission due to the failure rate of the F-111 in order to fly forty-five sorties a day. This meant that after the first day, I would no longer have the required crew rest to fly additional missions. I was going to ride with the maintenance flight line supervisor to decide which crews should fly which aircraft since many of the systems would not be available for use by the crew. There were always going to be aircraft discrepancies after each flight.

My job, therefore, was to match the aircrews that I knew had the capability of flying each mission with discrepancies that could not be cleared between the missions. To do this, I was on the flight line for 6:00 a.m. until 2:00 a.m. the next morning. I was able to get a couple of hours of sleep and then be back on the flight line at 6:00 a.m. to start the next day of sorties. It was similar to my schedule in Vietnam during the 1972 Spring Offensive. I had to depend on my operations officer to run the squadron while I was on the flight line. I was essentially matching aircrew capabilities to what systems were or were not available on each aircraft in order to maximize our best chance of completing a successful mission.

I know that God had to be guiding me because on one specific mission, I had to make a very critical decision as to whether to let one of my young inexperienced lieutenant crews fly a mission in an aircraft which was in need of serious repairs.

This particular mission was scheduled to be a live drop of twelve Mark 82 bombs (five-hundred-pound bombs) on a target at a small range in Colorado that I knew this aircrew had never been to. I also knew that a TAC flight examiner aircrew would be chasing the aircraft since this would be a live drop of bombs. The aircraft that had been scheduled for this mission needed repairs to the inertial navigation system (INS), the weapons radar, and the weapons release computer. All these systems are needed for the WSO to assist the pilot to complete the mission. Unfortunately, all these systems were inoperative, so the WSO would be along just for the ride. We did not have time to change aircraft because the bombs were already loaded on this aircraft. In order to make the time over target, this aircraft had to go. The crew that was scheduled for this mission was one of my young inexperienced lieutenant crews.

I was very familiar with both of these crew members. I had flown with each of them during their checkout to become combat ready. Without any of the technology in the right seat working, this F-111D was essentially a two-engine F-100 aircraft. The crew would have to navigate to the target area, and the pilot would have to drop the bombs manually without any technical support from the WSO.

I made the decision to send this young crew in this aircraft because we just did not have enough time to load another aircraft, and I did know this crew. This decision was fraught with all kinds of possible disasters that could go wrong. Even the maintenance supervisor knew what this decision meant if things went south.

I met my young crew at the aircraft as they arrived to begin their preflight of the aircraft. I started our conversation with, "I've got some good news and some bad news." I told my young crew that the bad news was that they would not have an INS, a radar, or a weapons delivery computer for this mission. I told the pilot that he would have to make a manual visual delivery of the bombs. I told them that the good news was that I knew that they could do it. They both looked at me with a noticeable disbelief on their faces. I then said to them, "I have flown with both of you, and I know you are capable of completing this mission." I then said to them, "You guys get into the aircraft, and I will do your preflight."

As the crew taxied out for takeoff, the maintenance supervisor and I just looked at each other, both thinking without saying it, *What have we done?* I had the same feeling that I had when I soloed my Iranian student Ammand in the T-37. I was again betting my wings.

The next two and one-half hours were very tense for us as we waited to hear the results of this mission. We could listen to the command post frequency in our truck to hear the results of the weapons delivery when the TAC flight examiner crew reported back the results of live-drop missions. While we were waiting, I had the same type of feeling I had when I lost the rear engine at night while flying the O-2A in MRII above clouds and mountains as I was trying to make it to the coast in Vietnam. It also was similar to the feeling I had when we were waiting for the Air Force Safety Office to decide which cause of the C-5A "Operation Babylift" accident that they were going to accept.

When we heard the radio call from the TAC flight examiner crew and they scored the mission as "bull" (bull's-eye), I also felt the same sort of relief as I had on all the previous major decisions that I had made that turned out good. Only God's hand could have been guiding all these events.

When the crew returned to Cannon AFB and got out of the aircraft, I had never seen any other crew have larger smiles on their faces and walked as tall as they both did as they returned to the Squadron. They knew they had done something very special. I was very thankful to God for all of his help on this mission.

At the completion of the ORI, which lasted for a week, we all waited to hear the results. With the ORI being the wing's report card and this being the first ORI for the F-111D aircraft, it was extremely important that we had to do well. A lot of careers were on the line.

The overall ORI results for the 27th TFW were "excellent." The results for the 522nd TFS were also "excellent." The results for the 523rd TFS, however, were "outstanding." I was extremely proud, and I knew that God had guided me to this point. As a result of the ORI, the wing commander made general, and both the 522nd Squadron commander and I were promoted to full colonel.

At the end of my two years as a squadron commander and having been promoted to full colonel, I also was selected to go to the Air War College (AWC) in residence. This, again, was an opportunity that God provided as not all colonels get selected to go to AWC in residence. The Air War College is like getting a PhD in Air Force doctrine. The Air War College is also located at Maxwell AFB in Alabama, where ACSC is located. It was 1985, and we were now on our way back to Maxwell AFB for the second time.

The Air War College (AWC), like the air command and staff college (ACSC), is also a yearlong course of study. Jan decided not to teach this time while we were at Maxwell AFB. She decided she would take the year off.

The Air War College is a stepping-stone to making general. However, one usually had to go to the Pentagon after graduation if one wants to try for the "brass ring" (make general). Assignments to the Pentagon, unfortunately, are very political in nature. One needs a sponsor to push one's career ahead at the Pentagon. I never was much for politics, and I did not have a sponsor that I knew of. In addition, the cost of living for military members in the Washington, DC, area is quite significant. Based on the above, I really did not want to go to the air staff at the Pentagon. I requested to go back to Kelly AFB in San Antonio, Texas, instead of going to Washington, DC. God must have agreed with my decision because my follow-on assignment from AWC was back to Kelly AFB.

It should also be noted that the last request for my deposition for the C-5A accident lawsuits occurred while I was at AWC. So for the time period from ACSC, my seven years at Cannon AFB, and my time at the AWC, I had been called to go to Washington, DC, at least ten to twelve times. I lost track of the total number of times that I was requested to go. The time period, however, was almost ten years from the first trip to the last trip. I do feel that it was God's plan to keep me in the States as part of his overall plan for this accident.

Since I had turned down my chance to go to the Pentagon and compete for a promotion to general, we just wanted to go back to San Antonio and retire from the Air Force. We had been stationed there two times, and San Antonio felt like home to us and was where we wanted to live after the Air Force. This must have also been God's plan for us because I did receive an assignment to Kelly AFB in San Antonio, Texas.

With our assignment in hand and before graduation, Jan went to San Antonio to buy our retirement home. I could not go with her because of school, so I told her to get the house that she wanted. She did exactly that, and we became owners of a house that I had never seen. She did a perfect job, and we still live in that house today.

I know that God was guiding her because the realtor that she found was the father of the wife of one of my flight commanders while we were at Cannon AFB. He was just super helping her, and they found the perfect house for us. The house was only nine months old and still under warranty. The original owners had just been transferred to Houston for job reasons. This to me was just more empirical evidence that God was guiding both of our lives.

When I arrived at Kelly AFB in June 1985, I did not know exactly what I would be doing. Upon arrival, I reported to the Air Logistics Center's (ALC) vice commander, who was a one-star general. He informed me that I would be going back to the Materiel Management (MM) Directorate where I would be the System Program Manager for all of the Air Force's small aircraft systems being managed by Kelly AFB. To me, this was great and just more evidence that God was behind this assignment. I became the division chief of the small aircraft division (MMS) of the Materiel Management (MM) Directorate for the Air Logistics Center (ALC).

I became the system program manager for the Air Force's fleet of T-37s, AT-37s, T-38s, F-5s, F-102s, F-106s, O-2As, and OV-10 aircraft systems. It was a great fit for me since I had flown essentially five of the weapon systems that I was now responsible for. The F-5 is essentially the fighter version of the T-38. The Air Force just added a gun and rocket pods to the T-38, and it became a fighter. The AT-37 is just an upgraded T-37 with T-38 engines without the afterburner. In addition, a minigun was added as well as wing pylons to carry small bomb loads. It was now also a fighter, and both were used in Vietnam. I did get a ride in an AT-37 in Vietnam when one of my fellow instructor pilots from Laughlin AFB received an AT-37 to Vietnam as his assignment. He was assigned to Bien Hoa, and we utilized the AT-37 in support of Cambodia.

I performed system program manager duties for approximately a year and a half when God provided me with an opportunity for advancement as far as job opportunities at Kelly AFB. I was selected to become the number two colonel in the Materiel Management Directorate. I was chosen to become the Resource Management division chief (MMM). This position put me in charge of all of the materiel management budget authority for Kelly AFB. I was responsible for approximately $5 billion of the Air Force's budget authority. My signature was the approval authority for the expenditure of funds based on purchase requests (PRs) developed by item managers at Kelly AFB. I had approximately five hundred item managers whose jobs were to procure spare parts for all the weapon systems being managed at Kelly AFB. In addition, I also had responsibility for the budget of the "black" programs that Kelly AFB was assisting in procurement for the Air Force. Only the two-star ALC commander and myself knew just how much budget authority I had for the "black" programs. At that time, the Air Force was procuring the F-117 and the B-2 aircraft weapon systems. This job elevated me to the level from which another opportunity to possibly make general was afforded me as a follow-on assignment after Kelly AFB.

I was being considered to go to McClellan AFB in Sacramento, California, to become the maintenance directorate commander for the F-111 aircraft weapon system. McClellan AFB was the Air Logistics Center (ALC) and depot repair facility for all of the Air Force's F-111 aircraft. This position was a one-star general position, and it was considered to be a great opportunity, if I accepted it. I also knew that if I turned it down, I would have to retire from the Air Force.

Since I had flown the F-111 for seven years, I knew just how much of a nightmare it was maintaining the F-111. It was a great aircraft to fly, but a real challenge to maintain. In fact, after I had been promoted to colonel while at Cannon AFB, I was required to give up the 523rd TFS commander's position. My class date for the Air War College, however, was six months away. Cannon AFB needed to find a position for me while I waited for my departure to the Air War College. It just so happened that the deputy commander for maintenance for the Twenty-Seventh TFW had just been fired. He was a full colonel and was retired immediately. This left an opening at the wing. Since I had just been promoted to colonel, the wing commander designated me to become the wing's deputy commander for maintenance. During those six months, I really learned firsthand just how hard it was to maintain the F-111 aircraft. This experience was an important factor in my decision.

A second factor in my decision involved the cost of living in California. The cost of living in California was very high compared to what Jan and I had always been familiar with. To me it was similar to the Washington, DC area and was one of the reasons I did not want to go to the Pentagon. In addition, I felt that God was leading me in a new direction.

I turned the job down and retired from the Air Force on June 30, 1989. I was very satisfied with my Air Force career, and I really did not have any aspirations to become a general officer. I knew that to be a general, you had to be political in all of your dealings. Being an engineer, I knew that I was not a politician by nature; and besides, Jan and I were in San Antonio, Texas, and this was home.

CHAPTER 6

Postmilitary Years

L IFE AFTER THE AIR Force was going to be a new experience for both of us. I was approaching this new phase of my life with some anxiety about just what I would do. God, however, had prepared me with all the pieces of the puzzle for my life's path that he had planned for me while I was in college and then the military. These pieces of the puzzle were now becoming clear to me.

He had led me to choose Iowa State University and study aerospace engineering and to choose advanced Air Force ROTC. In the Air Force, he provided me with the opportunity to get a master's degree in civil engineering and an MBA degree. He also provided me with the opportunity to work as an engineer and even have the opportunity to become a Texas-licensed professional engineer (PE).

Because of this, I was well prepared for my postmilitary career. It became obvious that God's plan for us was to retire in San Antonio after my second assignment to Kelly AFB.

After I retired from the Air Force, I began looking for an engineering position. I had a number of interviews with local San Antonio engineering firms. While I was looking for a job, God led me to the engineering firm that he had planned for me as part of my life after the Air Force. This firm was Chenn-Northern Inc., a geotechnical engineering firm with headquarters located in Denver, Colorado. They had a number of offices throughout the northwest portion of the United States. Their office here in San Antonio was the office farthest south and east of their headquarters in Denver.

The San Antonio Chenn-Northern office had just experienced a mutiny by the office manager and a number of employees. The office manager and some of the employees had decided to start their own engineering consulting firm and had quit Chenn-Northern very unexpectedly. When they left, they took a number of large clients like Exxon, Texaco, and Chevron with them. This had a significant impact on the San Antonio Chenn-Northern office, and they were looking for a new office manager. With a master's degree in civil engineering and being a Texas-licensed professional engineer, along with an MBA degree, I was a perfect fit for them. I was hired in August of 1989 as their new office manager. This is all just more empirical evidence of how God does have a plan for all of us.

After I was hired and began to see just how much damage had occurred to the business after the previous office manager and the employees left, I knew it was going to be a real challenge to recover the Chenn-Northern office. This is when God guided me as to what exactly I needed to do.

This was during the time period when national environmental concerns were coming to the forefront and the main focus of the Environmental Protection Agency (EPA). There was significant focus on gasoline underground storage tanks (USTs) at all gasoline stations. The State of Texas had just issued regulatory guidance requiring that all gasoline USTs had to be tested for leaks and even removed if over twenty-five years old. If leaks were found in the USTs that were less than twenty-five years old, then the site had to be evaluated for hydrocarbons. If a subsurface hydrocarbon impact was identified at the site and if those hydrocarbons were detected in the soil and/or groundwater above the established regulatory levels, the owners were required to remediate the site.

The saving grace for me was that the Chenn-Northern office had a drilling rig to perform drilling operations as part of its services as a geotechnical engineering firm. In addition, one of the technicians was a Texas-licensed water well driller. Since many of the geotechnical clients had left with the previous Office Manager and employees, I was left with a large void in business. Having this drill rig provided me the opportunity that I needed to rebuild the business for Chenn-Northern. I moved our business operations into the environmental consulting area by doing underground storage tank investigations and then site remediation services if gasoline leaks were identified. This gave me an advantage over those individuals who had left Chenn-Northern to start their own geotechnical firm since they did not have their own drilling rig.

With the number of Exxon and Chevron gasoline stations in the San Antonio and the surrounding area, it was not hard to get Exxon and Chevron back as clients. The state had established a time limit when all the gasoline stations had to be investigated and remediated if the site was found to have been impacted. Having our own drill rig allowed us to be able to respond a lot faster than the defecting office manager and his employees. They had to use a contract drilling firm to complete the required drilling operations. The local contract drilling firms were very busy as demand for their services was now great. We could also do the drilling more competitively as far as price. With these advantages, I was able to move the business into the environmental consulting side of operations, which offset the lack of geotechnical engineering projects that were no longer available.

It was not long before our office was doing very well with our environmental consulting services. We were doing about 80 percent of business in the environmental field and 20 percent in the geotechnical field of operations. I was able to grow the Chenn-Northern office back to the level it was before the desertion of the previous office manager and his employees in about a year and a half. I was learning just what the free market capitalistic economic society was all about. I learned that capitalism is a brutal and cutthroat operations environment that exists when conducting business operations. This, of course, was a much different environment than that I had been used to in the military.

The next challenge occurred when Chenn-Northern was bought out by a holding company based in Great Britain. This holding company was using a business model of rapid growth in order to advance their stock prices on the stock market.

Their model required a 50 percent growth rate in business operations each year, which resulted in their stock being very attractive for the stock market. They were achieving this by increasing business operations as much as possible at each office and then by overall expansion through acquisition of additional companies, like Chenn-Northern. This type of rapid-growth business model can work in the short term but cannot be sustained in the long term.

The difficulty with this type of business model occurs on the expansion side. When additional companies are acquired, the next company that is procured had to be twice as large as the previous one acquired. Chenn-Northern had seven office locations throughout the northwestern portion of the United States when it was acquired by the holding company. Therefore, to continue with this business model, the next acquisition would have to be twice the size of Chenn-Northern.

The holding company's next acquisition was Southwestern Laboratories Inc. (SWL), which had fifteen offices in the southwestern US. It was twice the size of Chenn-Northern and did fit with the holding company's business model.

The challenge for me was that there was a Southwestern Laboratory (SWL) office in San Antonio. This resulted in the Chenn-Northern office being in competition with the Southwestern Laboratories (SWL) office. They had been in San Antonio for a significantly longer period of time than Chenn-Northern. The SWL headquarters was located in Houston, Texas. The San Antonio SWL office concentrated on geotechnical engineering operations and had a solid client base. I was not sure what the holding company had in mind, and I was not sure if I was even going to be able to keep my job.

This is when additional empirical evidence was revealed to me that God had to be guiding my life's path. The decision being considered by the holding company was to combine the two offices under the name Southwestern Laboratories (SWL). The name SWL was kept since the SWL office was about twice the size of the Chenn-Northern office.

This meant that there would be no need for two office managers, and the SWL manager would, of course, have priority over me. He had been with SWL for a number of years and was doing a very good job.

The one good thing for me was that the SWL office business operations were primarily geotechnical services, and they also had their own drilling rigs. However, they were just getting into the environmental consulting side of business operations. Their business operations consisted of 80 percent geotechnical services and 20 percent environmental consulting services. Since the Chenn-Northern office was doing 80 percent environmental and 20 percent geotechnical, the holding company decided to beep both offices open with the SWL office performing geotechnical engineering services and the Chenn-Northern office performing environmental consulting services. We gave up our 20 percent geotechnical clients to the SWL office, and they gave up their 20 percent environmental clients to us at the Chenn-Northern office.

The old SWL office was then known as the Geotechnical Division Office, and our office was known as the Environmental Division of SWL. As such, both of us office managers were able to keep our positions as managers of our separate divisions. This had to be God's work in my life and just more empirical evidence that God does exist.

The rapid-growth model that the holding company in England was using worked for the next year and a half. The problem with trying to expand business operations at a 50 percent level each year is just not possible for individual offices. Expansion by acquisitions, therefore, had to be used to continue the desired growth rate. The problem for the holding company began when it became harder and harder to find larger engineering consulting firms to acquire. This is when the holding company began to require that each location increase their level of business operations by 15 to 20 percent each month. Anyone in the engineering consulting business knows that this level of growth is impossible to achieve. The holding company's main business was in pharmaceuticals, not engineering consulting. This all came to a head for me, three years after I had been hired by Chenn-Northern.

Our normal operations required that each SWL Division office issue a monthly profit and loss (P&L) statement. My boss was located in an SWL office in Austin, Texas. This is when the holding company decided to use "Enron" accounting methods to offset the lack of expansion opportunities through acquisition. My boss called me and directed me to add $250,000 to my P&L statement in a category called "work in progress." He said that this would represent work already accomplished on open projects, but the project had not been completed and billed. He said it would represent income that would be realized on our open projects that we had accepted proposals for but had not yet started or completed. He had no idea how many open projects we had or how many signed proposals we had. The $250,000 number was just a number he needed to meet the holding company's requirement with no basis in reality. I told him that I could not and would not do that because this was not considered to be a "generally accepted accounting principle (GAAP)." As a professional engineer with an MBA degree, I knew that this was just not ethical and was wrong. He said that I had to do it and hung up on me. The sad thing was, my boss was also a professional engineer.

My office accountant normally prepared our P&L statements and then mailed them to the Austin office. I told her what my boss had requested and that we were not going to comply. I told her to prepare our P&L statement without the $250,000 "work in progress" figure, and I would hand deliver it to the Austin office. I drove to Austin and handed our P&L statement to my boss and told him that I had not included the $250,000 figure because that figure was not real income earned and furthermore may not ever be generated. This, of course, did not go over well with him.

I departed the Austin office and returned to San Antonio. It was about an hour-and-fifteen-minute drive back to San Antonio. When I arrived back at the office, my accountant informed me that I had been fired. This is when God again stepped in and led me in a new direction.

One of the geologists had remained behind with the Chenn-Northern office when the previous office manager and some of the employees had left to start their own consulting firm. He stayed with Chenn-Northern, and he was the individual that had called the headquarters to inform them of what was happening. With my firing, he and I decided to start our own environmental consulting firm. He gave his two-week notice and quit, and we began the process of starting our own firm. God was providing a new path and opportunity for the both of us.

Both my MBA degree and my Texas PE License were of great benefit to us as I prepared our five-year business plan. The state of Texas requires a five-year business plan in order to incorporate a business in Texas. Both the MBA degree and my PE license were opportunities that God had provided me while I was in the military.

When atheists claim that there is no God, I just have to feel sorry for them. To me, there is just too much empirical evidence in my life that refutes their claims. I have previously discussed how God guided my life in the military, which resulted in a very successful military career. He also guided my life on the engineering path that he had planned for me during the military and then my postmilitary life.

God guided me to attend ISU and study aerospace engineering. As part of the aerospace engineering curriculum, we had to choose between structures and propulsion as areas of concentration for study in addition to the required core courses for the degree. There just was not enough time to study both of these areas in addition to all of the aerodynamic courses required for the degree. God led me to choose structures, which turned out to be what I needed to become the lead structural engineer for the C-5A fleet while I was in the military. He knew what I was going to need during that phase of my life.

Another excellent example of empirical evidence that God was guiding my life was revealed when he provided me the opportunity to go to AFIT while I was in the military and get a master's degree in engineering. The Air Force never asked me what field of engineering I wanted to study for my master's degree. After Vietnam, when I reported to the University of Denver, I found myself enrolled in the Civil Engineering Department. God had to have been behind this decision since he knew I would need a master's degree in civil engineering during his plan for me in my postmilitary life. He also knew I would need an MBA degree in my postmilitary life, so he guided me to get that degree also.

After I retired and was looking for a job, God led me to Chenn-Northern. The job opening for an office manager at Chenn-Northern had as part of the required qualifications included a master's degree in civil engineering, along with a Texas PE License. In addition, having an MBA degree was highly desirable, but not required. God knew exactly what I needed in order to be a perfect fit for the position with Chenn-Northern after I retired from the military. To me, the empirical evidence of the above only confirms that God had to be the one making all of this possible as part of his plan for me.

God had prepared me to be able to develop a business plan and be able to start my own engineering consulting firm after I was fired. My partner and I filed all the required paperwork, and STC Environmental Services Inc. was born during the second half of 1992. We rented office space, acquired some office furniture, and began business operations. We began business operations with four employees. Three of the employees were myself, my partner, the geologist, and his wife, who worked as our office receptionist. The fourth employee was the accountant who had worked for me at Chenn-Northern and at SWL.

I had hired this accountant when I was hired to manage the Chenn-Northern office. The previous accountant was one of the employees that left when the previous office manager left to start his own consulting firm. A total of seven people had left Chenn-Northern when the defection occurred.

On my departure from SWL, my accountant that I had hired for Chenn-Northern and now was working for SWL was also fired. She was fired just after I was because she complained to SWL management about the improper accounting procedure that she was being directed to do. This was the same procedure that I had refused to comply with. With her hiring as our accountant, we now had our nucleus for the start-up of STC Environmental Services Inc.

I know that God had to be guiding us because it is well known that approximately 75 percent of all small businesses fail within the first three years of operations. It was very tough getting our business started. My partner and I had both put in funds for start-up costs. With intense marketing efforts, we began to acquire clients. In the environmental consulting business, it takes some time to acquire clients and then complete projects. We had to prepare proposals, get them accepted, and then complete the project. This all had to be accomplished before the project could be invoiced and before cash could begin to flow.

As our workload began to increase, we needed to hire additional employees in order to be able to complete the work. This is when I know that God was guiding our efforts in our business operations. My partner and I did not receive a paycheck for the first three months that we were in business. It did not make sense for us to pay ourselves out of the start-up funds that we had put into the business. We needed those funds just to meet payroll for our employees and to pay operational costs.

The first year of business operations was very—and I mean very—tough. There were a number of times when payroll was due on the morning of payday, and we did not have sufficient funds in our checking account to cover payroll at the start of the day. The night before payday, if this was the case, I would wake up during the night wondering what we were going to do. When this would happen, I could not go back to sleep. I still had not learned that I should not have worried as the Bible states that God knows what we need, and he will provide it even before we pray for it. Each morning on those days when we were short of funds, when I got to work, I would pray for God's assistance. He never once failed me, and we never missed a payroll on payday. Only our accountant, my partner, and I knew just how close we came to missing payroll.

At our office location, the mail was always delivered by 10:00 a.m. each day. We normally issued paychecks at the end of the day. On those days when we were short on funds, our accountant would go out to the mailbox hoping that there would be checks in the mail. When the mailman delivered the mail, she would immediately go to the mailbox and then come back in. If she had a smile on her face, I knew that God had answered my prayer. There were a number of these days during the first year, and he never once let us down. By the end of the first year, we were on relatively firm financial basis for the firm.

I also know that Satan was hard at work. He used this opportunity to tempt us into doing the wrong thing just for money. As the Bible states in 1 Timothy 6:9–10 (NIV):

> People who want to get rich fall into temptation and a trap and into many foolish and harmful desires that plunge men into ruin and destruction. For the love of money is a root of all kind of evil. Some people eager for money have wandered from the faith and pierced themselves with many griefs.

Just after we started the business and we were working hard to get clients, we received a call from one of the well-known power brokers in San Antonio. He was the owner of one of the four largest San Antonio shopping malls. He invited us up to his office in his mall to discuss business opportunities. My partner and I both went to see what he had to say. His business would be a large plus if we could secure it.

Once we got to the meeting, it became very obvious to me that God was allowing Satan to tempt us to see how we were going to respond. This individual wanted us to provide him with environmental reports to satisfy all the new environmental regulations that had just been passed. These regulations required a significant number of environmental investigations that would be required for his shopping mall. Through his discussion, it became very clear that what he really wanted was for us to essentially "pencil-whip" these investigations in order to satisfy the regulations. As a local power broker in the city, he informed us that if we worked for him, he would ensure that we would receive all of the environmental work from the city that we could handle.

As a PE, I knew that I could not agree to work for this individual. My partner and I declined his offer and departed his office. It was soon after that, that our phone began to ring a lot at the office, and we began to acquire many new clients. God had tested us, and we had passed.

I should note that at the end of our first year of operations, the holding company that had acquired both Chenn-Northern and Southwestern Laboratories went bankrupt. Their stock prices plummeted when they were no longer able to continue with their rapid-growth business model. They had to sell off their companies that they had purchased for ten cents on the dollar.

In addition, after approximately five years, the power broker owner of the shopping mall passed away. His son tried to run the business, but soon failed and had to declare bankruptcy. When a buyer for the mall could not be found, the mall was torn down and the land sold off the settle the debt that remained. STC Environmental Services Inc. was doing just fine. God knew what was happening and took care of us.

I stayed with STC Environmental Services Inc. for eighteen years as the president and principal engineer. I worked until one day in November 2009, when I woke up thinking I was no longer having fun. I had always been a workaholic, and now I was tired and ready to retire for good.

My wife, Jan, had retired in 2002 from Taft High School in San Antonio, Texas, where she had been the head counselor. She always told me that I would know when it was time to retire. On that day in November, God led me to decide that it was time for me to retire for the second time. I was sixty-seven years old, and I was getting tired. I retired from STC Environmental Services Inc. on February 1, 2010.

I should also note that as of the date of this book, STC Environmental Services Inc. is still in business. That is over thirty-tree years of business operations. In addition to the holding company and all of their acquired companies that were no longer in business, the company that the defecting employees from Chenn-Northern started also went out of business. There is no one that can tell me that there is no God.

CHAPTER 7

The Retirement Years

I T IS NOW 2025, and I have been retired for fifteen years. I have never regretted my decision to retire. Jan and I are both enjoying our retirements, and we are very thankful for all the blessings that God has bestowed and continues to bestow on us throughout our entire lifetimes. I know without a doubt that he has guided our lives the entire time and continues to do so even in retirement. This was evidenced in one specific incident and a relationship that we have developed that can only be considered a blessing from God.

The specific incident that occurred was when, once again, God saved my life. I used to put out a lot of Christmas decorations in the front yard each Christmas. With each year, I would add more and more decorations to the yard display. The neighborhood Homeowners Association has a Christmas decoration competition contest each year. I finally had so many decorations that our house won the Christmas decoration contest three years in a row.

Between Christmases, I would store all of my decorations in our attic. The access to our attic is by a pull-down ladder from an opening in our hallway ceiling. I would have to climb up and down this ladder to get the decorations down each year and then put them back up after Christmas. The incident occurred during one of these Christmas-decoration events when I was putting the decorations back up into the attic.

I was wrestling with a large heavy container of decorations when I fell backward into the ladder opening while I was working in the attic. I know that it was God who saved me. When I fell backward, one leg was restrained on the opposite side of the opening while my head and shoulders were restrained on the other side. The other leg and the majority of my body were extending through the opening. If I had fallen through this opening, I would have landed on my head on the hallway floor below. I had absolutely no control over the falling motion, and I know it was only with God's helping hand that I did not fall through the opening that day. This incident really got my attention, and I now store all of my Christmas decorations in the garage. I do not even like going up into that attic anymore.

The relationship that Jan and I developed that we consider a true blessing from God concerns a young couple that moved in across the street from us. This couple had both graduated from Texas A&M University, and they were Aggies. Our oldest son, Doug, also had graduated from Texas A&M and was an Aggie. When the couple moved in, the wife was pregnant with her first child. With them being Aggies and with us being Aggie parents, we had a common bond to start. As they were moving in, Jan and I went over to welcome them to the neighborhood. This is when we found out they were Aggies.

Our oldest son, Doug, and his wife, who both are Aggies, had decided not to have any children. Our youngest son, Randall, is not married and, as such, does not have any children. This, of course, created the situation that Jan and I did not have any grandchildren, and the future did not look like this would change.

In addition to this couple being Aggies, we had a lot in common with them. The husband and I were both engineers. He had worked for NASA before moving to San Antonio. His wife and Jan had both been schoolteachers, which meant they had a lot in common. I know that God had led this couple to our neighborhood as part of his plan for them and us.

The couples' first son was born approximately two months after they moved in. Not having any grandchildren, Jan and I were very excited and happy to be able to help our new friends with their new son. To us, this young couple became family, and we became very close to them. I know that this was God's plan and a blessing to us because they have "adopted" us as "grandparents" to their children.

We are now the proud grandparents of their three awesome and wonderful children. I think everyone needs grandchildren during their retirement years in order to have a full and complete life. The sound of their young voices in our home makes our house a home and is a true blessing for Jan and me from God. Playing Santa Claus each Christmas is a true delight for me because of the looks on their young faces.

Retirement has given me the time to reflect back over my entire life. During this reflection, I have been able to truly realize just how God has guided me through my life. He guided me to write my first book titled *Hank: An Angel Dog*. This book was about Hank, our dog that our family had rescued from an animal shelter. Hank joined our family on the day that my mother-in-law passed away. Writing that book helped me realize just how God watches over all of his creation. Hank was truly an angel dog.

God also led me to write my second book titled *The Long Return*. This book was about my time in Vietnam and the difficulty I had when I returned from Vietnam. We Vietnam veterans were not welcomed home in a very pleasant manner. We were met with a significant amount of antiwar, antimilitary sentiment by the American society. Writing that book helped me understand how our American society had changed, and it helped me find peace within myself. Some of my friends that I gave copies of my book to who had been in Vietnam also said that the book had helped them. This book also allowed me to understand how God was guiding my life as a part of his plan for me while I was in the military.

It took approximately four years of my retirement to write and publish these two books. When I finished those two books, I felt that two books were enough. I never would have thought that I would ever write one book, let alone two. I do have to wonder just what the head of the English Department at Iowa State University would think now if he were still alive. He was the one that I am sure reviewed my third attempt at passing the senior English exam at ISU. I hope he would think he made the proper decision.

Writing the above two books really got me reflecting back over my life. That is when I really started to understand just how God had been watching over me and guiding me to make the decisions that I did in order to fulfill his plan for me. I was not planning to write any more books until God led me to decide that I needed to write this book. I figure he has a purpose, and I just need to do it.

As I reflected back over my life, and as I watched what was happening to our country, he led me to attempt to answer the questions, "Does God really exist?" and "Why does God let bad things happen to good people?"

While I was reflecting back over my life, I began to put the decisions and events that have occurred in my life into perspective. That is when all the empirical evidence that a higher power had to be present and is working for good in this world became undeniable. If a person only looks at each decision or event in isolation, they may not understand just how all these events and decisions are actually pieces of a puzzle, which is God's plan. These pieces all fit together to make up his plan for our lives. All we need to do is listen to him and obey.

I now know that my purpose and job for the remainder of my life that God has planned for me is to take care of my wife of sixty-two years. I had promised both God and her dad that I would take care of her. God has blessed me, and this is the very least that I can do until he calls me home.

As I now watch what is happening to our country, I became interested in just what the Bible says about the end of time, as we know it. Our society is so much different now than when I was a child growing up in the 1940s and 1950s. I began to wonder just what will happen to the United States when Jesus does return.

To answer this question, I decided to do research on the Bible prophecies to see if I could understand just what is happening and why. The following chapters document the results of that research.

It also provides a warning to atheists and other nonbelievers that *God really does exist!* This is why I do feel sorry for atheists and nonbelievers.

CHAPTER 8

The Prophecies

I N GOD'S BOOK, THE Bible, he provided many prophecies in both the Old and New Testaments about what must happen before the end of time as we know it. The end of time as we know it will occur during the time of what the Bible calls the *great tribulation.* As a Christian, I definitely have an interest in the events that are predicted to happen by these prophecies. Not being a minister or a pastor, I have to rely on individuals that are more knowledgeable in this area to help me understand these prophecies.

The best book that I came across was written by Dr. Ed Hindson in 1996 and is titled Final Signs. In 1996, Dr. Hindson was the minister of biblical studies at the nine-thousand-member Rehoboth Baptist Church in Atlanta, Georgia, and vice president of There's Hope. He was also a distinguished adjunct professor of religion at Liberty University in Lynchburg, Virginia. In his book, Dr. Hindson describes the Bible prophecies by discussing the Bible verses that describe what must happen before the end of the world as we know it. The end of days of our world is prophesized to occur at the time of the second coming of Christ.

Dr. Hindson points out that there are a number of passages in the Bible that warns of the time of the great tribulation when the end of our world as we know it will occur. In the Old Testament, in the book of Isaiah chapters 24 and 34, the prophet Isaiah warns of the day when God will judge the whole earth. Isaiah warns that this will occur during the great tribulation and will culminate in the battle of Armageddon.

Dr. Hindson also points out that some of the Bible prophecies that are prophesized have already been fulfilled. In addition to the prophecies that are revealed in the Old Testament, many of these prophecies are repeated in the New Testament with the teaching of Jesus during the three years that he taught while he was here on earth. These prophecies are documented in the New Testament books of Matthew, Mark, Luke, and John.

One of the first prophecies is noted in Matthew when Jesus directed that his Gospel message and growth of the Christian church be spread throughout the world. Matthew 24:14 (KJV) states, "And this gospel of the kingdom shall be preached in all of the world for a witness unto all nations; and then shall the end come." Matthew 24:21 (KJV) goes on to say, "For then shall be great tribulation, such as was not since the beginning of the world to this time, no, nor ever shall be."

When one considers our current continuing advancing computer technology and our satellite communications capability, there is no question in my mind that this prophecy either has been fulfilled or is very close to fulfillment. Our current technology makes it totally possible for every corner of the world to be interconnected by the large massive global computer network, which can transmit the Gospel of Christ around the world. There is, however, no assurance that all the people will heed or follow Christ. The fact is that there is no doubt that it is possible for this prophecy to have been fulfilled or soon will be.

In Genesis chapter 12 of the Old Testament, God chose the children of Israel to be his chosen people and gave them their land. This is also where God indicated that he will bless those that bless the children of Israel and punish those who curse them. This is documented in Genesis 12:1–3 (NIV), where it states:

> The Lord had said to Abram, "Leave your country, your people and you father's household and go to the land I will show you. I will make you into a great nation and I will bless

you; I will make your name great, and you will be a blessing. I will bless those that bless you and whoever curses you I will curse; and all people on earth will be blessed through you."

In Genesis 12:5 (NIV), it states that Abram listened to God and obeyed: "He took his wife Sarai, his nephew Lot, all the possessions they had accumulated and the people they had acquired in Haram, and they set out for the land of Canaan, and they arrived there."

In Genesis 12:7 (NIV), God gives Abram this land, which is documented by the following: "The Lord appeared to Abram and said, 'To your offspring I will give this land.' So he built an altar there to the Lord, who had appeared to him.'"

In Genesis 17:2–8 (NIV), God is speaking to Abram, and this is when God makes his covenant with Abram and the children of Israel. This is also when God gives them land forever and changes Abram's name to Abraham. This is documented in the following:

I will confirm my covenant between me and you and will greatly increase your numbers. Abram fell facedown, and God said to him, "As for me, this is my covenant with you: You will be the father of many nations. No longer will you be called Abram, your name will be Abraham, for I have made you very fruitful. I will make nations of you and kings will come from you. I will establish my covenant as an everlasting covenant between me and you and your descendants after you for the generations to come, to be your God and the God of your descendants after you. The whole land of Canaan, where you are now an alien, I will give as an everlasting possession to you and your descendants after you and I will be their God."

The Jewish people, however, were not always able to stay in their land after God gave it to them. As the struggle between the Arab nations and the Jewish people continued, the children of Israel found themselves displaced in Egypt at the time of Moses. This is when God intervenes and chooses Moses and Aaron to lead the Israelites out of Egypt and back to their chosen land. This was not completed in a simple manner, and it required God's assistance to convince the pharaoh of Egypt to allow the Jewish people to leave. This struggle is documented in the book of Exodus in the Old Testament.

The children of Israel lived in Egypt for a very long time. This is documented in Exodus 12:40–41 (NIV), where it states, "Now the length of time the Israelite people lived in Egypt was 430 years. At the end of the 430 years, to the very day, all of the Lord's divisions left Egypt." When they did finally get back to their land, they were able to stay there until the Romans destroyed Jerusalem in AD 70. The Israelites were once again displaced from their land.

A second prophecy that appears to now having been fulfilled is the return of the Jewish people for a second time to their land that God gave them. This happened on May 14, 1947, when the current nation of Israel was formed. This means that the Jewish people were absent from their land this time for approximately two thousand years. This prophecy is documented in the book of Amos in the Old Testament, chapter 9, verses 14–15 (NIV) where it states:

> I will bring my people Israel back from exile. "They will rebuild the ruined cities and live in them. They will plant vineyards and drink their wine; they will make gardens and eat their fruit. I will plant Israel in their own land, never again to be uprooted from the land I have given them," says the Lord your God.

The reason I feel that the prophecy for the Jewish people to have been returned to their land for good and the prophecy now fulfilled is documented in the book of Jeremiah in the Old Testament. As part of the covenant with Abraham, God promises to defend Israel against her enemies. In Jeremiah 30:16 (KJV), it states, "Therefore all they that devour thee shall be devoured; and all thine adversaries, every one of them, shall go into captivity; and they that spoil thee shall be a spoil, and all that prey upon thee will I give for a prey."

The evidence that this prophecy has been fulfilled was evident almost immediately after the nation of Israel was formed in 1947. When surrounding Arab nations attacked Israel, Israel was able to defeat the Arabs and force them to accept a truce. In 1956, Egypt attacked Israel and lost. In 1967, Nasser of Egypt again attacked

Israel, which started the Six-Day War. The results of this war was that Israel got the Sinai, the Old city of Jerusalem, the West Bank, and the Golan Heights. I would say that this is evidence that God means what he says. This to me is also just further evidence that the Bible is definitely non-fiction.

Another prophecy of what will happen before the end days is that there will be an increase in wickedness and the spread of evil. In 2 Timothy 3:1–4 (NIV) of the New Testament, the apostle Paul writes:

> But mark this: There will be terrible times in the last days. People will be lovers of themselves, lovers of money, boastful, proud, abusive, disobedient to their parents, ungrateful, unholy, without love, unforgiving, slanderous, without self-control, brutal, not lovers of the good, treacherous, rash, conceited, lovers of pleasure rather than lovers of God.

To me, the above could be an appropriate description of our current society and not so much of our society past decades.

The above prophecy is also repeated in Matthew 24:36–39 (NIV) by Jesus when he was describing what the world would be like just before he comes back again:

> But about that day or hour no one knows, not even the angels in heaven, nor the Son, but only the Father. As it was in the days of Noah, so it will be at the coming of the Son of Man. For in the days before the flood, people were eating and drinking, marrying and giving in marriage, up to the day Noah entered the ark, and they knew nothing about what would happen until the flood came and took them all away. That is how it will be at the coming of the Son of Man.

The twentieth century was riddled with evidence of an increase in wickedness and evil in our world on a global scale. Joseph Stalin, an atheist leader, formed the Soviet Union in 1917. The political system he championed was communism. This system is the most brutal form of Marxism/socialism. Joseph Stalin is reported to have murdered millions of Russian people during his harsh tenure as the leader of the Soviet Union. The Communist Soviet Union really only lasted until December 25, 1989, when the Berlin Wall was torn down. This was only seventy-two years, but the system was extremely brutal and evil.

Another prime example of the increase in evil on the world stage was Adolph Hitler in Germany in the 1940s. Adolph Hitler exterminated at least six million Jewish people. The political system that Hitler championed was fascism. This system also has no belief in God and is not based in God's teachings. Adolph Hitler's reign did not last long.

Since the Jewish people are God's chosen people, it is no wonder that God would not let Hitler achieve his goal of world dominance. It also is not difficult to understand why the Jewish people got their land back in 1947 as fulfillment of that prophecy. God does exist, and the Bible is nonfiction.

Adolph Hitler was not the only evil leader in the world at that time. Benito Mussolini was the Italian strongman leader that was an evil, brutal leader in Italy at the same time as Hitler. In addition, Japan tried to use the opportunity of the evil disorder that was going on in the world to expand their imperialism during Hitler's assault on Europe. While all of this was happening, there is no doubt that wickedness and evil in the world was on the increase.

A question that is often asked is, why does God let bad things happen? Since God created man with a free will to choose, the Bible clearly states that God will not always strive to be with man. This is documented in Genesis 6:3 (KJV), which states, "And the Lord said, 'My spirit shall not always strive with man, for that he also is flesh: yet his days shall be an hundred and twenty years.'" To me, Satan is the one that causes all the bad things that occur as part of his continuing battle against God.

The Bible also indicates that God would prefer not to interfere with how we humans choose to govern ourselves. This is evident in Matthew 22:21 (KJV), when Jesus was teaching, and he stated, "Then saith he unto them. 'Render therefore unto Caesar the things which are Caesar's; and unto God the things that are God's.'"

It is evident, however, that, at times, God had to intervene in man's affairs as part of his overall plan for mankind. When wickedness and evil get to a level that God can no longer tolerate, he does step in to stop evil. This was evidenced during the time of Noah. God destroyed the entire earth and its inhabitants with the flood because of man's wickedness and evilness. He also destroyed the cities of Sodom and Gomorrah because of man's wickedness. He also intervened against the pharaoh of Egypt to force him to release his chosen people from their bondage.

It is also evident that he had to intervene in the twentieth century against the evil caused by Hitler, Mussolini, and Japan. All the governing systems of these leaders did not believe in God or his principles. When God's people were being subjected to the Holocaust and murdered at concentration camps such as Auschwitz, he stepped in just like the prophecies predicted in the Old Testament. He greatly assisted the United States and its allies to defeat Germany and the Axis powers during WWII. God blessed the United State because we were supporting the Jewish people, which led to the creation of the nation of Israel as fulfillment of the prophecy of returning his chosen people to their land. This is a lesson that I hope we have not lost in our present day of governing system for the United States.

At that time, Russia happened to be allied with the United States and the free world. This to me illustrates just how evil Hitler really was. As such, communism was not defeated until 1989. It should still be noted that communism was eventually defeated after only seventy-two years. I attribute this fact to communism's nonbelief in God and his principles. This is another lesson I hope we have not lost in our current political system and the path that we seem to be on.

At the end of the twentieth century and at the beginning of the twenty-first century, evil has continued to increase in the world in the form of radical Islamic terrorism. Terrorist attacks on innocent individuals like the attack on the World Trade Center on September 11, 2001, can only be considered as pure evil. This is the worst kind of evil because the terrorists use a perverted form of the Muslim religion to justify their actions. We should not be too surprised, however, as the Bible warns us of false prophets and apostate religion before the end days. To me, radical Islam may be one of those apostate religions.

As far as false prophets, the Bible warns us that many false prophets will rise. This is documented in Matthew 24:4–11 (KJV) when Jesus was asked about the end of days. Jesus responded with the following:

> Take heed that no man deceive you. For many shall come in my name, saying, I am Christ, and shall deceive many. And ye shall hear of wars and rumors of wars: see that ye be not troubled: for all these things must come to pass, but the end is not yet. For nation shall rise against nation, and kingdom against kingdom: and there shall be famines, and pestilences, and earthquakes in diverse places. All these are the beginning of sorrows. Then shall they deliver you up to be afflicted, and shall kill you: and ye shall be hated of all nations for my name's sake. And then shall many be offended, and shall betray one another, and shall hate one another. And many false prophets shall rise and shall deceive many.

In the Old Testament, the prophet Ezekiel predicts an invasion of Israel by a number of Arab nations in the last days. This is documented in Ezekiel 38:14–16 (NIV):

> This is what the Sovereign Lord says: In that day, when my people Israel are living in safety, will you not take notice of it? You will come from your place in the far north, you and many nations with you, all of them riding on horses, a great horde, a mighty army. You will advance against my people Israel like a cloud that covers the land. In days to come, Gog, I will bring you against my land, so that the nations may know me when I show myself holy through you before their eyes.

In verses 18–23, Ezekiel goes on to say:

> This is what will happen in that day. When Gog attacks the land of Israel, my hot anger will be aroused, declares the Sovereign Lord.

In my zeal and fiery wrath I declare that at that time there shall be a great earthquake in the land of Israel. The fish of the sea, the birds of the air, the beasts of the field, every creature that moves along the ground, and all the people on the face of the earth will tremble at my presence. The mountains will be overturned, the cliffs will crumble and every wall will fall to the ground. I will summon a sword against Gog on all my mountains, declares the Sovereign Lord. Every man's sword will be against his brother. I will execute judgment upon him with plague and bloodshed; I will pour down torrents of rain, hailstones, and burning sulfur on him and on his troops and on the many nations with him. And so I will show my greatness and my holiness, and I will make myself known in the sight of many nations. Then they will know that I am the Lord.

The Bible mentions Gog and Magog on a limited basis. I was not able to learn whom Gog and Magog actually represent. Ezekiel does predict that Israel will be invaded by a host of Arab nations at the time of the end days. He also does provide some names of these Arab nations that will join together. These nations include Persia (now Iran), Cush (now Sudan/Ethiopia), Put (now Libya), as part of the invading forces. In addition, he also names Gomes (now part of Russia) and Beth Togarmah (now Turkey) as being from the north. Gog, who is noted to be the "chief prince" of Magog, heads this alliance of nations. Dr. Hindson indicates that there have been many attempts to identify Magog.

In his book, Dr. Hindson indicated that some of these attempts to identify Magog included an ancient Jewish historian named Josephus. He indicated that Magog was the name of barbarians from the north. In addition, Alfonso III of Spain (AD 866–910) interpreted Ezekiel's prophecy as the depiction of the defeat of the Moors (Muslims) in Spain. Other historians have seen Magog as the Huns, Mongols, Magyars, Turks, or Russians.

Based on the above, we just do not know whom Magog represents. What we do know is that Magog—along with Persia, Cush, Put, Gomes, and Togarmah—will invade Israel in the last days as predicted in Ezekiel 38 and 39 and will be destroyed. In Luke 21:20–24 (NIV), Jesus describes a sign of the end days in a similar manner to Ezekiel's prophecy by the following:

> When you see Jerusalem being surrounded by armies, you will know that its desolation is near. Then let those who are in Judea flee to the mountains, let those in the city get out, and let those in the country not enter the city. For this is

the time of punishment in fulfillment of all that has been written. How dreadful it will be in those days for pregnant women and nursing mothers! There will be great distress in the land and wrath against this people. They will fall by the sword and will be taken as prisoners to all the nations. Jerusalem will be trampled on by the Gentiles until the times of the Gentiles are fulfilled.

In verses 25–28, Jesus goes on to describe additional signs:

There will be signs in the sun, moon and stars. On the earth, nations will be in anguish and perplexity at the roaring and tossing of the sea. People will faint from terror, apprehensive of what is coming on the world, for the heavenly bodies will be shaken. At that time they will see the Son of Man coming in a cloud with power and great glory. When these things begin to take place, stand up and lift up your heads, because your redemption is drawing near.

This to me clearly indicates that the end of the world as we know it will start in the Middle East with an attack on Israel from the north. Some of the nations named that will be part of the attack include the current nations of Iran, Sudan/Ethiopia, Libya, Turkey, and either Russia or some elements of Russia. There are six small areas or provinces in Russia that are Muslim Republics.

These are Kazakhstan, Uzbekistan, Turkmenistan, Tazbekistan, Kyrgyzstan, and Azerbaijan.

The Bible also predicts that the Roman Empire will be reconstituted during the end days by a union of ten nations that will represent the last major world system. The attack on Israel is what will start the battle of Armageddon as documented in Revelation 16:16 (NIV): "Then they gathered the kings together to the place that in Hebrew is called Armageddon."

The prophet Daniel in the Old Testament provides additional insight concerning how this all comes about. Daniel prophesied that a world leader will establish a peace agreement with Israel and then break the agreement. In addition, Jerusalem will be destroyed during the referenced end-times of the Gentiles as predicted in

Luke 21:20–24 (NIV) and previously noted. Daniel's prophecy is documented in Daniel 9:25–27 (NIV) and states the following:

> Know and understand this: From the time the word goes out to restore and rebuild Jerusalem until the Anointed One, the ruler, comes, there will be seven "sevens," and sixty-two "sevens." It will be rebuilt with streets and a trench, but in times of trouble. After the sixty-two "sevens," the Anointed One will be put to death and will have nothing. The people of the ruler who will come will destroy the city and the sanctuary. The end will come like a flood: War will continue until the end, and desolations have been decreed. He will confirm a covenant with many for one "seven." In the middle of the "seven," he will put an end to sacrifice and offering. And at the temple he will set up an abomination that causes desolation, until the end that is decreed is poured out on him.

A "seven" is thought to represent 7 years, for a total of 483 years. The last "seven" is considered to be the agreement for seven years that is broken after three and one-half years.

The prophet Daniel was blessed with visions that God wanted his people to know. When he did not understand a vision, however, he would ask God to explain it to him. This happened when he had a vision of a ram and a goat. In Daniel 8:19–26 (NIV), God sends the angel Gabriel to explain the vision about the ram and goat to Daniel as being the prophecy of the end days. In verses 19–26, Gabriel explains the vision to Daniel in the following manner:

> He said: "I am going to tell you what will happen later in the time of wrath, because the vision concerns the appointed time of the end. The two-horned ram that you saw represents the kings of Media and Persia. The shaggy goat is the king of Greece, and the large horn between its eyes is the first king. The four horns that replaced the one that was broken off represent four kingdoms that will emerge from his nation but will not have the same power. In the latter part of their reign, when rebels have become completely wicked, a fierce-looking king, a master of intrigue, will arise. He will become very strong, but not by his own power. He will cause astounding devastation

and will succeed in whatever he does. He will destroy those who are mighty, the holy people. He will cause deceit to prosper, and he will consider himself superior. When they feel secure, he will destroy many and take his stand against the Prince of princes. Yet he will be destroyed, but not by human power. The vision of the evenings and mornings that has been given you is true, but seal up the vision, for it concerns the distant future."

To me, this passage predicts the false prophet and Antichrist that will be present at the time of the end days, as Jesus warns us of during his teachings.

The Bible also teaches us that there has been a heavenly battle going on between good and evil since the beginning of time. We know that evil (Satan) and his followers have been at work since the beginning of time as we know it when he tempted Eve as a serpent in the Garden of Eden. In the New Testament, the apostle Paul refers to this heavenly struggle between God and Satan in Ephesians 6:11–12 (NIV):

Put on the full armor of God so that you can take your stand against the devil's schemes. For our struggle is not against flesh and blood, but against the rulers, against the authorities, against the power of this dark world and against the spiritual forces of evil in the heavenly realms.

Both the Old and the New Testaments warn us about Satan and his efforts in this world. In Isaiah 14:12 (NIV) of the Old Testament, Isaiah discusses Lucifer (Satan) and how he will fall from heaven and work against God by weakening nations of the earth. Isaiah describes this by the following, "How you have fallen from heaven, O morning star, son of the dawn! You have been cast down to the earth, you who once laid low nations!" Isaiah explains the reason that he was cast out of heaven in verses 13–15 where he writes:

You said in your heart, "I will ascend to the heavens; I will raise my throne above the stars of God; I will sit enthroned on the mount of assembly, on the utmost heights of Mount Zaphon. I will ascend above the tops of the clouds; I will make myself like the Most High." But you are brought down to the realm of the dead, to the depths of the pit.

In the New Testament and the book of Revelation 12:7–9 (KJV), this heavenly struggle between good and evil is documented by the following:

> And there was war in heaven: Michael and his angels fought against the dragon; and the dragon fought and his angles, and prevailed not; neither was their place found any more in heaven. And the great dragon was cast out, that old serpent, called the Devil, and Satan, which deceiveth the whole world, he was cast out into the earth, and his angels were cast out with him.

To me, this answers the question, "Why does God let bad things happen to good people?" It is Satan and his angels that cause bad things to happen as the struggle between good and evil continues even to the end of time. This battle will continue until the end days and will lead to the Great Tribulation.

In Revelation 12:12 (KJV), a warning to the inhabitants of the earth is provided: "Therefore rejoice, ye heavens, and ye that dwell in them. Woe to the inhabitants of the earth and of the sea! For the devil is come down unto you, having great wrath, because he knoweth that he hath but a short time." When God does expel Satan and his allies from heaven, we do not have to assume that he will increase his evil efforts here on earth because Satan will know that his time is short. This is consistent with Jesus's teaching that evil and wickedness will greatly increase in the end days, which will lead to the great tribulation.

The good news for Christians is that just before the great tribulation occurs, the prophecy that will then be most likely fulfilled is that the Christian church will be raptured and removed from the earth with the second coming of Jesus. The Christian church is the church that Jesus started while he was here on earth. This is documented in Revelation 3:10 (NIV), where Jesus states, "Since you have kept my command to endure patiently, I will also keep you from the hour of trial that is going to come upon the whole world to test those who live on the earth."

The Bible also predicts that this rapture will occur in the twinkling of an eye. This is documented in 1 Corinthians 15:49–52

(NIV), where it also indicates that our bodies will also be changed into the bodies of a heavenly likeness. This is stated by the following:

> And just as we have borne the image of the earthly man, so shall we bear the image of the heavenly man. I declare to you, brothers and sisters, that flesh and blood cannot inherit the kingdom of God, nor does the perishable inherit the imperishable. Listen, I tell you a mystery: We will not all sleep, but we will all be changed—in a flash, in the twinkling of an eye, at the last trumpet. For the trumpet will sound, the dead will be raised imperishable, and we will be changed.

In 1 Thessalonians 4:14–17 (NIV), the rapture prophesy is further explained by the following:

> For we believe that Jesus died and rose again, and so we believe that God will bring with Jesus those who have fallen asleep in him. According to the Lord's word, we tell you that we who are still alive, who are left until the coming of the Lord, will certainly not precede those who have fallen asleep. For the Lord himself will come down from heaven, with a loud command, with the voice of the archangel and with the trumpet call of God, and the dead in Christ will rise first. After that, we who are still alive and are left will be caught up together with them in the clouds to meet the Lord in the air. And so we will be with the Lord forever.

In the Old Testament, the prophet Zechariah prophesized the same thing at the time of the great tribulation when God steps in. This is documented in Zechariah 14:3–5 (NIV) by the following:

> Then the Lord will go out and fight against those nations, as he fights on a day of battle. On that day his feet will stand on the Mount of Olives, east of Jerusalem, and the Mount of Olives will be split in two from east to west, forming a great valley, with half of the mountain moving north and half moving south. You will flee by my mountain valley, for it will extend to Azel. You will flee as you fled from the earthquake in the days of Uzziah king of Judah. Then the Lord my God will come, and all the holy ones with him.

After rapture occurs and the Church has been removed, the Jewish people will remain. We must remember that the Jewish people did not accept the fact that Jesus was the Son of God when he came to earth the first time. Jesus's purpose with his first coming was to provide a path to salvation when he formed the Christian church as God's way to eternal life. God now, however, needed a way to convince his chosen people that Jesus is the Son of God. It would seem that God's plan is to use the great tribulation as his way to convince his chosen people that Jesus is the Son of God and was the Messiah that was prophesized in the Old Testament.

When rapture occurs, all moral restraint will disappear from the face of the earth. This is when the Antichrist and the false prophet will rise and be at their peak in their efforts working against God. This is described in the New Testament, which the Jewish people do not follow, and is documented in 2 Thessalonians 2:3–12 (NIV):

> Don't let anyone deceive you in any way, for that day will not come until the rebellion occurs and the man of lawlessness is revealed, the man doomed to destruction. He will oppose and will exalt himself over everything that is called God or is worshiped so that he sets himself up in God's temple, proclaiming himself to be God. Don't you remember that when I was with you I used to tell you these things? And now you know what is holding him back, so that he may be revealed at the proper time. For the secret power of lawlessness is already at work; but the one who now holds it back will continue to do so till he is taken out of the way. And then the lawless one will be revealed, whom the Lord Jesus will overthrow with the breath of his mouth and destroy by the splendor of his coming. The coming of the lawless one will be in accordance with how Satan works. He will use all sorts of displays of power through signs and wonders that serve the lie, and all the ways that wickedness deceives those who are perishing. They perish because they refused to love the truth and so be saved. For this reason, God sends them a powerful delusion so that they will believe the lie and so that all will be condemned who have not believed the truth but have delighted in wickedness.

The rise of the Antichrist and the false prophet will occur with his false promises of peace and his persecution of believers. This will result in the great tribulation and war with God, which culminates at Armageddon. All of this occurs after Satan and his followers are expelled from heaven.

The Bible describes the Antichrist and the false prophet in Revelation 13 as a beast coming out of the sea and a beast coming out of the earth. The Bible describes the beast coming out of the sea as having been injured during the war in heaven, and the battle resulted in the expulsion of Satan and his followers from heaven. This is described in Revelation 13:1 (NIV), which states, "And I saw a beast coming out of the sea. He had ten horns and seven heads, with ten crowns on his horns, and on each head a blasphemous name." In verse 3, it goes on to state, "One of the heads of the heads of the beast seemed to have had a fatal wound, but the fatal wound had been healed. The whole world was astonished and followed the beast." This beast from the sea is considered to be the Antichrist and is described in Revelation 13:5–8 (NIV):

> The beast was given a mouth to utter proud words and blasphemies and to exercise its authority for forty-two months. It opened its mouth to blaspheme God, and to slander his name and his dwelling place and those who live in heaven. It was given power to wage war against God's holy people and to conquer them. And it was given authority over every tribe, people, language and nation. All inhabitants of the earth will worship the beast—all whose names have not been written in the Lamb's book of life, the Lamb who was slain from the creation of the world.

The second beast seen as coming out of the earth is considered to be the false prophet and is backed by Satan. Revelation 13:12–18 (NIV) describes this beast as follows:

> It exercised all the authority of the first beast on its behalf, and made the earth and its inhabitants worship the first beast, whose fatal wound had been healed. And it performed great signs, even causing fire to come down from heaven to the earth in full view of the people. Because of the signs it was given power to

perform on behalf of the first beast, it deceived the inhabitants of the earth. It ordered them to set up an image in honor of the beast who was wounded by the sword and yet lived. The second beast was given power to give breath to the image of the first beast, so that the image could speak and cause all who refused to worship the image to be killed. It also forced all people, great and small, rich and poor, free and slave, to receive a mark on their right hands or on their foreheads, so that they could not buy or sell unless they had the mark, which is the name of the beast or the number of its name. This calls for wisdom. Let the person who has insight calculate the number of the beast, for it is the number of a man. That number is 666.

This false prophet will try to convince the remaining Jewish people that he is the long-awaited Messiah that was predicted in the Old Testament. He will do this by performing "great and miraculous signs." In addition, he will also convince the remaining false church, or an apostate religion that is remaining after rapture, that he is the true Christ. He will definitely be able to deceive the remaining inhabitants of the earth.

It is important to note that in Matthew 24, when Jesus is describing the signs of the end days, he refers to the prophecy of Daniel. Daniel had prophesized that a world leader would break his seven-year agreement that he makes with Israel after three and one half years and attacks Israel. This is consistent with the prophecy of the beast form the sea as previously described in Revelation 13:5 (NIV) and who is considered to be the Antichrist, which states, "The beast was given a mouth to utter proud words and blasphemies and to exercise his authority for forty-two months." Forty-two months is three and one-half years. In Matthew 24:15(NIV), Jesus states, "So when you see standing in the holy place the abomination that causes desolation, spoken through the prophet Daniel—let the reader understand—then let those who are in Judea flee to the mountains."

This is when God steps in and defeats the false prophet and the Antichrist. This is documented in Zechariah 12:9 (NIV), where is states, "On that day I will set out to destroy all nations that attack Jerusalem." This also reinforces the prophecy that the Jewish people will not be driven out of their land again as previously noted in Jeremiah 30:16.

Also in Matthew 24, when Jesus is speaking about the day when God steps in, he indicates that there will be tremendous distress and destruction going on in the world. Jesus says that if God does not step in, no one will survive. This is documented in Matthew 24:21–22 (NIV): "For then there will be great distress, unequaled from the beginning of the world until now—and never to be equaled again. If those days had not been cut short, no one would survive, but for the sake of the elect those days will be shortened."

In Matthew 24:29–31 (NIV), Jesus provides us with additional insight when he describes just how that day will start when God steps in:

> Immediately after the distress of those days "the sun will be darkened, and the moon will not give its light; the stars will fall from the sky, and the heavenly bodies will be shaken." Then will appear the sign of the Son of Man in heaven. And then all the peoples of the earth will mourn when they see the Son of Man coming on the clouds of heaven, with power and great glory. And he will send his angels with a loud trumpet call, and they will gather his elect from the four winds, from one end of the heavens to the other.

When one thinks about the amount of evil that was in the world during Hitler's time and the fact that God did not step in then, it is hard for me to imagine the level of evil, distress, and destruction that will be present at the time that he does intervene.

In Revelation 19:19–21 (NIV), the apostle John describes the battle of Armageddon when God does step in to defeat evil:

> Then I saw the beast and the kings of the earth and their armies gathered together to wage war against the rider on the horse and his army. But the beast was captured, and with it the false prophet who had performed the signs on its behalf. With these signs he had deluded those who had received the mark of the beast and worshiped its image. The two of them were thrown alive into the fiery lake of burning sulfur. The rest were killed with the sword coming out of the mouth of the rider on the horse, and all the birds gorged themselves on their flesh.

John then goes on to describe what happens next in Revelation 20:1–4 (NIV):

> And I saw an angel coming down out of heaven, having the key to the Abyss and holding in his hand a great chain. He seized the dragon, that ancient serpent, who is the devil, or Satan, and bound him for a thousand years. He threw him into the Abyss, and locked and sealed it over him, to keep him from deceiving the nations anymore until the thousand years were ended. After that, he must be set free for a short time. I saw thrones on which were seated those who had been given authority to judge. And I saw the souls of those who had been beheaded because of their testimony about Jesus and because of the word of God. They had not worshiped the beast or its image and had not received its mark on their foreheads or their hands. They came to life and reigned with Christ a thousand years.

This to me indicates that God does not destroy the earth when he steps in at the time of the great tribulation and the battle of Armageddon.

This is also prophesized in the Old Testament in Zechariah 14:16 (NIV), where it states, "Then the survivors from all the nations that had attacked Jerusalem will go up year after year to worship the King, the Lord Almighty, and to celebrate the Feast of Tabernacles."

As previously noted in Revelation 20:3 (NIV), the devil must be set free from the abyss for a short time. After the thousand years and Satan is released, he again will deceive the nations remaining on the earth. At this time, however, God will defeat Satan once and for all. This is described in Revelation 20:7–10 (NIV) by the following:

> When the thousand years are over, Satan will be released from his prison and will go out to deceive the nations in the four corners of the earth—Gog and Magog—and to gather them for battle. In number they are like the sand on the seashore. They marched across the breadth of the earth and surrounded the camp of God's people, the city he loves.

But fire came down from heaven and devoured them. And the devil, who deceived them, was thrown into the lake of burning sulfur, where the beast and the false prophet had been thrown. They will be tormented day and night forever and ever.

After this event, God comes to earth and passes final judgment on the earth. This is when heaven is revealed and the earth and sky pass away. This is documented by Revelation 20:11–15 (NIV) by the following:

Then I saw a great white throne and him who was seated on it. The earth and the heavens fled from his presence, and there was no place for them. And I saw the dead, great and small, standing before the throne, and books were opened. Another book was opened, which is the book of life. The dead were judged according to what they had done as recorded in the books. The sea gave up the dead that were in it, and death and Hades gave up the dead that were in them, and each person was judged according to what they had done. Then death and Hades were thrown into the lake of fire. The lake of fire is the second death. Anyone whose name was not found written in the book of life was thrown into the lake of fire.

After this final judgment, a new heaven on earth, with a new Jerusalem, will be created. This is documented in Revelation 21:1–4 (NIV) by the following:

Then I saw "a new heaven and a new earth," for the first heaven and the first earth had passed away, and there was no longer any sea. I saw the Holy City, the new Jerusalem, coming down out of heaven from God, prepared as a bride beautifully dressed for her husband. And I heard a loud voice from the throne saying, "Look! God's dwelling place is now among the people, and he will dwell with them. They will be his people, and God himself will be with them and be their God. He will wipe every tear from their eyes. There will be no more death or mourning or crying or pain, for the old order of things has passed away."

Based on all of my study of the Bible and all the additional information that I have been able to find, I do agree with Dr. Hindson that there is no doubt that the end days for the earth as we know it will start in the Middle East. To me, this is not too surprising since God started his creation with Adam and Even in the Middle East. In addition, God's chosen people are the Jewish people, and Jesus was born to Jewish parents. God's focus has always been on the Middle East and especially Jerusalem.

In 1996 and in his book Final Signs, Dr. Hindson argues that at the time of the great tribulation, there will be a one-world government and a global economy. He also argues that a pseudo-false religion that does remain will team with the one-world governing power. The two beasts, he explains, represent this, which he feels are the Antichrist and the false prophet. In addition, Dr. Hindson points out that both the first President Bush and President Clinton talked about a new one-world order. In fact, I even heard that Bill Clinton wanted to be the first world president. Even more recently, the second President Bush and President Obama have both talked about a new world order during their presidencies.

In 1996, there was significant evidence that the world was moving toward a possible one-world order based on the rise of globalism and a global economy. This was evidenced by the increase in trade agreements between nations across the globe. For example, the European Economic Community (EEC) was formed on December 31, 1992, and many more trade agreements have been made since. Even the formation of the World Trade Organization (WTO) tends to support this type of movement. The world environment at that time was more conducive to this trend than now in 2025.

The thing that I feel changed the world environment from what Dr. Hindson was observing was the unanticipated rise of radical Islamic terrorism. The destruction of the World Trade Center towers on September 11, 2001 (9/11), immediately changed the world environment for all nations. The world environment in 2025 is significantly different than it was in 1996 when Dr. Hindson was writing his book.

In 1996, the United States had not yet understood that radical Islamic terrorist had declared war on the United States and its allies.

I think both the first President Bush and President Clinton viewed a new-world order as something similar to the United States. Because of a world economy, globalism was on the rise, and it would only be natural for all nations to come together to foster world trade and prosperity for all nations. I think they felt that the world would unite under a single governing power as part of this new-world order.

In 2025, because of 9/11 and similar terrorist attacks across the world, I feel that the radical Islamic terrorists pointed out that many nations of the world have totally different cultures and histories and, as such, are just too different to accept a one-world governing system like the United States. I also feel that there is sufficient evidence that this idea of a single one-world governing system just will not work, nor will it be accepted by all nations.

For example, the League of Nations was formed as a prelude to this idea but was unsuccessful in the past. Even the current United Nations does not appear to have achieved the results that were intended when it was formed. Nations across the globe just do not want to give up their sovereignty totally. This, unfortunately, is just the nature of man.

Dr. Hindson also discussed that a pseudo-religion will be present during the end days and will team with a political governing system at that time. He describes this possibly as the Catholic Church in Rome, along with the Bible's prophecy that the Roman Empire will be resurrected. He describes what he feels that this pseudo-religion will be like. I am not sure that this pseudo-religion would be anything like what we consider religion to be in our day. In fact, I think it may well be radical Islam or even the worship of a political system such as socialism.

My impression of religion is based on the Bible, and with the evidence of the perversion of Islam by the radical Islamic terrorists, I just am not sure of what religion will look like during the end days. I do feel that it will be different than what we see today just based on the evidence of the widespread sexual abuse that has occurred in the Catholic Church. In addition, we are now hearing about significant sexual abuse occurring in the Southern Baptist Church. My impression of the Methodist religion was changed when I was attending the University of Denver in 1973.

When my wife and I were attending a Methodist church one Sunday, the pastor described the meaning of being born again. The pastor said, "Being born again was when you decide what you want to do as your lifetime career." After the service, my wife and I just looked at each other, and I said, "Did I hear what I thought I heard about being born again?: She responded with a yes. That is not what I believe being born again means. I would like to believe that this was just this pastor and not the entire Methodist belief. Denver was a very liberal city then and now.

As far as the pseudo-religion during the end days, I will defer to Dr. Hindson. Religion is his area of expertise, and I am sure he knows a lot more than I. My efforts have been to answer my questions about what the end days will look like.

As a result of my studies, I can understand why Dr. Hindson felt about his interpretations of the end days when he wrote his book in 1996. In 2025, however, I feel that the world environment has changed significantly during the time period since then. For example, technology has advanced tremendously in the use of computers and the internet.

In 1996, the initial mobile phones were just coming on line. Pagers were being used as a way of communicating with others. Since then, mobile phones have progressed to cell phones and now to smartphones. A smartphone nowadays has more computer capabilities than the computers utilized by our first astronauts and their first rockets. In 2025, computers have advanced to a level of self-driving cars and artificial intelligence. This technology is expanding exponentially so fast that it is extremely difficult to even dream of what is coming next. We now have smart TVs, smart homes, and so many other smart devices and appliances that it seems that the only limitation is ourselves and what we can think of. Social media seems to dominate our total society and relationships. This is true worldwide.

In addition, the rise of radical Islamic terrorism has increased the level of evil throughout the world. I attribute this to the work of Satan. There also seems to be a focus to increase the spread of socialism around the world. This is now even occurring in the United States by the radical, liberal, progressive left wing of the Democratic Party. I also attribute this to the work of Satan.

The problem with socialism is that it does not work in the long term. It may sound good in theory, but it has failed everywhere it has been tried. Since socialism does not believe in God, it will never work. This is why I feel that this is all part of Satan's work and is all part of his battle against God.

As Dr. Hindson theorized in his book, I do feel that there will be a world economy and a pseudo-religion of one type or another during the end days. As far as a one-world order, I do not feel that a single governing system will occur. I feel that there will be regions around the world where groups of nations will unite in some form for a common goal for them, but not under a single governing system. I base my conclusion on what is occurring in the world currently and the Bible prophecies.

The prophecies of the Old Testament contained in the books of Daniel and Ezekiel describe the time of the great tribulation and why the end days will occur in the Middle East. I feel this is all part of God's overall plan on how he will get the attention of his chosen people, the Jewish people, since they have not accepted Jesus as the Messiah that was prophesized in the Old Testament. It is very clear in the Bible that the Jewish people are God's chosen people.

Dr. Hindson did mention in his book that the Antichrist might be linked to the computer/internet and not necessarily a person. I have to agree that I think the Antichrist is the internet and why there will be a global economy, which will be controlled by the internet. The reference to the mark of the beast as 666 as a requirement to buy or sell seems to be right in line to our current internet and the use of the computer.

We can now buy and sell almost everything on the computer. Our credit cards have computer chips installed so now all we have to do is tap the card on a computer device that allows people to pay for items with no cash required. In fact, there currently is a push to do away with cash with companies actually refusing to accept cash for payment. In addition, there is now computer currency being used instead of money. It also was just reported on the news media that an individual was having a computer chip installed in his forehead so that he doesn't even have to carry a credit card to conduct business. Does this sound like the mark of the beast being on the right hand or forehead in order to conduct business? I hate to say it, but I do.

As a result of my research and studies, I do not have much optimism for the United States. I did not find any evidence in the Bible prophecies that indicated that the United States will be a factor or even a consideration during the end days. This to me suggests that the radical, liberal, progressive left-wing of the Democratic Party will succeed and "fundamentally change the United States," as President Obama indicated as his agenda while he was president. His agenda and his supporters want socialism to be the governing system for the United States instead of capitalism.

Since socialism does not believe in God, God has to be removed from all aspects of our society. This is the obvious agenda currently of the radical, liberal, progressive left-wing Democratic Party. In the 2018 election, there were forty-seven self-proclaimed socialists running for office. There already was a large number of socialist Democrats currently serving in our government. When the United States turns its back on God, God will turn his back on the United States. Since there was no mention of the United States in the end-days prophecies, I had to assume and conclude that they will be successful.

It is also interesting to note that the Bible prophecies do not mention anything about China. With China being a communist/socialist country as far as their governing system, they also do not believe in God. No wonder they are not mentioned or referenced in the Bible prophesies during the end days.

What this all means to me is that, as a Christian, we can expect that the conditions of our world will continue to deteriorate in order to fulfill the Bible prophesies. As Jesus stated in Matthew 24, "There will be great distress unequaled from the beginning of the world until now and never to be equaled again." He also went on to say that if God does not step in, no one will survive.

Even though this is a bleak forecast for our world, Jesus did tell us what we need to do as Christians. This is documented in John 14:1–4 (NIV) by the following:

Do not let your hearts be troubled. You believe in God; believe also in me. My Father's house has many rooms; if that were not so, would I have told you that I am going there to prepare a place for you? And if I go and prepare a place for you, I will come back and take you to be with me that you also may be where I am. You know the way to the place where I am going.

In Matthew 24:36–39 (NIV), as previously noted and repeated here, Jesus also tells us that no one, not even he, knows when God will have his Son return to claim his church. Jesus stated this by the following:

But about that day or hour no one knows, not even the angels in heaven, nor the Son, but only the Father. As it was in the days of Noah, so it will be at the coming of the Son of Man. For in the days before the flood, people were eating and drinking, marrying and giving in marriage, up to the day Noah entered the ark; and they knew nothing about what would happen until the flood came and took them all away. That is how it will be at the coming of the Son of Man.

Through my research and studies, I think God purposely made sure that the Bible prophesies did not reveal the exact date. I arrived at this conclusion because the Bible is not specifically clear when Jesus will return to claim his church. This is when rapture will occur. It is not clear if Jesus's return occurs before the one thousand years, when the beast and the false prophet (Satan) are locked up in the abyss as described in Revelation, or after the one thousand years, when Satan must be released as described in Revelation.

Bible scholars have been arguing over this for many years. As a result, three theories have been developed. These three theories are known as *postmillennial, amillennial, and premillennial.* Here again is where I have to rely on Dr. Hindson to help me understand the difference in these three theories.

Dr. Hindson describes postmillennial as a school of thought that believes that the thousand-year reign of Christ (the millennium) is interpreted symbolically as synonymous with the church age. This assumes that only after Christianity succeeds on earth and Christ will return and announce that his kingdom has been realized.

Dr. Hindson describes amillennial as an approach that sees no millennium of any kind on the earth. Instead, amillennialists tend to view the so-called millennial prophesies as being fulfilled in eternity. The amillennialists see no specific future for the nation of Israel.

Dr. Hindson describes the premillennial view as Christ returning at the end of the church age to set up his kingdom on earth for a thousand-year period. He goes on to say that most premillennialists also believe that there will be a period of great tribulation on earth prior to the return of Christ. Premillennialists also generally believe in the restoration of the state of Israel and the eventual conversion of the Jewish people to Christianity. Dr. Hindson also points out that most evangelical Christians hold to the view that rapture is the next major prophetic event to occur. This view believes that this will end the church age and prepare the way for tribulation and the return of Christ.

I am one who accepts the premillennialist's point of view. I base my acceptance of this on 1 Thessalonians 4:16–17 (NIV), which was previously noted and states:

> For the Lord himself will come down from heaven, with a loud command, with the voice of the archangel and with the trumpet call of God, and the dead in Christ will rise first. After that, we who are still alive and are left will be caught up together with them in the clouds to meet the Lord in the air. And so we will be with the Lord forever.

Since no one knows the date or time of the second coming, Jesus told us what we should do. In Matthew 25:13 (NIV), Jesus tells us to do the following, "Therefore keep watch, because you do not know the day or the hour."

In summary, I do have to feel sorry for atheists who do not believe in God or his Son, Jesus Christ. This includes all of those people and governments who believe in socialism, communism, Marxism, and fascism. They obviously do not have a very bright future awaiting them.

God sent Jesus to this earth to provide a way to salvation and achieve eternal life. He did this so that he would not have to destroy the earth again when wickedness and evil get out of hand as a result of Satan battling against God. It is unfortunate that God's chosen people did not accept Jesus as the Son of God. Jesus made it perfectly clear in John 14:6–7 (NIV) when he states: "Jesus answered, 'I am the way and the truth and the life. No one comes to the Father except through me. If you really know me, you will know my Father as well. From now on, you do know him and have seen him.'"

Atheists will have a big problem on judgment day. In Matthew 10:32-33 (NIV), Jesus tells us what to expect for non-believers. Jesus states the following, "Whoever acknowledges me before others, I will also acknowledge before my Father in heaven. But whoever disowns me before others, I will disown before my Father in heaven."

My study of the Bible prophesies has led me to conclude that God's Word does provide significant warning to nonbelievers as well as the United States. This warning answers the question, does God exist? The fact is that God does exist, and a final judgment will occur during the end of time, as we know it. God will judge all on what they did during their lifetime. Atheists will not like the results, but they made their choice. As such, they will have to suffer with it forever and ever.

CHAPTER 9

What About the United States?

As I noted earlier, I did not find any mention of the United Sates as being part of the end days. I also did not find any parable in the Bible by any of the prophets that even suggested that a Western nation would be present as part of the end days. There are, however, references to nations from the north and south during the end days. It should also be noted that in addition to no mention of a Western nation, there also is no mention of any nation from the east. This would suggest that China also would not play a role during the end days, even though China has a history of over four thousand years. This to me suggests that the United States and China will fall from their present positions of being leading, prominent nations within the world system of nations at the time of the great tribulation. This caused me to want to try and understand why this will happen as part of God's overall plan.

As I think back over history, I can understand why China would fall from its current position due to its governing system, which is a communistic/socialistic approach to governing of its people. History tells us that all systems that do not believe in God are doomed to failure. The Bible also confirms this to be a fact. This is why I have a great concern about the United States.

The United States was founded on Judeo-Christian principles; however, the United States now appears to be turning its back on God. The current radical, liberal, progressive left wing Democratic party appears to be focused on replacing capitalism with socialism as the governing system for the United States. This is evidenced by so much of their focus is on removing God from our society. If they are successful, this will doom the United States. This may be what happens and why the United States is not mentioned in the parables of the end times.

During the history of our world, many nations have developed and then eventually disappeared from the world's landscape. Two of the most prominent empires or nations during the time period that the Bible was being written included the Egyptian empire ruled by Pharaohs and the Roman empire ruled by Caesars. Both of these governing systems did not believe in God and had a lot to do with God's chosen people. There were also many other groups of people that formed nations and governing systems and then were taken over by other nations or groups of people through wars and conflicts as a result of power expansion goals. These groups of people tended to worship idols and not God.

Jesus was born of Jewish parents, which would be expected since the Jewish people are God's chosen people. Unfortunately, God's chosen people did not accept Jesus as the Messiah that was prophesized in the Old Testament. This had to be a great disappointment to God. Jesus did teach that God would prefer not to interfere with how mankind chooses to govern themselves, but he does prefer that nations do believe in him. He has made it perfectly clear that he will protect his chosen people and punish those who curse the children of Israel.

Wars between nations and other small groups of people under different governing systems have been going on since the beginning of time. It seems that humans just have a thirst for power and earthly riches. I think this is what Satan likes to use as he wages his war against God. It appears to me that it is the nonbelievers in God who are the ones that are normally behind the start of any war. Satan spreads his evil as he tempts these nonbelievers to pursue their selfish goals. Wars are examples of good versus evil and, as the Bible predicts, will continue until the end of days. This is why I do not see a one-world order as far as a governing system for this world. Satan is just too powerful, and only God will be able to defeat him, as is predicted in the Bible.

The Bible does indicate that God will intercede when it affects his chosen people. As previously noted, God interceded to cause the release of his chosen people from the pharaoh of Egypt. There is no evidence that he intercedes when nonbelievers attack other nonbelievers. This was evidenced by the fact that the Roman Empire fell to barbarians, who continually attacked the Romans until they were defeated. He did not come to the rescue of the Romans.

This provides the evidence that God does not bless nations that do not believe in him and who worship idols. This is also evidenced by the Mayan civilization that once was present in Central America. They existed for approximately 1,200 years, after which they just seemed to disappear. I recently heard that the Mayan civilization disappeared due to a water shortage. Evidently, their water source was a very large lake, which dried up and resulted in their civilization ceasing to exist.

Archeological studies of their ruins suggest that they were advanced and knowledgeable, as far as their civilization, when compared to other civilizations during that time period. It would not have been any problem for God to provide a water source if they had believed in God. This should provide a lesson for all of us.

The United States was formed in 1776 and was based on Judeo-Christian principles. This is why I feel that God blessed the United States to become a superpower and leader of the free world. I feel that he assisted the United States in winning the Revolutionary War against a much stronger opponent of Great Britain. I also feel that God also blessed the United States during World War II to defeat Hitler and the Axis powers of evil. He made sure that Hitler did not annihilate his chosen people. With the defeat of Hitler, the Jewish people were given back their land in 1947, which fulfilled the biblical prophecy that this would happen. The Judeo-Christian principles are based in the belief in God and his Son, Jesus Christ.

The Bible does provide evidence of why God did not help the Romans or the Mayans in their time of need but did bless the United States to help defeat Hitler. In the Old Testament, in Psalms 33:10–16 (NIV), it states:

> The Lord foils the plans of the nations; he thwarts the purposes of the peoples. But the plans of the Lord stand firm forever, the purposes of his heart through all generations.
>
> Blessed is the nation whose God is the Lord, the people he chose for his inheritance. From heaven the Lord looks down and sees all mankind; from his dwelling place he watches all who live on earth— he who forms the hearts of all, who considers everything they do. No king is saved by the size of his army; no warrior escapes by his great strength.

God also provides us with a warning to any nation that turns its back on God. If a nation does turn its back on God, God will turn his back on that nation. This is documented in Proverbs 14:34 (NIV), which states, "Righteousness exalts a nation, but sin is a disgrace to any people." What this means to me is that people or nations cannot just ignore God's laws and live their lives as they please and expect to be happy and blessed by God. Turning your back on God is a sure path to destruction and the final judgment.

Since my educational background is in engineering and not history, I once again had to rely on others while researching what our founding fathers actually believed about religion when they formed our country. I had to look to others who are historians and who have the knowledge of history in this matter.

I was able to find an excellent source in a recently released DVD by Citizens United and Citizens United Foundation. The DVD is titled *Rediscovering God in America*. Newt and Callista Gingrich narrate this DVD. Newt Gingrich is a well-known historian and author. This DVD is based on the New York Times bestseller *Rediscovering God in America*. This DVD provided tremendous insight into our nation's founding fathers' belief in God and explains just what they were trying to do when they wrote our Constitution.

In 1776, our nation's founders authored the Declaration of Independence. Thomas Jefferson drafted this document with input from others. It provides us with strong evidence that our nation's founders held a very strong belief in God. This is evidenced by the second sentence of the second paragraph of the Declaration of Independence. This sentence states the following, "We hold these truths to be self-evident that all mean are created equal, that they are endowed by their creator with certain inalienable rights, that among these are life, liberty, and the pursuit of happiness." Thomas Jefferson also expressed his strong belief in God by other writings. One example is evidenced by this writing by Thomas Jefferson:

> God who gave his life gave us liberty. Can the liberties of a nation be secure when we have removed the convictions that these liberties are the gift of God? Rights and freedom come not from a king or government, but a creator.

The American Revolution was fought to stop taxation by England and to provide freedom for all individuals to exercise their right to worship as they choose to do so. One of the arguments that we hear continuously from the radical, liberal, progressive left-wing Democratic politicians so much nowadays is the need for "separation of church and state." Based on my research, I have come to the conclusion that this idea has been manipulated by the radical, liberal, progressive left-wing Democrats in a way that was never intended by our founding fathers.

My conclusion is that our nation's founders were not trying to keep religion out of government but were trying to keep government out of religion. I think that our founding fathers actually felt that religion should have a significant role in government based on the beliefs of its leaders and should influence how they govern. Their intent was that government should not legislate any specific religion on its people, but religion should influence how they govern the people. This to me is the real meaning of the "separation of church and state" and what our founders were trying to achieve, not the reverse. I have come to this conclusion based on examples of writings of other members of our founding fathers.

For example, James Madison wrote the following when he was discussing the American revolution and what he saw as the intervention of a higher power, which led to the final victory in the Revolutionary War. He wrote the following: "It is impossible for the man of pious reflection not to perceive that a finger of that almighty hand, which has been so frequently and simply extended to our relief in the critical stages of the revolution."

George Washington also expressed his belief as to how religion and morality must be part of the underlying government structure in order to be successful when governing a nation. He wrote the following: "Of all the dispositions and habit which lead to political prosperity, religion and morality are indispensable supports."

Our nation was formed in the nineteenth century with the Declaration of Independence. A strong religious belief in God carried on well into the twentieth century and is evidenced by many of our government structures located in Washington, DC. For example, in the National Archives Building, there is an image of the Ten Commandments engraved in bronze on the floor of the entryway. On top of the Washington Monument, the phrase "Praise be to God" is inscribed. At the top of the facade of the Supreme Court Building, there are figures of religious icons and/or leaders of different faiths present. There are figures of Moses, Confucius, Mohammad, and other well-known religion leaders. The Library of Congress building also has an image of Moses holding the Ten Commandments and images of Jewish women praying. In addition, the Tomb of the Unknown Soldier, which was constructed in 1933, has the following inscription: "Here rests in honor and glory an American Soldier known but to God."

In 1934, Franklin D. Roosevelt had the Jefferson Monument established. There are four panels present in this monument with inscriptions present. God is referenced on three out of the four panels. In addition, in the Lincoln Memorial, there is also an inscription of President Lincoln commenting on the Civil War. This inscription reads as follows: "We were highly resolve that these dead shall not have died in vein, that this nation under God, shall have a new birth of freedom." President Lincoln also used this phrase in his famous Gettysburg Address. It is obvious that our founding fathers held a strong belief in God as part of their core beliefs.

Additionally, in the early 1800s, religious services were allowed to be held in the Capitol building. Both Thomas Jefferson and James Madison attended these services during their presidencies. I cannot even imagine what the current radical, liberal, progressive left-wing Democrats would say about this today if this were to occur or even how they would react.

To me, all of the above evidence says that our founding fathers did believe in God and felt that religion was a very important aspect needed to support the nation's governing leaders. It also supports the idea that the "separation of church and state" was meant to prohibit government from establishing a national religion, not to keep religion out of government.

When I look at what is happening today in our country, I see a constant onslaught by the radical, liberal, progressive left-wing politicians trying to remove God from our government, our schools, and every facet of our lives. I have also seen a significant decline in the morality of our society. This has resulted in an increase in evilness and division across our country. The actions by the radical, liberal, progressive left-wing Democratic senators during the confirmation hearing for Justice Brett Kavanaugh simply highlighted just how far left many members of the Democratic Party have gone. Their actions were a direct assault on our Constitution and our Judeo-Christian principles of the rule of law and the presumption of innocence until proven guilty. How Justice Kavanaugh was treated by these radical, liberal, progressive left-wing Democratic senators was truly an abomination. If this is how these current Democrats will govern our nation, if they return to power, I know why the United States is not mentioned in the Bible prophecies as being a factor during the end days.

The radical, liberal, progressive left-wing portion of the Democratic Party have been pushing for the appointment of progressive liberal activist judges to all courts throughout our land for some time now. They appear to have decided that the best way for them to advance their socialistic agenda is through the courts. What they cannot achieve at the ballot box, they plan on achieving through activist judges at all levels, but especially through Supreme Court justices. This is why they fought so hard to block Justice Kavanaugh's appointment. Their long-term goal is to get rid of our Constitution in its present form.

I clearly remember President Obama expressing his great disdain for our Constitution when he declared that our present

Constitution states what he cannot do, not what he can do. This is why the current radical, liberal, progressive left-wing socialistic-minded Democrats want to change the Constitution. They claim that the Constitution should be a living and breathing document that should change to reflect what they consider to be the current view of our society. These socialistic Democrats say that the Constitution is outdated since it was created in 1776. Since the Constitution was founded on Judeo-Christina principles, this is also why they are continuing to push to get God removed from our society.

They feel that the best way to nullify the Constitution is through activist judges on the Supreme Court. These radical, liberal, progressive left wing Democrats want only activist judges on the Supreme Court who will make law, not interpret the law based on our Constitution. Judge Kavanaugh is a Constitution originalist; therefore, he had to be blocked at all costs. With liberal activist judges, the Democrats can push their socialistic agenda and avoid ballot box defeats. If they do regain power, our nation surely is doomed.

Unfortunately, this to me does suggest that eventually these radical, liberal, progressive left-wing Democrats will gain power. The easiest way for them to change our Constitution is to appoint five liberal, progressive, socialistic judges to the Supreme Court. They will then have the means to destroy our Constitution, which will result in the end of the United States as we now know it. This would explain why the United States in not a factor during the end days of the great tribulation.

John Adams understood how a nation must be made up of moral and religious people in order to function under our Constitution. Our Constitution is not a living and breathing document that requires change. John Adams expressed this when he wrote, "Our Constitution was made for a moral and religious people. It is wholly inadequate to the government of any other." Socialism is not a moral system and certainly not a religious system.

Ronald Reagan also knew how important religion and belief in God are to a nation. In one of his speeches, he stated the following: "If we ever forget that we are one nation under God, then we will be a nation gone under."

When President Obama stated that the United States was no longer a Christina nation, this caused me to have a significant concern about the future of our country. He also promised that he was going to "fundamentally change America." It is now 2025, and I have never seen so much deviousness in our country between Republican and Democrats. I have to wonder if he indeed succeeded in his efforts. If he did, what does this mean for our country? A look at the histories of democracies of the past may be able to tell us something about our future.

One historian that studied past democracies was Alexander Tyler, a Scottish history professor at the University of Edinburgh. In 1887, Professor Tyler came up with the following conclusion after studying the Athenian Republic that existed two thousand years earlier:

> A democracy is always temporary in nature; it simply cannot exist as a permanent form of government. A democracy will continue to exist up until the time that voters discover that they can vote themselves generous gifts from the public treasury. From that moment on, the majority always votes for the candidates who promise the most benefits form the public treasury, with the result that every democracy will finally collapse over loose fiscal policy, (which is) always followed by a dictatorship. The average age of the world's greatest civilizations from the beginning of history has been about two hundred years. During those two hundred years, these nations always progressed through the following sequence:
>
> > From bondage to spiritual faith,
> > From spiritual faith to great courage,
> > From courage to liberty,
> > From liberty to abundance,
> > From abundance to complacency,
> > From complacency to apathy,
> > From apathy to dependence,
> > From dependence back into bondage.
> > I would say that we are in the apathy to dependence phase.

Being 2025, we have been a nation now for 249 years. We are the only nation in the world that has been under a single document, the *Declaration of Independence*, for over two centuries. If the radical, liberal, progressive left-wing socialistic-minded Democrats regain power and the presidency in the 2020 elections, the United States obituary may well be written as the following: "Born 1776—Died 2020."

I am now eighty-two years old, and I have a tremendous concern about the future of the United States. My research for this book has led me to the conclusion that eventually the radical, liberal, progressive left-wing socialistic-minded Democrats will regain power; and when they do, we will be able to write the obituary. This will also fulfill the Bible prophecy of the end days in which the United States appears not to be a factor. Whenever the end days do arrive, I feel that rapture will have already occurred, and only the atheist and nonbelievers will remain in our nation These remaining nonbelievers, along with the other world nonbelieving survivors of the great tribulation, will then be judged during the final judgment by God. As a warning to atheists—God does exist!

CHAPTER 10

So What Happened: 1900 to the 1960s

T HE QUESTION NOW IS, How did we get from a country that was founded on Judeo-Christian principles and a strong belief in God in 1776 to where we are today? At one time, there really was not much difference between the Republican and Democratic parties. The majority of the leaders in both parties appeared to have a strong belief in God and a religious morality of character.

Franklin Delano Roosevelt (FDR), a Democrat, was president from 1933 to 1945. He is considered to be the father of the progressive movement in our country. Even as a progressive Democrat, however, he still believed in God and was religious. This indicates to me that the current radical, liberal, progressive left-wing Democrats of today are not really like the first progressives. Since FDR had polio and was in a wheelchair, he indicated that he prayed to God to stay strong. In addition, just prior to the D-Day invasion of Europe, FDR led a prayer on national radio to rally the American people during World War II. He ended his prayer with, "Thy will be done, Almighty God. Amen." Even though he may have been a progressive, this tells me that he was a religious man and did believe in God. Can you even imagine a current radical, liberal, progressive left-wing Democrat doing this today? I cannot even imagine them praying.

From 1933 to the present (2025), we have had sixteen presidents. We have had eight Democrats and eight Republicans. During the initial portion of this time period from 1933 to 1993, there was not much difference in Republicans and Democrats and their belief in God. There were ten presidents during this time period with five being Republicans and five being Democrats. During this time period, we fought World War II, Korea, Vietnam, and the first Gulf War in Kuwait. In addition to these wars, we also had the Cuban Missile Crisis and the Bay of Pigs.

FDR was president when World War II started, and Harry S. Truman was president when the war ended. Both of these presidents were Democrats. Harry S. Truman was president when the Korean War started, and Dwight D. Eisenhower, a Republican, was president when the cease-fire occurred. Eisenhower was president when the Cuban Missile Crisis and the Bay of Pigs started. John Fitzgerald Kennedy (JFK), however, was president when it ended. Once again, one Republican and one Democrat. The Vietnam War was started when Lyndon Baines Johnson, a Democrat, was president and carried through the presidency of Richard Nixon and ended during the presidency of Gerald Ford. Both President Nixon and President Ford were Republicans.

As noted earlier, even though FDR is considered to be the father of the progressive movement, he still believed in God as was evidenced previously. I assume that President Truman, a Democrat, also believed in God. I base this on the fact that he was from the Midwest part of our country. President Eisenhower, a Republican, also believed in God. This was evidenced in 1954 when he was president, and he added the words "Under God" to our Pledge of Allegiance. We also know that JFK believed in God because of his religious Catholic faith, which was somewhat of a controversy during his election. This is also evident by the fact that he stated the following in one of his speeches: "I believe that the rights of man come not from the generosity of the state but the hand of God."

So at least through the early 1960s, there is sufficient evidence that our leaders, both Republican and Democrat, believed in God. This even includes FDR, a progressive Democrat. When we compare the leaders during that time period to today's leaders, especially the radical, liberal, progressive left-wing Democrats, we have to wonder, What happened? What changed?

If we look at the United States from the 1900s through the 1960s, we can get an indication of just what did change. Our leaders during 1933 through 1963 were born either just before 1900 or in the years just after that. That means these leaders grew up during World War I and the Great Depression. The environment and conditions in the United States during this time period had to have a large impact on their beliefs and attitudes as how they would govern.

World War I was a very brutal war, and all nations were impacted tremendously. National patriotism and a strong belief in God were prevalent in the United Sates. This belief in God, as well as the high level of patriotism, was similar to the beliefs and attitudes of our founding fathers. After World War I ended, our country entered into the Great Depression. The focus of our national leaders during this time period had to be winning the war and then leading our nation back to prosperity from depression. When conditions are difficult in the environment that we are living in, it is normal to find hope with a strong belief in God. As the old saying goes, "There are no atheists in foxholes." This was the environment that the future leaders of 1933 to 1963 grew up in. This naturally had to shape their attitude and beliefs.

When World War II occurred, our leaders, who had come from an environment that fostered a strong belief in God and a strong sense of patriotism for our country, governed with this type of attitude. Looking at the environment that these leaders grew up in, it is not hard to see why there was not much difference between Republicans and Democrats. Their focus was on the survival of our nation.

World War II was fought against Adolph Hitler and the other Axis powers. Adolph Hitler had two goals: one goal was to impose fascism on the world as the governing system, and the other was the extermination of the Jewish people. Fascism is defined as "an autocratic and an extreme nationalistic governing system and social organization that is brutally intolerant of different points of views and/or practices." As far as Hitler's second goal of extermination of the Jewish people, he was able to exterminate six million Jews before he was defeated.

As far as the other Axis powers, when Hitler started his push to take over Europe, Benito Mussolini in Italy joined with Hitler as he had similar belief on how to govern. In addition, while Hitler and Mussolini were causing trouble in Europe, Japan decided that it had a chance to expand their empire in the world and attack the United States at Pearl Harbor. This resulted in the United States and our leaders facing a war on two fronts.

To me, this was an excellent example of the continuous battle between good and evil and Satan's battle with God. When Hitler started exterminating God's chosen people, the Bible clearly indicates that God is not going to let that happen. As when God intervened for his chosen people in Egypt to get them set free, it is not too surprising that he surely was going to intervene to stop Hitler.

With the United States being a Judeo-Christian nation with religious leaders that believed in God, there is no question in my mind that God did intervene and blessed the United States to help us and our allies to defeat Hitler. With the defeat of Hitler, the Bible's prophecy as stated in Amos 9:14 was fulfilled. This is the prophecy previously noted where God promised his chosen people that they would return to their land and never again be displaced. World War II ended in 1945, and as previously noted, the nation of Israel was established in 1947.

God had to be helping the United States during World War II. The United States and its allies were both outmanned and outgunned, but God made sure that we were able to develop the atomic bomb before the Germans did. The first atomic bomb was detonated on July 16, 1945. President Truman authorized the first of two atomic bombs that had been developed to be dropped on Hiroshima, Japan, on August 6, 1945. After the second atomic bomb was dropped on Nagasaki, Japan, on August 9, 1945, Japan said enough was enough and surrendered unconditionally. With the development of the atomic bomb, the world environment was changed forever. With Hitler, Mussolini, and Japan defeated and the end of World War II, the United States emerged as a world superpower through God's help and blessing.

World War II was known as the *war to end all wars*. We know, however, as the Bible tells us, that wars will continue until the end days. But what is important is that with the development of the atomic bomb, the world environment was changed drastically, and now the world would have to contend with the threat of nuclear war. We also know that Satan was going to continue his battle against God and that the battle between good and evil would continue.

The problem now was that Russia, under Joseph Stalin, had been one of the allies of the United States against Hitler. In 1917, with the takeover of Russia by the Bolsheviks and Vladimir Lenin, communism was instituted as the governing system in Russia. Communism is a political theory derived from Karl Marx, which advocates class warfare and a nonbelief in God. This system leads to a society in which all property is publically owned by the government, and each person works and is paid according to their ability and needs. It is the most brutal form of socialism, which is defined by the following:

> Socialism is a political and economic theory of a social organization that advocates the means of production, distribution, and exchange and should be owned and/ or regulated by the community organization as a whole. Governing policies and practices are based on Marxist theory, which is thought to be a transitional social state between the overthrow of capitalism and the realization of communism.

The United States had developed their atomic bomb in 1945. By 1949, Russia, which had become the Soviet Union after World War II ended, when Joseph Stalin claimed a large portion of Eastern Europe for his own. He also secured many of the German engineers that had been working on their atomic bomb and used them to develop an atomic bomb for the Soviet Union. This was realized in 1949. The world now had two nuclear-capable superpowers in the world with two totally different governing ideologies.

The world environment was now such that the two superpowers in the world had dramatically opposing visions of what the world should look like. The Soviet Union had the ideology of communism, which championed a Marxist/socialist form of a centrally controlled government. On the other side was the United States, which was the champion of free markets and democratic free societies as its ideology. The world was again at war, but now a very different war—a war of ideologies.

This was as a war of opposing ideologies as both countries tried to expand their influence in the world. Since both the United States and the Soviet Union possessed nuclear weapons, it became obvious that the use of these types of weapons would result in total destruction of both countries and most likely the world. This forced the leaders of both the United States and the Soviet Union to accept and adopt a policy of Mutually Assured Destruction (MAD). This new war became known as the Cold War because a "hot war" with nuclear weapons was unthinkable.

As a result of the blessing of God on the United States during World War II and its success, the generation of people that fought the war along with our leaders became known as the greatest generation. The environment that this generation grew up under included World War I and the Great Depression, which was previously discussed. The fact is that this environment had a very significant unifying impact on their beliefs, both in religion and their patriotic feelings and their approach to governing our country. The last president from the "greatest generation" was George Herbert Walker Bush, who was president from 1989 to 1993.

Because of the policy of Mutually Assured Destruction (MAD) and the fact that any war between the United States and the Soviet Union was unthinkable, the Soviet Union began to employ a policy of using proxies to pursue their goal of spreading communism. The Soviet Union began to back smaller communist countries and encourage them to be more aggressive toward others as a way to spread communism. The United States was then forced to back the countries that were being targeted by the communist aggression. The Cold War was being fought between the Soviet Union and the United States by proxies who could fight a "hot war" but at the conventional weapons level. It was hoped that through this means, a direct confrontation between the United States and the Soviet Union could be avoided. This "Cold War" policy resulted in the type of military actions which resulted in the Korean War (1950–1953), the Bay of Pigs and the Cuban Missile Crisis (1961–1962), and the Vietnam War (1965–1975).

The Korean War lasted from 1950 to 1953, when communist North Korea attempted to take over democratic South Korea. This war occurred just five years after the end of World War II. The major difference between a proxy war and conflicts like World War I and World War II is that the goal of the world wars was total defeat of the enemy. In a proxy war, the goal is a limited goal of convincing the aggressor to abandon its goal of a takeover and is not total defeat of the enemy. The limited goal in the Korean War resulted in a cease-fire armistice without a clear winner. Both North and South Korea remained intact with no formal peace treaty signed when hostilities ceased. No peace treaty has ever been signed, even to this day.

There is a very important aspect that needs to be considered when fighting proxy wars, which only has a limited goal. In a world war, the goal is and has to be total defeat of the enemy. There are two ways to affect a total defeat of an enemy. Carl Von Clausewitz defined these two ways in 1832 in his book On War. This book is considered to be the Bible on military actions.

Mr. Clausewitz indicates that the first way to achieve total defeat of an enemy is to destroy the enemy's capability to wage war. The second way to achieve total defeat is to destroy the enemy's will to wage war. True defeat is to destroy both the enemy's capability and their will to wage war. This is what happened in World War II to both Germany and Japan.

As a retired twenty-five-year Air Force veteran, fighter pilot, and combat veteran, I learned why a nuclear war was unthinkable between superpowers. I learned both in Air Command and Staff College (ACSC) and the Air War College (AWC) through war gaming exercises that the only way to defeat a superpower is to go nuclear. This is why a direct confrontation between the Soviet Union and the United States had to be avoided.

The problem with a limited goal during proxy wars, like the Korean War, is that when hostilities do end and total defeat of the enemy is not obtained, the enemy still remains intact. In order to ensure that the limited goal is not lost, a very critical step must be utilized to keep the enemy from not just pausing for a period of time, just waiting for conditions to change and then pursue their goal. In Korea, this was accomplished by the United States, leaving twenty-five thousand American troops in South Korea as a tripwire if the North ever decided it could achieve its goal of taking over South Korea. Our leaders from the "greatest generation" knew this, and we still have American troops stationed in South Korea as of today.

In Korea, since the goal was not total defeat of the enemy and limited to just stopping the communist North from taking over the South, many people in the United States were not totally behind this war effort. They did not see this as a vital national security threat to the United States. Our leaders, therefore, did not have the full support of the majority of the American population to fight this war. This was totally different from the American population's attitude and support during World War II.

In 1959, Fidel Castro and his guerilla army were able to overthrow the American-backed dictator, Cuban president General Batista. In 1960, Castro established diplomatic relations with the Soviet Union. This, of course, was a distinct problem for the United States. The US was going to have a communist country approximately ninety miles from its shores. The time period between 1961 and 1962 was probably the closest time in which the world was on the brink of a nuclear war as a result of a miscalculation by leaders in either the US or the Soviet Union.

In 1961, the US attempted the Bay of Pigs invasion of Cuba, which resulted in a complete disaster. Then in 1962, the Soviet Union, seeing a possible opening as a result of this US disaster, attempted to place nuclear capable missiles in Cuba. Under President John F. Kennedy, a Democrat, it became a test of wills to see who was going to blink first.

Thankfully, the Soviets blinked first and removed the missiles from Cuba.

The generation after the "greatest generation" is known as the *baby boomers*. This is the generation that was born just after World War II and grew up during the late 1940s and 1950s. Their early adulthood years occurred during the Vietnam War years of the 1960s and 1970s. This is when the policy of Mutually

Assured Destruction (MAD) was shaping our political policies and the environment when these baby boomers were entering their young adulthood.

The Vietnam War was being fought similar to the Korean conflict with a limited goal of stopping North Vietnam from taking over South Vietnam. Once again, this war was not supported by all the American people and especially the baby boomers. The threat of nuclear war was always present, especially during and after the Cuban Missile Crisis.

This resulted in the younger generation in the United States, the baby boomers and our future leaders, growing up under the uncertainty of the possibility of world annihilation due to the use of nuclear weapons. If a conflict between the United States and the Soviet Union resulted due to a miscalculation on the part of their leaders or our leaders, it could escalate into a nuclear war. This could happen as each country tried to expand its respective views while simultaneously expanding its influence in the world. As a result, this generation became antiwar and antimilitary in their thinking due to the possibility of world annihilation from the use of nuclear weapons.

The Cuban crisis in the early 1960s was when I believe the attitudes of the younger generation were changed from that of the "greatest generation." That is when the "hippies, yuppies, and peaceniks" became very active in their protest against war. This was the incident that created the environment for the development of the current radical, liberal, progressive left-wing, antiwar, antimilitary component of the Democratic Party. This totally shaped their approach and attitude toward life, and they became self-centered and less concerned about what was good for the country. They adopted the attitude that society should take care of them, and they had the attitude "if it feels good, do it." The 1960s were when these baby boomers became old enough to begin expressing their sense of self-interests.

As they became active in politics and began to voice their ideas, they were significantly different than those of the "greatest generation." The environment that they grew up in was totally different than the environment that the "greatest generation" grew up under.

These baby boomers began using the tactics of protests and marches and antiwar, antimilitary rallies against the Vietnam War. Through the use of these tactics and with the help of the news media, they were able to turn the national attitude against the Vietnam War. As they became politically active, they began to run for political office. Once in office, they were able to turn the political tide against the Vietnam War, which resulted in all funding for the South Vietnamese government to be cut off in February of 1975.

The Vietnam War started during President Johnson's, a Democrat, administration. The antiwar movement became so strong that President Johnson did not seek a second term. President Nixon, a Republican, campaigned on ending the war with the slogan of "Peace with Honor" and the promise to bring all of our troops home. This was accomplished by President Nixon's policy of Vietnamization of the war. He was able to bring all of our combat troops home in 1973. The fighting was left to the South Vietnamese to fight for themselves. The United States was still providing funding and advice, but no combat troops.

The difference now between Korea and Vietnam was that due to the political environment in the United States, no combat troops were left in South Vietnam as a tripwire like in Korea. The Vietnamese were left on their own. Even though our leaders were still part of the "greatest generation," the younger baby boomers were beginning to gain power. Their political orientation was antiwar and antimilitary.

It should be noted that in 1972, during the time that President Nixon was bringing our troops home, North Vietnam tried to embarrass the United States. Our troop levels on January 1, 1972, were down to 140,000 combat troops. The plan was to be down to 70,000 troops by April 1, 1972. On March 30, 1972, North Vietnam launched what was called the Spring Offensive of 1972. Even though the Paris peace talks were ongoing, it became obvious that the limited goal of changing the minds of North Vietnam from taking over the South had not been achieved.

The only significant combat troops remaining in South Vietnam at that time were some special forces and military advisors that were with the South Vietnamese Army Units. We did, however, have significant air power still available present from both the Navy and Air Force. These remaining American troops were essentially the tripwire that was needed to stop the 1972 Spring Offensive. North Vietnam came very close to being successful in taking over the South during this 1972 Spring Offensive. The month of April and May of 1972 were very critical. If it had not been for air power, they would have been successful in 1972. I know! I was there in 1972 as a forward air controller (FAC) during this Spring Offensive. I was flying the O-2A as previously noted.

We were able to stop the North about 50 miles north of Saigon. They were, however, able to essentially cut the country in half as well as takeover a significant portion of the northern section of South Vietnam before we were able to stop them. This kept the North from embarrassing the United States as we continued to withdraw our forces.

The attitude of the American population about the Vietnam War was even more different than the attitude of the American people during the Korean War. Even though there was not as much support for the Korean War as during World War II, our leaders were able to continue support of South Korea after hostilities ceased. We were able to take the critical step of leaving troops in South Korea to act as a tripwire if North Korea changed their mind and decided to continue with their goal of taking over the South. The American attitude was much different concerning the Vietnam War, when we ceased combat operations in Vietnam, which ended our participation in that war.

Our leaders did not have enough support to leave troops in South Vietnam like we did in South Korea. The liberal, progressive Democrats had gained sufficient power in Congress by February 1975 to get all funding to South Vietnam cut off. This is when the Vietnam War was lost. This is when it became obvious that the military win the battles, but the politicians lose the wars. The action by our congressional leaders doomed South Vietnam.

When the North Vietnam leaders saw what our congressional leaders had done about funding of the South, they saw an opportunity to achieve their goal of taking over the South. By this time, President Nixon had resigned, and President Ford was now president.

In early 1975, North Vietnam decided to again attack the South and to pursue their goal of taking it over. In February 1975, when the North again attacked the South, President Ford requested $720 million as emergency aid to South Vietnam. At that time, there were sufficient liberal, progressive Democrats in Congress to get this funding rejected. The baby boomers had finally secured sufficient power in Congress to begin to push their liberal, progressive agenda. Without a tripwire of American troops and no financial aid, South Vietnam was doomed.

When North Vietnam initiated their takeover of the South in 1975, they used the same battle plan they had used during the 1972 Spring Offensive. Without our aid and air power, they were doomed. South Vietnam fell to the North on April 30, 1975. The first example of how politicians lose wars.

As I look back over the time period of the 1950s, when our country was under the leadership of the "greatest generation," it is obvious to me that this is when the United States society was enjoying its best days. I hear politicians keep saying the best days for the United States are ahead of us. I do not believe it. I grew up in the 1950s. As a youth, I can remember that we never had to lock our doors at night. I also had a 1955 red Ford convertible. I could leave the top down and the keys in the ignition at night and never had to worry about it being stolen. People then respected one another and one another's property. Neighbors helped one another and had respect and integrity in their relationship with others.

In the 1960s when the baby boomers were growing up under the threat of nuclear war and the possibility of world annihilation, the environment changed. This to me is when, I believe, the moral decline in the United States also began, and we started on the path that will lead to our destruction as a nation.

This started when the baby boomers became a generation of inward-looking individuals who were more concerned about self-interests and less concerned about the good of the country. This is when the "if it feels good, do it" philosophy became somewhat of a norm for this generation. This is when I feel that the liberal, progressive left-wing component was born and began to take over the Democratic Party.

I think the prime examples of these types of leaders are Bill and Hillary Clinton. They grew up under the MAD policy that created the environment of the possibility of world annihilation as a result of a nuclear war. This was the seed of their antiwar, antimilitary philosophy. In addition, drug use became a major factor in this generation's approach to life and self-satisfaction. Their ideas about sex changed, and a moral decline began to occur. The importance of the family unit was no longer as significant as it had been in the past.

As Dr. Hindson points out in his book *Final Signs*, in 1960, married couples made up 75 percent of US households. By 1995, married couples made up only 45 percent of US households. In addition, one out of every eight children was born out of wedlock. With the increase in drug use, crime rates went up.

As the baby boomers grew up under this type of permissive environment, they began to develop their own agenda through the formation of the liberal, progressive left-wing approach to government. This is when these baby boomers began to entertain socialism as the solution to our nation's problems. This is when the United States began to turn its back on God and his laws and teachings. They at first tried to disguise their true agenda by resenting anyone calling them socialists. I think Hillary Clinton said it best when asked if she was a socialist. She answered the question by saying she was more in line with the progressive nature of FDR's positions as opposed to being a socialist. We now know that was totally false.

FDR believed in God while socialists do not. I think it was an insult that Hillary Clinton would call her beliefs similar to FDR when they are obviously more in line with Saul Alinsky's vision of socialism. Even JFK was considered to be liberal, but he also believed in God and even cut taxes while he was president. I also feel that neither FDR nor JFK could get the Democratic Party's nomination for president today under the current radical, liberal, progressive left-wing Democratic Party. Neither of them turned their backs on God. This led me to want to research why the United Stated decided to turn its back on God. This is the time period from the 1970s to the present.

CHAPTER 11

1970s to 2019

T HE LIBERAL, PROGRESSIVE, LEFT-WING politicians of the 1960s
and 1970s began to try to remove God from our schools and
government agencies by claiming the need for "separation of church
and state." They pursued policies such as legalization of abortion,
claiming gay and lesbian activities are normal relationships, and
that marriage should no longer be defined as just being between
one man and one woman. When a nation or people turn their backs
on God's laws and teachings, he will step in and punish them. The
Bible clearly illustrates what happens when a nation or a group
of people turn away from God. When the Jewish people, God's
chosen people, turned their backs on God, he sent them into the
wilderness for forty years. He destroyed the cities of Sodom and
Gomorrah due to the wickedness of their inhabitants. If we are no
longer a Christian nation, as President Obama has claimed, God
will no longer bless us as he has in the past.

The baby boomers of the liberal, progressive, left-wing segment
of the Democratic Party advanced their power by running for and
getting elected to office. There still were, however, many moderate
Democratic leaders in the Democratic Party remaining from the
greatest generation. The new liberal, progressive, left-wing Democrats
still had not advanced to the point that they could win the presidency.

In 1977, with the loss of the Vietnam War, which was the first loss of a war by the United States, our country turned from the Republican Party to the Democratic Party. This occurred with the election of James Earl Carter Jr. (Jimmy Carter), who was known as a liberal Democrat, but not in the mold of the new liberal, progressive, left-wing Democrats of today. He was more in the progressive mold of FDR and JFK. I think the difference was because Jimmy Carter was still part of the greatest generation, and he had served in World War II, just like JFK. He was a liberal Democrat on social issues, but not to the point that he did not believe in God. I know this to be a fact because one of my Air Force pilot training class members attended the same church as the Carters in Alabama.

With the election of Jimmy Carter, he became the first president from a new kind and changing Democratic Party. This new and emerging Democratic Party was changing its view on the military and its use. As I mentioned earlier, the Democratic Party had changed so much that I truly doubt if JFK could have received the Democratic nomination for president in 1976. With the liberals focusing on social issues, not many of the new Democrats were heard expressing comments like President Kennedy's statement on January 1961, when he said, "Ask not what your country can do for you, ask what you can do for your country."

Another example of why I do not think that President Kennedy could now get the new Democratic Party's presidential nomination was evident in his January 20, 1961 inaugural address. When talking about our adversaries, he said, "We dare not tempt them with weakness. For only when our arms are sufficient beyond doubt can we be certain beyond doubt that they will never be employed." Have you ever heard any of the current liberal, progressive, left-wing Democrats voice a similar statement?

Under President Carter, the military budget was drastically cut to the point that the American military combat capability was adversely affected. I know this to be a fact because I personally experienced the impact to our military combat capability when I was flying the F-111D aircraft.

When I was assigned to fly F-111s at Cannon AFB in Clovis, New Mexico, in the late 1970s, there was visible evidence of the impact of Jimmy Carter's drastic cuts in the military budget and its resulting impact on our combat capability. At that time, Cannon AFB had 72 F-111D aircraft assigned to the Twenty-Seventh Tactical Fighter Wing. These aircraft were assigned to four squadrons that made up the Tactical Fighter Wing (TFW) located at Cannon AFB. These squadrons consisted of two combat squadrons, one replacement training unit squadron for F-111s stationed in England, and one training squadron for crews assigned to Cannon AFB to man the two combat squadrons.

When I arrived at Cannon AFB, if a person walked down the flight line and looked at the front of the F-111 aircraft, there were nineteen holes where there should have been engines present. There was such a shortage of engine spare parts that there were not enough engines available to fill all the aircraft present. This resulted in not having sufficient aircraft in a flyable condition to do the required training or to maintain the combat capability of the combat squadrons.

This lack of flyable aircraft resulted in my training to learn to fly the F-111 to take twelve months to complete instead of the six months that the training course should have taken. In addition, neither of the two combat squadrons was considered combat-ready if called upon to deploy. The lack of spare parts for the F-111D aircraft system due to President Carter's drastic military cuts manifested itself in the F-111D program as just one example of the significant impact on combat capability throughout the Air Force. Additionally, at the same time, the Army was having difficulty keeping their combat divisions capable to conduct combat operations if called upon by a national emergency.

After four years of President Carter's liberal, progressive, left-wing policies, the American public became discouraged with high interest rates and a bad economy and the so-called misery index. This was the combination of high interest rates and inflation, which totaled approximately 18 percent. In 1981, Ronald Reagan, a Republican from the "greatest generation," was elected president.

President Reagan believed in a strong military and immediately began to rebuild the military back to the level needed to deter the Soviet Union from expanding their influence in the world.

President Reagan believed that a strong military makes a safer world for all. Because of his belief in a strong military, President Reagan increased the Department of Defense's (DOD) budget to make up for all the harm done to the military during the Carter years and liberal policies of his administration.

When I left Cannon AFB in 1985, the bases' combat capability was such that the Twenty-Seventh Tactical Fighter Wing of F-111D aircraft could deploy both of its combat squadrons within twenty-four hours if called upon to do so. These two deployed squadrons could provide the required number of combat sorties as required by United States war plans.

President Reagan implemented conservative policies as he rebuilt the military. He cut taxes, which always causes our economy to grow and expand. He also knew exactly how to defeat communism/socialism in the Soviet Union. His policies essentially attacked the major weakness of socialism, which is a planned and centrally controlled economy.

An economy that is planned and centrally controlled by the government cannot respond or adapt to an unforeseen change in the environment. This is due to the planned limited-resource allocation capability of a socialist economy. President Reagan attacked this weakness of a socialized economy by stating that the United States was going to build a military defense weapon system called Star Wars. This system would be designed and built in order to be able to defend the United States and our allies against intercontinental ballistic missiles. This caused the Soviet Union to have to respond by building a new weapon system that could defeat the Star Wars system.

Because the Soviet Union's governing system of communism was based on socialism, a planned government-controlled system of production, distribution, and exchange that is regulated by the government, it cannot adapt rapidly and efficiently to unforeseen change. When the Soviets channeled more of the government-controlled limited assets into the military side of their economy, they had to divert limited assets from the other aspects of their regulated economy. This resulted in a serious decline in their ability to provide enough of their limited resources to keep their basic economy on a solid basis. They were not able to increase their military spending while maintaining their economy at a sufficient level to satisfy the people's needs. President Reagan essentially forced the Soviet Union into bankruptcy.

On June 12, 1987, President Reagan challenged the Soviet Union's general secretary Gorbachev during a speech at the Berlin Wall. President Reagan challenged Secretary Gorbachev "to tear down this wall!" Because the Soviet Union's economy was in such a decline, Secretary Gorbachev had no choice but to do so.

On December 25, 1989, the Berlin Wall came down and Soviet Communism lay dead in the streets of Berlin. The Soviet Union's style of socialism (communism) had failed after seventy-two years. The Cold War ended, and Western Europe was freed form the Soviet Union's grip on these people. It was hoped that the world would become a much safer place.

The United States enjoyed prosperity and peace during the eight years (1981–1989) of conservative policies under President Reagan. As such, in the 1988 election, George Herbert Walker Bush, a Republican and vice president to Ronald Reagan, was elected president. President Bush was also part of the "greatest generation" and also fought in World War II. He was part of the generation that believed in God and had a strong patriotic belief in the United States.

With the failure of the Soviet Union, it seemed that the world would be safer and more stable. This hope was soon dashed when a new world threat surfaced in the form of terrorist attacks. Religious fanatics on many different fronts and locations began conducting terrorist attacks. This included Muslims attacking Muslims as well as attacks on all forms of governments. These attacks had their basis in a perverted fanatic religious ideology that opposed any type of government control that was in place that did not agree with them. This was a new and very different kind of enemy. Once again, a significant change had occurred in the world environment.

The next threat to world peace occurred when Saddam Hussein of Iraq invaded Kuwait. Since the United States did have a strong military, due to President Reagan's efforts, President Bush was able to stop Saddam Hussein and force him back into Iraq. This was known as the First Gulf War and lasted from August 2, 1990, until February 28, 1991. It is unfortunate that President Bush only had a limited goal (once again) of stopping Saddam Hussein from taking over Kuwait. The goal was not to remove Saddam Hussein's regime from Iraq but only to keep him from taking over Kuwait.

I think that President Bush had to limit the goal to just stopping Saddam Hussein due to not being able to garner enough support from Congress to be able to topple his regime, which would have been a far better solution to the problem. What was happening is that the baby boomers from the 1960s and the 1970s and their liberal, progressive, left-wing, antiwar, antimilitary views were gaining strength as they gained in numbers of elected officials in our government. This forced President Bush to have to put together a coalition of forces from thirteen different countries even to do what he did. This coalition included Muslim as well as Democratic countries. It was the largest military alliance established since World War II.

President Bush's next unfortunate misstep occurred when he campaigned on his pledge that he would not raise taxes when he said, "Read my lips, no new taxes." When he then was required to actually have to raise taxes on the American people, this opened the door for the now ever-increasing numbers and supporters of the rapidly-changing Democratic Party's shift to an even further liberal, progressive, left-wing position. This resulted in the election of the first baby-boomer president—William Jefferson Clinton—in 1992.

As the first baby-boomer president, Bill and Hillary Clinton were now in power. The Clinton administration was the initial step for the liberal, progressive left-wing agenda to have a chance to become reality and take over the Democratic Party. This to me is when the seeds for the current "radical," liberal, progressive left-wing policies were first planted.

The Clintons bragged about the idea that his election gave the United States two leaders for the price of one. Hillary soon made her presence known when she was put in charge of developing a new health-care system for our country. Thankfully, she was not successful, or we would have had "Obamacare" much earlier.

The seed, however, was planted for the later effort during the Obama administration.

President Clinton's liberal, progressive, left-wing antimilitary attitude was evidenced when he dramatically cut the military budget similar to what President Carter had done. He called the cuts a "peace dividend" as a result of winning the Cold War. In addition, the moral decline in our government leaders' attitudes toward God and religion became more evident.

This was evidenced when one of the very first presidential actions that President Clinton took was when he issued his "don't ask, don't tell" policy to the military. This policy addressed gay and lesbian members serving in the military. Prior to this policy, gay and lesbian individuals were prohibited from serving in the military and were discharged if their sexual preference became known.

It was also during the Clinton administration that it became more and more evident that the Democratic Party was moving even further to the left as more and more baby boomers were elected to office. Many Democrats of the "greatest generation" were insulted if you called them a socialist or even a liberal to their face. The title socialist was considered to be representative of a communist approach to government. The term liberal, by definition, means open to a new behavior of opinion and willingness to discard traditional values. They preferred to be called "moderates" and considered themselves to be moderate on social issues. Some Republicans also consider themselves to be moderate on social issues but conservative on fiscal policies. To me, however, these Republicans are considered to be RINOs (Republicans in name only) rather than conservative Republicans.

As previously noted, Hillary Clinton was one of the first Democrats to express her thoughts as to whether she was a socialist or a liberal when asked the question. She never really answered the question but gave a response that she considered herself to be more of a progressive in the vein of the Progressive Party that was formed under Theodore Roosevelt in 1912. Her definition of a progressive is a person that advocates or wants implementation of social reform based on new liberal ideas. A progressive liberal is one that believes that many traditional behaviors and beliefs are dispensable and are invalidated by modern thought and, as such, are subject to change. This belief is the same idea that our Constitution should be a living breathing document and open to change based on current ideas and morals that may be different than those of our founding fathers. The only problem is that her definition of a progressive is based more on the writings and ideas of Saul Alinsky.

Saul Alinsky, who died on June 12, 1972, wrote a book titled *Rules for Radicals*. It is known that during Hillary Clinton's college years, she was a proponent of Saul Alinsky's ideas. In fact, she wrote a ninety-two-page college senior honors thesis on the radical "community organizer." It has been reported that she met with Alinsky several times while she was writing her thesis. It has also been reported that after Alinsky's death in 1972, Hillary maintained a relationship extending into the 1990s with Saul Alinsky's main community organizing group called the Industrial Areas Foundation (IAF).

When I look at Saul Alinsky's *Rules for Radicals*, I just do not think that the Progressive Party of 1912 was as radical as Saul Alinsky's ideas are in his book. I believe that Hillary's interpretation of those early progressive ideas have been perverted to suit her needs similar to the perversion that has occurred with the idea of the "separation of church and state."

Saul Alinsky essentially developed a guide or plan on how to go about creating a new socialistic state. He outlines eight rules that he said are needed to be followed in order to create a new social state. These eight rules are really levels of control that have to be established in order to create this new social state. It appears to me that the radical, liberal, progressive left-wing Democrats are using Saul Alinsky's rules as their handbook to take over America's government, education, news, and entertainment institutions in order to create a new socialistic America. This may be what President Obama meant when he declared that he would "fundamentally change America." In his book, Saul Alinsky listed these eight rules in the order of importance. What Alinsky essentially did was to simplify Vladimir Lenin's original scheme for world domination by communism under Russian rule.

The following are the eight rules, in the order of importance, that Alinsky said must be followed in order to be successful in creating a new social state:

1. *Health care.* Alinsky said control health care, and you control the people.

2. *Poverty.* Alinsky's next important rule is to increase the poverty level as high as possible. He said it is easier to control poor people, and they will not fight back if you are providing everything that they need to live.

3. *Debt.* Alinsky's rule on debt is to increase debt to an unsustainable level. This way, you will be able to increase taxes, which in turn will produce more poverty.

4. *Gun control.* Alinsky says that you have to remove the ability for individuals to defend themselves from the government. This will allow you to create a police state

5. *Welfare.* Alinsky believes you must take control of every aspect of individual lives to include food, housing, and income..

6. *Education.* Alinsky says you have to control what people read and listen to and what our children learn in school by taking over the education system.

7. *Religion.* Alinsky insists that you must remove the belief in God from the government and the schools.

8. *Class warfare.* Alinsky's last rule is to divide the people into the wealthy and the poor. This will cause more discontent, and it will be easier to tax the wealthy in order to support the poor.

Based on Saul Alinsky's eight rules for radicals, it is no wonder why Hillary Clinton was put in charge of developing a new health-care system for our country when Bill Clinton was elected president. This also provides evidence of just how Hillary Clinton's ideology had been shaped by Saul Alinsky. Instead of just being a liberal progressive, she is a "radical" liberal progressive in her beliefs.

It should be noted that President Obama also wrote about Saul Alinsky in his book. This is also not surprising since Saul Alinsky was also a "community organizer." It would seem that this is what he meant when he said that he would "fundamentally change America." It again is no wonder that President Obama and the Democratic Party pushed so hard for Obamacare when he was elected president since Hillary Clinton's plan failed.

As the activist baby boomers from the 1960s and 1970s leaders were progressing upward in the hierarchy of the Democratic Party, it became obvious that additional Alinsky rules were in play. This is when the old Democratic Party from the "greatest generation" was beginning to be taken over by these activists and radical-thinking liberal progressive left-wing baby boomers." Their power base was expanding as they gained power.

That additional Saul Alinsky rules were in play was evidenced by rule 7 and the need to remove God from the government and the schools. This is when we began to hear about the "separation of church and state." This became the basis for the attack on our traditional values about the freedom of religion.

These efforts included banning prayers from schools and after-school programs. This has forced many teachers and athletic coaches to have to hide their faith. Atheist groups began to sue to have such things as "Under God" removed from our Pledge of Allegiance and to ban Christmas nativity scenes from public places. There also have been efforts to remove crosses from public view and to outlaw the display of the Ten Commandments in courthouses throughout our country. There even have been efforts to remove "In God We Trust" from our money. These efforts have continued to increase right up to the current day.

In addition, Saul Alinsky's rule 6 concerning what we listen to has been implemented quite well when you consider who has control of what we read and listen to. I remember when I came home from Vietnam in 1972. Walter Cronkite was on television every night criticizing the Vietnam War and President Nixon. It was very obvious that the so-called mainstream news media was pushing the antiwar, antimilitary agenda daily to sway the American population. This—along with all the antiwar protests, marches, and demonstrations—was very effective.

Using these methods, the activist baby boomers were successful in destroying American support for the Vietnam War along with the destruction of President Nixon's presidency. Since these methods were successful then, it is no wonder that the current and even more radical, liberal, progressive left-wing Democratic leaders are supporting the same tactics today. There is no doubt that today's so-called mainstream news media is extremely biased against conservatives and is in total support of the radical, liberal, progressive left-wing agenda.

Alinsky's rule 6 also addresses the education of our children. There is no doubt that these new radical, liberal, progressive left-wing activists have taken over our colleges so that their radical views are instilled in our future teachers and leaders. Their goal is to control what is taught in our schools so that our children are educated in the radical, liberal, progressive left-wing agenda from a young age. A good example of this is "common core." This policy has been implemented in our public schools in order to indoctrinate our children to believe and think along the lines of the radical, progressive, socialist agenda.

Another good example of Alinsky's rule 6 being implemented can be seen in the entertainment sector of our society and what Hollywood is turning out. So much of the entertainment today that is in movie theaters and on television supports the radical, liberal, progressive left-wing agenda and ideas. It is almost impossible nowadays to watch a movie or a television program that does not have homosexuality in it being portrayed as a normal human activity for our society—all this is contributing to the moral decay of our society and the erosion of our Christian beliefs and teachings.

In addition, Alinsky's rule 4, concerning gun control, has been on full display since the mid-1960s with the constant attack on Article 2 of our Constitution. This article is about our right to own and bear arms. Every time there is a shooting, all we hear about from the left is the need for more gun control. There are plenty of gun-control laws in place now; they just need to be enforced. Criminals do not obey the law; that is why they are criminals. All of this focus on gun control has been on the increase since the late 1960s and continues through the present by the left.

It is interesting to note that the United States essentially has always had at least two major political parties. There have been other political parties present and still are, but not to the degree that they could challenge the two major parties. George Washington really did not have a political party per se. By the time our second president, John Adams, was elected, there were two major parties that were known as the Federalists and the Democratic/Republican parties. Then offshoots began to appear such as the Whig Party, Whig/Democratic Party, and finally just the Democratic and Republican Parties. Andrew Jackson, our seventh president, was considered to be the first Democratic president, and Abraham Lincoln, our sixteenth president, was considered to be the first Republican president.

In addition to the above-mentioned parties, the previously noted Progressive Party was present in 1921 during the presidency of Theodore Roosevelt. There also have been additional parties present such as the Libertarian Party, the Green Party, and the Communist Party. All these parties have fielded candidates for election to the presidency at one time or another. In fact, the Communist Party used to nominate a candidate to run for president in the elections of the 1940s and 1950s.

None of the above candidates, however, garnered much support, but they did have enough support to field a candidate.

The fact that the Communist Party did have enough support is somewhat disturbing. This may have been due to the fact that Communist Russia was our ally during World War II, but the Soviet Union was our main adversary after World War II. One had to wonder what happened to the American Communist Party after the 1960s.

In his book Real America: *Messages from the Heart and Heartland*, Glenn Beck addresses this question. In chapter 6 of his book, Mr. Beck discovered some very interesting information that was buried in the congressional record. Florida congressman Albert Herlong Jr. had submitted the information to the congressional record in the mid-1960s. The information was titled "Communist Goals of 1963."

This document listed the goals that the Communists had decided they needed to achieve in order to dismantle our way of life and to defeat the United States. This, of course, was during the time of the policy of Mutually Assured Destruction (MAD). This list of goals provided evidence that the Soviet Union was out to destroy the United States in any way possible including from within. Mr. Beck theorized that as we were watching for our enemy at our gate, he might be already inside. He expressed this by writing, "Our enemy may have already arrived in a Trojan horse known as liberalism." I have to agree, and in fact, I think the radical, liberal, progressive left-wing Democrats of today are the current enemies that we face.

The following is that list of communist goals that Mr. Beck found. As you read the list, just think about which of our political parties (Democrat or Republican) seem to actually support many of these goals as part of their agenda for our country. To me, it is not hard to decide.

1963 Communist Goals

1. US acceptance of coexistence as the only alternative to atomic war.

2. US willingness to capitulate in preference to engaging in atomic war.

3. Develop the illusion that total disarmament by the US would be a demonstration of "moral strength."

4. Permit free trade between all nations regardless of Communist affiliation and regardless of whether or not items could be used for war.

5. Extension of long-term loans to Russia and Soviet Satellites.

6. Provide American aid to all nations regardless of Communist domination.

7. Grant recognition of Red China, and admission of Red China to UN.

8. Set up East and West Germany as separate states in spite of Khrushchev's promise in 1955 to settle the Germany question by free elections under supervision of the UN.

9. Prolong the conferences to ban atomic tests because the US has agreed to suspend tests as long as negotiations are in progress.

10. Allow all Soviet Satellites individual representation in the UN.

11. Promote the UN as the only hope for mankind. If its charter is rewritten, demand that it be set up as a one-world government with its own independent armed forces. (Some Communist leaders believe the world can be taken over as easily by the UN as by Moscow. Sometimes these two centers compete with each other as they are now doing in the Congo.)

12. Resist any attempt to outlaw the Communist Party.

13. Do away with loyal oaths.

14. Continue giving Russia access to the US Patent Office.

15. Capture one or both of the political parties in the US.

16. Use technical decisions of the courts to weaken basic American institutions, by claiming their activities violate civil rights.

17. Get control of the schools. Use them as transmission belts for socialism and current Communist propaganda. Soften the curriculum. Get control of teachers' associations. Put the party line in textbooks.

18. Gain control of all student newspapers.

19. Use student riots to foment public protests against programs or organizations which are under Communist attack.

20. Infiltrate the press. Get control of book-review assignments, editorial writing, policymaking positions.

21. Gain control of key positions in radio, TV, and motion pictures.

22. Continue discrediting American culture by degrading all forms of artistic expression. An American Communist cell was told to "eliminate all good sculpture from parks and buildings, substitute shapeless, awkward and meaningless forms."

23. Control art critics and directors of art museums. "Our plan is to promote ugliness, repulsive, meaningless art."

24. Eliminate all laws governing obscenity by calling them "censorship" and a violation of free speech and free press.

25. Break down cultural standards of morality by promoting pornography and obscenity in books, magazines, motion pictures, radio, and TV.

26. Present homosexuality, degeneracy, and promiscuity as "normal, natural, healthy."

27. Infiltrate the churches and replace revealed religion with "social" religion. Discredit the Bible and emphasize the need for intellectual maturity which does not need a "religious crutch."

28. Eliminate prayer or any phase of religious expression in the schools on the ground that it violates the principle of "separation of church and state."

29. Discredit the American Constitution by calling it inadequate, old-fashioned, out of step with modern needs, a hindrance to cooperation between nations on a worldwide basis.

30. Discredit the American Founding Fathers. Present them as selfish aristocrats who had no concern for the "common man."

31. Belittle all forms of American culture and discourage the teaching of American history on the grounds that it was only a minor part of the "big picture." Give more emphasis to Russian history since the Communists took over.

32. Support any socialist movement to give centralized control over any part of the culture—education, social agencies, welfare programs, mental health clinics, etc.

33. Eliminate all laws or procedures which interfere with the operation of the Communist apparatus.

34. Eliminate the House Committee on un-American activities.

35. Discredit and eventually dismantle the FBI.

36. Infiltrate and gain control of more unions.

37. Infiltrate and gain control of big business.

38. Transfer some of the powers of arrest from the police to social agencies. Treat all behavioral problems as psychiatric disorders, which no one but psychiatrists can understand (or treat).

39. Dominate the psychiatric profession and use mental health laws as a means of gaining coercive control over those who oppose Communist goals.

40. Discredit the family as an institution. Encourage promiscuity and easy divorce.

41. Emphasize the need to raise children away from the negative influence of parents. Attribute prejudices, mental blocks, and retarding of children to suppressive influence of parents.

42. Create the impression that violence and insurrection are legitimate aspects of the American tradition; that students and special-interest groups should rise up and use "united force" to solve economic, political, or social problems.

43. Overthrow all colonial governments before native populations are ready for self-government.

44. Internationalize the Panama Canal.

45. Repeal the Connally Reservation so the US cannot prevent the World Court from seizing jurisdiction over domestic problems. Give the World Court jurisdiction over domestic problems. Give the World Court jurisdiction over nations and individuals alike.

When I first read these communist goals, I was able to understand an interview I heard on television a number of years back, when one of the candidates from the Communist Party was being interviewed. This candidate had run at least twice in our elections, but had not run in the latest presidential election at that time. The reporter asked him why he had not run for election this time, and his response took me totally by surprise. His answer was, "There was no need to run since the Democratic

Party had essentially adopted the majority of his election platform." After I read the list of these 1963 communist goals, I completely understood his answer.

This list helped me understand the liberal, progressive policies of Bill and Hillary Clinton. It is also interesting to note that, at that time, it seemed that Bill Clinton tried to govern from a slightly left of center position, which was more of a moderate position than from the hard left-wing, liberal, progressive position that we now know that the Clintons actually believe in. Bill Clinton was trying to keep the Democratic Party as a moderate to liberal party as opposed to a hard-left party. Their true hard-left attitude and agenda was not truly revealed until later by their actions.

This is especially true of Hillary's actions. I think they knew that there were still too many Americans from the "greatest generation" alive, and they could not get enough support to implement their true socialist, liberal, progressive agenda. The current radical, liberal, progressive left-wing socialistic agenda of the Democratic Party was forced to remain in the closet until more support could be garnered to push their true agenda on the American people.

In addition, Bill Clinton tarnished the office of the president by all the sexual allegations that surfaced against him. These allegations revealed two major areas of concern. The first was his actions toward females, which revealed his true attitude toward morality. The second concern revealed his focus on power. Many of the allegations were from women that were in positions that Bill Clinton had power over. This was true while he was governor of Arkansas and during his presidency.

The most egregious of these allegations was the Monica Lewinsky case. Bill Clinton was president of the United States, the most powerful person in the world, while Ms. Lewinsky was a twenty-two-year-old intern. His continuous denials of what happened between them just pointed out his true attitude toward women. He obviously thought he could do whatever he wanted because of his position and power and get away with it. He only admitted what he had done when undeniable evidence was provided that proved Ms. Lewinsky's allegation. This to me is strong evidence that he does not have any respect for women or respect for the office of president.

As further evidence of his true attitude and beliefs, the same type of behavior was well documented by his actions while he was governor of Arkansas. He was using his position of power for his own selfishness and gratification with no thought of how it would reflect on the office of the governor. This type of behavior truly reflects the 1960s baby boomers' attitude of "if it feels good, do it."

Hillary Clinton's true self also became evident when she supported her husband against all of his accusers. It would seem that most wives would not have stayed with their husbands, especially after Bill Clinton was impeached. This tells me she was more interested in power than what is right or wrong. It became evident why she stayed with Bill when she later ran for president herself. Power and money has always been the focus for both of them, not what is best for our country.

During the time period that Bill Clinton was president, the world was relatively quiet and peaceful. This was more than likely a result of the actions of the first President Bush's actions against Saddam Hussein. There were, however, occasional terrorist attacks and discourse in the Middle East. This discourse actually started during President Carter's presidency when Iran took over our embassy in Tehran. They held our people for a year. President Carter seemed to not want to challenge Iran after the failed attempt to rescue our hostages occurred. This was also probably another reason why the American people turned away from the Democrats and elected President Reagan.

In contrast, when Colonel Muammar Gaddafi sponsored a terrorist attack on the La Belle discotheque in West Berlin on April 5, 1986, in which two American servicemen were killed, President Reagan ordered a punitive attack on Colonel Gaddafi in late April 1986. This attack did quiet down Colonel Gaddafi somewhat on his eagerness to sponsor terrorism.

As previously noted, the first President Bush did use the military to stop Saddam Hussein from taking over Kuwait in 1990 and 1991 in the action known as the First Gulf War. However, it should be noted that the first terrorist attack on United States soil did occur during President Clinton's presidency. This first terrorist attack occurred in 1993 in the basement of the World Trade Center's parking garage. The American attitude at that time, however, was such that we had not realized that war had been declared on the United States by radical Islamic terrorists.

After the two presidential terms of Bill Clinton and his liberal, progressive left-wing policies, the American people again turned back to the Republican Party. George W. Bush, the son of George H. W. Bush, was elected president in 2000.

Then on September 11, 2001, the world dramatically changed for the US with the attack of the Twin Towers of the World Trade Center and the Pentagon. This attack was not completed by a specific government against the United States but by a group of radical Islamic terrorists using highjacked civilian airliners. This terrorist action was based in a radical Islamic belief and ideology that transcends all borders. The terrorists' goal is to convert the world to their form of radical Islamic belief under Sharia law and their interpretation of the Qur'an. Islam the religion was not the enemy, but radical Islam is.

President George W. Bush had no choice but to go after the terrorist responsible for the attacks on the Twin Towers and the Pentagon. A fourth aircraft was stopped from getting to its target, but all souls aboard this aircraft were lost when it crashed in Pennsylvania. Once Osama bin Laden had been identified as the leader behind the attack, the use of the military was once again needed.

Since terrorist groups are not specific governments, they will live and exist wherever they can. This makes it very difficult to confront them directly. They are free to move from country to country, and they find it relatively easy to recruit fighters for their cause. This is especially true in poor underdeveloped countries in the Middle East.

To address this new threat, this President Bush put together another coalition of forces in 2001 to fight terrorism, wherever it was found. Because evidence that many of the terrorists were known to be in Afghanistan, US military forces were deployed to Afghanistan to fight terrorist groups like the Taliban and al Qaeda. This was the start of the Afghan War.

Then in 2003, President Bush initiated an invasion of Iraq to go after Saddam Hussein under the pretense that Saddam Hussein had weapons of mass destruction (WMDs). Many people, especially on the left, felt that President Bush had made a huge mistake going into Iraq in 2003 in what became known as the Second Gulf War. He did, however, make the decision, and now the US had military forces involved in conflicts in both Afghanistan and Iraq. This President Bush had grown up under the influence of his father, who was part of the "greatest generation." This President Bush was also a F-102 pilot in the National Guard and understood the military and its proper use.

In the 2008 presidential Election, Barack Obama, who was born in 1961 and was raised as a Muslim as a child, entered the presidential race. Mr. Obama had never been in the military and had worked as a community organizer before entering politics. His political orientation was far-left-wing progressive, liberal, and he focused his campaign on ending the wars in both Afghanistan and especially Iraq. He promised to bring our troops home and to "fundamentally change America."

With his promise to "fundamentally change America," the radical, liberal, progressive left-wing socialist Democrats felt that they now had sufficient power in order for them to come out of the closet and pursue their agenda in full view. This is when the full onslaught of the war against our traditional American values of Judeo-Christian principles really came into prime focus by the radical, liberal, progressive left-wing socialistic Democrats.

Even though the Clintons did not like President Obama, they decided that the goal of the radical, liberal, progressive left-wing socialistic Democratic policies was far more important than whether they liked each other. Hillary Clinton felt that Barack Obama had stolen the Democratic presidential nomination from her in 2008. She and Bill felt that it was her right and that she deserved to be the president, and Barack Obama had cost her the opportunity to become the first woman president of the United States. When the Clintons decided that it was more important to work with President Obama in order to advance the radical, liberal, progressive left-wing socialistic agenda, they joined forces.

President Obama appointed Hillary Clinton to be the secretary of state. This, I am sure, was accomplished to try and enhance

Hillary Clinton's chances of becoming president at the end of the two terms of President Obama. The only problem was that her performance as secretary of state was not very sterling.

Her first problem was her handling of the Benghazi terrorist attack, which resulted in the killing of Ambassador Christopher Stevens and three other Americans. Then she lied about the cause of the attack to attempt to cover up the fact that she had disregarded Ambassador Steven's request for additional security measures for Benghazi. She also did not order any rescue forces to try and assist these individuals.

Her second problem occurred when the information became public about her disregard for the security of classified information and her use of a private server for her e-mails surfaced. The American people were not impressed. These actions simply highlighted her true beliefs that the law does not apply to her and Bill, and she could do whatever she wanted to do.

Unfortunately for the radical, liberal, progressive left-wing socialistic members of the Democratic Party, this was going to be a significant problem to get Hillary Clinton elected as president. Since the radical, liberal, progressive left-wing socialistic Democrats had begun to come out of the closet under Bill Clinton and were fully out of the closet under President Obama, this was a major setback to their radical agenda. This, to me, is when the Deep State under President Obama decided that they had to take action in order to preserve this opportunity to "fundamentally change America." We must remember that President Obama had also studied Saul Alinsky's Rules for Radicals, and he was raised as a Muslim during the first five years of his life. For the radical, liberal, progressive left-wing socialistic agenda to succeed, Hillary Clinton had to be protected so that she could be elected president.

The "Deep State," which consists of a number of President Obama appointees and others, aggressively came to Hillary Clinton's rescue to protect her from any possible fallout from her actions as Secretary of State. When Donald J. Trump became the Republican Party's nominee for president for the 2016 election, the Deep State radicals felt there would be no problem to get Hillary Clinton elected president. In the minds of these radical, liberal, progressive far-left-wing Democrats, there was no way the American people would ever elect someone like Donald J. Trump. All they had to do was protect Hillary Clinton. To me, this shows just how far out of step these radical Democrats are with the current majority of the American society.

The 2016 election of Donald J. Trump as President completely shocked the radical left to the point they just could not help themselves from the continuous fanatical opposition to President Trump. In their minds, the American people had made a tremendous mistake, and it was now up to them to correct this mistake. These radical, elite Democrats feel that they know better than the American people, and it is up to them to fix the problem. They believe that "truth is whatever you want it to be."

The radical, liberal, progressive left-wing Democrats had worked so hard to obtain power in order to accomplish their goal of turning the United States into a socialistic society with them in control. They had worked hard to take over the mainstream news media, health care, education in our schools and colleges, the entertainment sector of our society, and getting rid of God. They just could not accept that Donald J. Trump won the presidency. In their eyes, this was the absolute worst thing that could occur. They became absolutely livid because now President Trump would be the one filling the vacated seats on the Supreme Court, one of which was currently vacant at the time of the election.

When a seat did open up on the Supreme Court in the last year of President Obama's term and the Republicans were able to delay filling that seat until after the 2016 election, this turned into a major crisis for the radical left. Instead of President Hillary Clinton, President Donald J. Trump would be the one who would be filling that seat.

For the radical, liberal, progressive far-left-wing Democrats, they know that the only way they can accomplish their radical agenda is through the Supreme Court. They know that they had to get liberal, progressive activist judges appointed to the Supreme Court in order for the court to make law, not just interpret law based on our Constitution. They had to change the Constitution in order to implement their agenda. This is why a major crisis now existed, and President Trump had to be stopped. President Trump now represented the greatest threat to them in order for them to be able to achieve their ultimate goal of socialism.

This is why the radical, liberal, progressive far-left-wing Democrats have declared war on President Trump. Their total and singular goal since his election has been to force him out of office one way or the other. This is what we have been witnessing since the elections of 2016 when President Trump became the president.

Soon after President Trump took office, he nominated Judge Neil Gorsuch to the Supreme Court to fill the seat that was vacant. Judge Gorsuch was known to be a constitutionalist and, as such, was exactly not the type of judge that the liberal, progressive left-wing Democrats wanted on the Supreme Court. They fought hard, but with the Republicans controlling the Senate, Judge Gorsuch was confirmed.

When the second seat on the Supreme Court opened up, the radical, liberal, progressive far-left-wing Democrats literally became hysterical because President Trump was going to be able to nominate a second Supreme Court justice. When President Trump nominated Judge Brett Kavanaugh to fill this seat, the radical, liberal, progressive left-wing Democrats essentially went ballistic in their attempt to stop Judge Kavanaugh's nomination. Judge Kavanaugh was also known as a constitutionalist. The actions of the radical, liberal, progressive left-wing Democrats on the Senate confirmation committee were truly disgraceful.

During the confirmation hearings, these radical, liberal, progressive left-wing Democrats were willing to do whatever they could to stop Judge Kavanaugh's confirmation. This included using every delaying tactic possible and even disregarding the "rule of law" in order to delay the confirmation of Judge Kavanaugh until after the 2018 elections. Their hope was that the Democrats would regain control of the Senate and the House of Representatives in the 2018 midterm elections. I truly believe that their disgraceful efforts to stop this confirmation actually helped the Republicans to gain seats in the Senate during the 2018 midterm elections.

The radical, liberal, progressive left-wing Democrats were able, however, to take control of the House of Representatives during this election. Because of this, I see nothing but an increase in efforts to get rid of President Trump with very little being accomplished for the country between now and the 2020 presidential election.

The question now is, what does all of this mean for our country? To me, if the United States continues to follow a course of turning away from God that is being pushed by the radical, liberal, progressive far left-wing Democrats, we can expect God to turn his back on the United States. Based on my research of the Bible and the biblical prophecies, I am not very optimistic that the country will return to God. This is the only way that I feel we can actually save our country. Unfortunately, Satan is busy at work, and I feel that the American society is changing to the point that it will not be long until these radical Democrats will succeed in implementing their radical, liberal, progressive socialistic agenda. When they do, they will have achieved President Obama's goal of "fundamentally changing America." When this happens, I can understand why the United States is not mentioned as a factor during the end days of this world as we know it. The Bible prophecies will be fulfilled.

CHAPTER 12

"Fundamentally Changing America"

T HE REASON FOR MY pessimism about the future of the United States is based on the abundance of evidence presented by the actions of the radical, liberal, progressive, far-left-wing activists of the Democratic Party. As I have watched each presidential election since Jimmy Carter's election, Democrats have been able to get elected by campaigning as "moderates." After they get elected, their true focus and loyalty to the far left becomes apparent.

The election of President Reagan after Jimmy Carter was essentially a revolt against liberal, progressive policies that President Carter pursued. I feel this is true even thought I do not think President Carter was a card carrying extreme far-left radical, progressive, liberal member of the Democratic Party. I would even consider both of the Bush presidents to be "moderates," even though they both were Republicans. Both of the Bush presidents, along with Bill Clinton, seemed to have a desire to see more progress toward a one-world-order system. This is why I feel that Dr. Hindson in his book Final Signs felt that we were progressing toward a one-world order and a global economy. Bill Clinton, however, seemed to lean more toward a one-world order than both of the Bushes.

When Bill Clinton was elected president and Hillary was put in charge of developing a new health-care system for the United

States, it became obvious that they were part of the far left-wing, socialistic-minded Democrats. As I have previously noted, Hillary Clinton was a strong proponent of Saul Alinsky's Rules for Radicals. Her actions revealed her true motives and agenda. The radical far-left-wing agenda to install socialism on America was still in the closet but was gaining power rapidly.

I also feel that the election of President Clinton, and with Hillary becoming the First Lady, is the point at which actions were set in motion to begin to implement Saul Alinsky's Rule for Radicals. At the same time, some of the 1963 communist goals were beginning to be initiated or at least pursued.

I have previously discussed how Hillary attempted to create a program to control our nation's health care as part of Alinsky's rules, but this failed. I am sure, however, we all remember Hillary's emphasis on our children. I clearly remember Hillary pushing the idea of, "It takes a village to raise a child." This to me is evidence that an attempt to adopt some of the 1963 communist goals began in the earnest by members of the Democratic Party.

This is when I feel that communist goals number 40 and 41 were being pursued. The 1963 communist goal 40 states, "Discredit family as an institution. Encourage promiscuity and easy divorce." Goal 41 states, "Emphasize the need to raise children away from the negative influence of parents. Attribute prejudices, mental blocks, and retarding of children to suppressive influence of parents."

I do not know if Bill and Hillary Clinton's goal was to also implement communist goal 15, but it seems that a natural evolution to convert the country to socialism was initiated by the Clintons. Communist goal 15 states, "Capture one or both of the political parties in the US." When President Obama declared that he would "fundamentally change America" and that "the United States was no longer a Christian nation," it became clear that his goal was to turn the United States into a socialist nation. His policies of "the redistribution of wealth" became a strong focus for his administration.

It was during President Obama's administration when the Obamas and the Clintons decided to team up to push their socialistic agenda and when the "deep state" was created. The "deep state" are members of the radical, liberal, progressive, far-left-wing, socialistic Democrats who have obtained high levels of positions in our government and now felt they had sufficient power to come out of the closet and push their socialist agenda to fruition. They now felt that they could no longer be stopped. There is evidence when this change occurred.

When President Obama was first elected president, there was a national debate going on over gay marriage. President Obama initially supported that a marriage was defined as one man and one woman as defined in the Bible. In Matthew 19:4–6 (NIV), when Jesus was speaking to some Pharisees, he said:

> "Haven't you read" he replied, "that at the beginning the Creator made them male and female and said, for this reason a man will leave his father and mother and be united to his wife, and the two will become one flesh so they are no longer two, but one. Therefore what God has joined together, let no man separate."

When the true radical, liberal, progressive, left-wing, socialist agenda came out of the closet into full view, President Obama instructed his Justice Department to no longer defend the Judeo-Christian belief that a marriage is considered to be between one man and one woman. On June 26, 2015, the Supreme Court of the United States legalized gay marriage. I am sure God took notice of this and not in a pleasing way. To me, this was a death sentence for the United States, based on God's actions when you consider the flood and Sodom and Gomorrah in the Old Testament.

This, however, illustrates why the radical, liberal, progressive, left-wing, socialist Democrats feel they need to control the nominations to the Supreme Court. This is why the current-day radical, liberal, progressive, left-wing socialist Democrats fought so hard against the two most recent nominations to the Supreme Court by President Trump. This also is why President Obama was so upset that he did not get to nominate the individual that he wanted at the end of his second term, which was Merrick Garland. He did become the Attorney General (DOJ) under President Biden.

President Obama is also the one that had a problem with our current Constitution. President Obama said our current

Constitution told him everything he could not do and nothing about what he could do. This sounds awfully similar to communist goal 29, which states, "Discredit the American Constitution by calling it inadequate, old-fashioned, out of step with modern needs, a hindrance to cooperation between nations on a worldwide basis." We continually hear this mantra by the current radical, liberal, progressive, left-wing, socialist Democrats.

In the 2016 presidential election and with the radical, liberal, progressive, left-wing, socialist Democrats coming out of the closet, the "deep state" under President Obama only had to get Hillary Clinton elected. With her election, these radical, liberal, progressive, left-wing, socialist Democrats would be able to complete the "fundamental change of America" to socialism. They felt comfortable that Donald J. Trump could not possibly get elected. There was now no need for them to hide their actions or their true agenda of implementing socialism on America. The election of Hillary Clinton had to be achieved by any means necessary. This, to me, is what led to the greatest abuse of power that the United States has ever seen in its entire history.

With this as their mind-set, the "deep state" individuals felt that they no longer had to conceal their true agenda or their actions. They had the support of the then current President Obama, and with the election of Hillary Clinton, no one would ever investigate their actions on how they got Hillary Clinton elected. All they had to do was stop Donald J. Trump from being elected.

They felt very comfortable that they could do this since they knew they had the support of the mainstream news media, and they had been in control of the majority of the colleges and universities and what was being taught to our students.

They also had control of the entertainment sector of our society by the Hollywood elites. They completely believed that they had moved the American society far enough away from the Judeo-Christian principles and values and that it was now time for a full court press to complete their socialist agenda to "fundamentally change America."

Let's look at the empirical evidence that is available as to why these radical, liberal, progressive, left-wing socialist Democrats felt that the time was ripe for execution of their final push. The best way to do this is to look at Saul Alinsky's Rules for Radicals and the 1963 communist goals.

Rule 1—health care. Hillary Clinton tried to implement a socialist health-care program when Bill Clinton was elected president in 1992. This was defeated by the Republicans at that time. The radical left now felt that sufficient time had passed, and since they were in control, they could again push to implement Saul Alinsky's most important rule: rule 1—health care.

The Affordable Care Act known as Obamacare was passed in 2010 with only Democratic votes. Not one Republican voted for it. This was extremely important since health-care accounts for one-seventh of our economy. As Saul Alinsky said, "If you control health care, you control the people."

I should note, however, that I think the most ridiculous and ignorant comment I ever heard from a politician was when the Speaker of the House Nancy Pelosi said, "We have to pass this bill in order for us to find out what is in it." Do you really think she cared or thought the bill was the best thing for our country?

Rule 2—poverty. I think the best way to illustrate how President Obama contributed to implementing rule 2 is to list the results of President Obama's policies on our economy while he was president. The best was to do that is to use the list that Sean Hannity uses on his TV show. The following is Sean Hannity's list of President Obama's negative impact of his policies on our economy, which definitely definitely contributes to the increase in poverty and the implementation of rule 2:

- America had its lowest labor participation rate since the 1970s.

- There were almost ninety-five million Americans who were considered out of the labor force.

- The US economy had its worst recovery since the 1940s.

- American home ownership was at its lowest rate in fifty-one years.

- At the end of his administration, there were almost thirteen million more Americans on food stamps.

- During President Obama's administration, eight million more Americans were added to the number of Americans living in poverty, which increased the total to over forty-three million.

- President Obama was the only president to never reach 3.0 percent on gross domestic product (GDP) growth.

As Saul Alinsky said, "Poor people are easier to control and will not fight back if you are providing everything for them to live."

Rule 3—debt. President Obama did extremely well implementing this rule. He added $9 trillion to our national debt during his administration. This is more debt added than all the previous presidents before him combined. Again, as Saul Alinsky says, "If you increase the debt to an unsustainable level, you will be able to increase taxes, which in turn will produce more poverty." I would give President Obama a grade of A+ on implementing this rule.

Rule 4—gun control. After each horrific mass or school shooting, all we hear from Democrats is a call for more gun control. It should be noted that in Illinois, which has some of our nation's strictest gun control laws, we continually hear about all the shootings in Chicago every weekend. Chicago has been under Democratic rule for more than eighty years. Between 2011 and 2018, 4,046 murders occurred in Chicago. When you compare this to the Iraqi Freedom War, which occurred between 2003 and 2010, we only lost 3,481 American soldiers in that war. It would appear that it is safer in a war zone than in Chicago.

The fact is that there are plenty of gun-control laws on the books, but the Democrats appear to not want to enforce them. They would rather have gun control as an issue for debate during each election. What the Democrats really want is what Saul Alinsky said about gun control when he said, "If you remove the ability for citizens to defend themselves, it is easier for the government to create a police state."

Rule 5—welfare. As pointed out during the discussion of rule 2—poverty, there were almost thirteen million more Americans added to the rolls for food stamps as well as eight million more Americans living in poverty during the Obama administration. President Obama's policies were also very effective in implementing Saul Alinsky's rule 5.

Rule 6—education. There is an abundance of evidence regarding the implementation of this rule along with some of the 1963 list of communist goals. Goal 17 states, "Get control of the schools. Use them as transmissions belts for Socialism, and current Communist propaganda. Soften the curriculum. Get control of teacher associations. Put the party line in textbooks." Goal 18 states, "Gain control of all student newspapers." Goal 19 states, "Use student riots to foment public protests against programs or organization which are under Communist attack." Goal 20 states, "Infiltrate the press. Get control of book review assignments, editorial writing, and policy-making positions." One can see just how important this rule is just based on the number of communist goals that address this issue.

For many years, the radical, liberal, progressive, left-wing, socialistic-minded Democrats have been working hard to take over our colleges and universities in order to control what our children learn. Their goal has been to train and provide as many liberal, progressive-minded teachers as possible to teach in our elementary, middle, and high schools in order to further their radical, liberal, progressive, left-wing, socialist agenda. They have been very successful in their implementation of this rule and associated communist goals. Recently, there was additional empirical evidence provided of the above with the implementation of the Common Core Program. This attempts to control all school district curriculums across our nation. Conservative ideas are not popular in the Common Core Program.

As further evidence of how strong and pervasive their grip is on ensuring that they stop any attempt to undermine their agenda with conservative ideas, we all too frequently witness protest and demonstrations occurring on our campuses. These seem to occur whenever a conservative speaker or some other conservative activity is scheduled to occur on a college or university campus. These universities and colleges profess to be for free speech, but it seems only if that speech agrees with their liberal, progressive agenda. They simply do not tolerate conservative views being expressed on their campuses by guest speakers or others.

When protests and demonstrations do occur, this simply provides the evidence that communist goal 42 is being implemented. They use this goal as justification of why they have to demonstrate. Goal 42 states, "Create the impression that violence and insurrection are legitimate aspects of the American tradition; that students and special interest groups should rise up and make a 'united force' to solve economic, political or social problems."

In addition to the education aspect of rule 6, it also states that you must take control of what people read and listen to. As far as what people read, the New York Times and the Washington Post are prime examples of the radical, liberal, progressive left-wing socialist agenda being forced upon our society by the printed news media. There is obvious left wing bias against Republicans and conservatives by both of these newspapers. This has been especially true on their reporting on President Trump.

As far as gaining control of what we listen to or watch, communist goal 21 emphasizes how this is to be implemented. Goal 21 states, "Gain control of key positions in radio, TV, and motion pictures." I think they have been extremely successful at accomplishing this goal. The radical, liberal, progressive left-wing socialistic agenda is being projected daily by the mainstream news media. This includes the national networks and especially the cable networks like CNN and MSNBC. They have essentially become the propaganda arm of the radical left-wing Democratic Party. This has been evidenced daily since President Trump decided to run for president in 2015.

This radical left-wing bias has been constantly on display since he was elected president in 2016. After he was elected president, the negative reporting on all things related to President Trump has been evaluated to be at a level of 92 percent negative. The only news media that attempts to give President Trump a fair shake is Fox News. With their motto of "We Report, You Decide," they do make a genuine effort to report both side of an issue. I have to agree with Sean

Hannity about the mainstream mews media and their reporting on President Trump. Sean Hannity has said that even if President Trump cured cancer, the mainstream media would spin it somehow to be a negative. They would complain that it took too long for him to do it. This is why President Trump calls them "fake news." I have to agree.

It is no wonder that this is occurring since it has been reported that 90 to 95 percent of journalists are Democrats. It is very obvious that the radical left-wing Democrats have done well implementing communist goals 20 and 21.

When we look at the entertainment segment of our society, this too depicts just how successful the Hollywood radical left-wing elites have been in implementing the radical hard-left-wing agenda. They continually push the LGBTQ agenda in their movies and television programs. This is totally in line with communist goals 25 and 26. Communist goal 25 states, "Break down cultural standards of morality by promoting pornography, and obscenity in books, magazines, motion pictures, radio and TV." Goal 26 states, "Present homosexuality, degeneracy, and promiscuity as 'normal, natural, and healthy.'" If this does not indicate that Satan is at work, I do not know what does.

I am sure that God really liked a recent TV program titled Midnight Texas. One of this program's main characters is a fallen angel that is gay. The radical left has been extremely successful in implementing Saul Alinsky's rule 6 and many of the 1963 communist goals.

Rule 7—religion. We have discussed some of the radical left-wing attempts at removing God from our society. We also do hear some reporting of their efforts in the news, but I was truly shocked when I learned just how prevalent their efforts have been. My eyes were definitely opened by a letter written by Governor Mike Huckabee on behalf of Mr. David Bossie, president of the Citizens United Foundation.

In his letter, Governor Huckabee points out how these groups have been attacking our traditional Judeo-Christian principles and values since the 1960s and 1970s. It is totally obvious that these types of groups are working diligently to implement rule 7 of Saul Alinsky's *Rule for Radicals*, which addresses religion. It also provided evidence that their efforts are in total support of communist goals 27 and 28. Goal 27 states, "Infiltrate the churches and replace revealed religion with 'social religion.' Discredit the Bible and emphasize the need for intellectual maturity, which does not need a 'religious crutch.'" Goal 28 states, "Eliminate prayer or any phase of religious expression in the schools on the grounds that it violates the principle of 'separation of church and state.'"

Governor Huckabee's letter pointed out just how significant the radical left wing has been pursuing their goal of removing God from our society. One of the groups pointed out by Governor Huckabee is known as the Freedom from Religion Foundation. Through the rulings by activist judges and ridiculous lawsuits, they have been able to achieve some horrific victories toward their overall goal of removing God from our society. This is evidenced by the following.

They have been able to ban prayer from our public schools, outlaw the Ten Commandments from courthouses all over the country, and even win the Supreme Court decision on Roe vs. Wade in 1973. This decision opened the door for abortion on demand. This had to be a direct affront to God.

This Freedom from Religion Foundation has now launched a new campaign against our traditional religious values. This campaign is known as the Campaign for an Atheist America. Their goal is to remove God totally from the public square. In the last few years, they have sued to remove "under God" from the Pledge of Allegiance, and they have achieved a ban on prayers from after-school programs. They are now launching new lawsuits to further remove God from America. These lawsuits attempt to ban Christmas nativity scenes in public places, stopping students in public schools from learning about the Bible, and removing crosses from public view.

The following evidences some additional examples of the efforts of the Freedom from Religion Foundation. In Kentucky and Michigan, this foundation forced two school districts to prohibit all employees from playing Christmas music when students are within hearing distance of the source of the music. In California, at the Turlock Unified School District, they forced the school to shut down the school's chaplain program because it supposedly violated the civil rights of atheists.

In Mercer County in West Virginia, the foundation lawyers are suing local schools to stop the seventy-five years tradition of holding Bible classes. According to the Freedom from Religion Foundation, even just holding these optional classes violates the "civil rights" of students and parents. In Ohio, the foundation is suing to prohibit the Star of David from being displayed at a new Holocaust Memorial, saying that the star was a dishonor and exclusionary.

I am sure that, like me, there are many Americans that are unaware of all the efforts of such groups as the Freedom from Religion Foundation. The above information was very shocking to me as far as the extent of these efforts and the type of efforts that are being pursued by just this single foundation. This does not even consider what the total effort is when added to the other similar organizations that are pushing the radical far-left-wing, liberal, progressive agenda.

If we do nothing about all these efforts to attack our Judeo-Christian principles and traditional Christian values, we may soon live in a country where ministers and pastors may be arrested for "discrimination" if they refuse to officiate at homosexual weddings. In addition, all crosses will be required to be hidden from view, even at places like Arlington National Cemetery. There may also be a day when simply quoting the Bible might get an individual arrested and placed behind bars if these atheists succeed in having the Bible labeled as "hate speech."

There is already an effort in Christian schools and hospitals to prevent them from Christian teachings and services under the scheme of the need to be more "inclusive." David Horowitz of the Freedom Center pointed out the following efforts by the radical left and their assault on God. Mr. Horowitz noted the following:

> In a Florida school, students had to design and create Muslim prayer rugs. Recently, a federal judge prohibited public prayer at a school graduation ceremony and even banned the words *prayer and amen*. In Maryland, students had to write out the Salada, which states, "There is no God but Allah, and Muhammad is the messenger of Allah." In Texas, a seventh-grade assignment taught kids that God was a myth and not a fact.

Texas, a seventh-grade assignment taught kids that God was a myth and not a fact.

In addition, countless schools around the country force children to learn and recite the five pillars of Islam. In New Jersey, the ACLU forced a school to cover up all religious symbols during a graduation ceremony. We Christians must be ready to fight back when these type of actions take place in our locations throughout the country.

Rule 8—class warfare. This Saul Alinsky's rule is meant to divide people into groups and then pit the groups of people against one another. For example, they divide the people into groups such as wealthy versus poor, blacks versus whites, liberal versus conservative, LGBTQ versus heterosexual, and sectarians versus Christians.

When the conservative right criticizes the liberal, progressive left, the radical left immediately calls them racists. The mainstream news media is a very willing, active arm of the radical, liberal, progressive, socialistic left wing in assisting the left as much as they can. This is evidenced daily by the mainstream news media negative reporting on President Trump's actions. As previously noted, a number of polls have reported that at least 92 percent of the reporting by the mainstream media has been negative during President Trump's first two years. This relates back to rule 6 and the controlling of what people listen to and how they get their information about what is going on in the world.

A recent poll conducted between October 25 and 30 of 2018 titled "Politico Morning Consult Poll" asked people who was more to blame for the divisiveness in our country: the news media or President Trump? The results of this poll were that 64 percent of the respondents thought that the news media have done more to divide the country rather than uniting the country. When compared to the results for President Trump, 56 percent blamed the president.

In September of 2014, ABC News conducted a similar poll during President Obama's administration. This poll asked respondents if President Obama was doing more to divide the country as opposed to uniting it. The respondents indicated that President Obama was doing more to divide the country at a 55 percent level rather than uniting it. What is unusual about this poll is that ABC News is part of the liberal, progressive, left-wing arm of the Democratic Party. It is surprising that they would even report this. I am also sure that this poll did not ask about themselves.

The Hollywood elites have also been very prevalent in trying to divide the country against President Trump. For example, on January 21, 2017, after the 2016 election and Donald Trump won the presidency, Madonna was on television and stated, "Yes, I have thought an awful lot about blowing up the White House." On February 3, 2017, while on the TV program The View, Robert De Niro stated, "Of course, I want to punch him in his face," referring to President Trump. On June 22, 2017, while in Somerset, England, Johnny Depp was being interviewed and stated the following: "When was the last time an actor assassinated a president? I want to clarify, I'm not an actor. I lie for a living. However, it's been a while, and maybe it's time." This to me is evidence of just how biased the Hollywood elites are as they push the hard-left-wing, liberal, progressive agenda. I also think that at least two of these statements should have caused the Secret Service to investigate these individuals.

Even during the 2018 midterm elections, the Hollywood elites continued to push the radical left-wing agenda and employ Saul Alinsky's rule 8 of class warfare. Rapper Common teamed up with the ACLU and stated that our current criminal justice system was born out of racism and white supremacy. Actor James Cromwell warned that there would be "blood in the streets" if Democrats did not win the midterm elections.

On November 7, 2018, Adam Serwer wrote an article for The Atlantic, which I think sums up exactly how the radical left is implementing Saul Alinsky's rule 8. The articles states:

> If Republicans ran on their policy agenda alone, they would be at a disadvantage. So they have turned to the destructive politics of white identity, one that seeks a path to power by deliberately dividing the country along racial and sectarian lines. They portray the nation as the birthright of white, heterosexual Christians. America's problem isn't tribalism— it's Racism.

To me, it is interesting to note that when the radical left-wing Democrats accuse the Republicans of something, they are the ones actually doing what they are accusing the Republicans of doing. Now that the 2018 midterm elections are over, and the Democrats won the House of Representatives, it is interesting to note just what will be the Democrats' agenda of the House of Representatives. When you listen to Nancy Pelosi, Adam Schiff, and Jerry Nadler, I agree with Sean Hannity. He says the Democratic agenda for Congress after the 2018 elections will consist of the following:

- Impeach Trump
- Keep Obamacare
- Block any Trump Supreme Court nominees
- Open borders
- Kill off any "deep state" investigations
- Rescind the Trump tax cuts

In my opinion, none of the above seems to have the good of the American people in mind. Their agenda seems to be focused on getting and then keeping power as they pursue their goal of "fundamentally changing America" into a socialist nation.

Recently, Newt Gingrich was on Mark Levin's TV program *Life Liberty & Levin*. He made the statement that he now felt that the radical, liberal, progressive, hard-left-wing, socialistic-minded Democrats now represent approximately 60 percent of the Democratic Party after the 2018 midterm elections. This is consistent with the fact that at least forty-two radical left-wing socialists had been running for office. It would appear that the radical left-wing arm of the Democratic Party is well on its way to accomplishing goal 15 of the 1963 Communist goals, which states, "Capture one or both political parties in the United States."

There is also evidence that these socialistic-minded politicians have made inroads into the Republican Party. There are a few socialistic-minded moderate Republicans whom I consider RINOs (Republican in name only). It is quite obvious that there have been significant efforts to infiltrate the Republican Party as well.

It has been obvious for a long period of time that the radical, liberal, progressive, far-left-wing of the Democratic Party is represented primarily by the east and west coast segments of our country along with Chicago. States like California, Washington, Oregon on, the West Coast and New York and the states located on the northeast portion of our country along with Chicago have traditionally voted Democratic. The "flyover" portion of our country between the East and West Coasts is where the majority of what I consider the commonsense, God-fearing people reside. These states are where the hardworking middle-class people live and work and where many do not agree with the radical hard-left wing of the Democratic Party and their leaders. There is evidence that supports this belief and also provides a glimpse of the effect of long-term liberal, progressive, left-wing policies governing these areas.

Professor Joseph Olson of the Hamline Law School located in St. Paul, Minnesota, did an analysis of the 2008 presidential election when Mitt Romney ran for president against Barack Obama. He looked at the states and counties won by each candidate in terms of square miles of land that was represented and the population present. He then looked at the murder rates per 100,000 residents in these counties of the states won by each and compared the results. The following table depicts the results of that study.

Candidate	States Won	Square Miles	Population of Counties Won	Murder Rate Per 100,000 Residents in Counties Won
Obama	19	580,000	127 million	13.2
Romney	29	2,427,000	143 million	2.1

When you look at the results of this study, Barack Obama only won 39.4 percent of the states with Mitt Romney winning 60.4 percent of the states. As far as square miles, the states that Obama won only represented 19.3 percent of the total square miles represented. This means that the area of the states that Romney won represented 80.7 percent of the total. As far as population represented by the study, Obama's number was 47.0 percent of the population versus 53.0 percent of the population represented by Romney. The problem is that the murder rate per 100,000 residents was 6.28 times greater for the area and population represented by Obama versus the population and area represented by Romney.

In addition, a map of the territory won by Romney was mostly land owned by taxpaying citizens of the country. The territory of the land won by Obama consisted mostly of those citizens living in low-income tenements who were living off various forms of government welfare. This led Professor Olson to believe that the United States is somewhere between the "complacency and apathy" phase of the previously noted hierarchy of the fall of any Democracy as outlined by Professor Alexander Tyler in 1887. Professor Olson concluded that the United States was located between "complacency and apathy" phase since an estimated 40 percent of the nation's population has already reached the "governmental dependency" phase. The radical left has been very successful in implementing Saul Alinsky's Rules for Radicals as well as a number of the 1963 communist goals.

When we consider Professor Tyler's sequence of the downfall of democracies after the "government dependency" phase, the nation progresses into bondage under a governing system that resembles a dictatorship. Does this sound like a Marxist/socialistic system that is ruled by an elite few over a population of citizens dependent on the government? This is just exactly the result Saul Alinsky anticipated that his Rules for Radicals would produce.

When one looks at today's radical, liberal, progressive, socialistic-minded hard-left-wing Democrats, it is easy to understand that this is just what their agenda is all about. They are doing this with the help of the "deep state" and the left-wing-biased mainstream news media. The question is—will they succeed in "fundamentally changing" America?

CHAPTER 13

George Soros and the Deep State

THE "DEEP STATE" WAS created when a sufficient number of baby boomers and other antiwar, antimilitary, and anticapitalism politicians reached high levels of positions in our governments. This became evident during the Clinton administration and even more evident during the Obama administration. To me, this became evident when both of these administrations began to openly push their radical, hard-left-wing, progressive agenda. The deep state was essentially created when the Clintons and the Obamas joined together in order to achieve their socialist agenda for the United States. All they needed was money. This is when George Soros entered the picture as a billionaire financier of the socialist agenda.

George Soros was born in Hungary and became a naturalized United States citizen in 1961. He made his fortune managing hedge funds and investments worldwide. According to Forbes magazine in their February 2017 issue, Soros's net worth was estimated to be $25.2 billion. This ranked him as the nineteenth wealthiest individual in the world.

According to Judicial Watch, George Soros began his direct political activity during the 2004 campaign cycle. He contributed just over $25 million to various liberal and progressive Democratic Party groups working to defeat President George W. Bush's reelection effort. He has continued to make large personal contributions to both Hillary Clinton and Barack Obama during their presidential aspirations and campaigns. He not only has contributed to far-left-wing, radical groups and presidential candidates in the United States, but he is also known to support far-left-wing political and socialistic views throughout the world.

His interest in advancing a worldwide left wing radical agenda began in 1979 when George Soros created his "Open Society Foundation." In fact, according to the group's website, the organization has contributed $1.5 billion to various like-minded groups in the United States alone. These groups that receive funds from the "Open Society Foundation" all represent a "progressive" philosophy of promoting "reform" in our governmental system. These groups that are funded cover the full spectrum of progressive and radical causes. Some of these groups include the American Civil Liberties Union (ACLU), Planned Parenthood, The Brookings Institution, Common Cause, and the Center for American Progress. It is estimated that his Open Society Foundation may fund as many as 200 organizations in the United States alone.

In addition to the above organizations, Soros's Open Society Foundation also funds many anti-Christian activists groups. According to the Congressional Prayer Caucus Foundation (CPCF), some of these include the Rockefeller Foundation, Carnegie of New York, the Tides Foundation, the Democracy Alliance, the Hewlett Foundation, the Gill Foundation, and the Ford Foundation.

To illustrate just how determined George Soros is on imposing his philosophy of the radical hard-left-wing progressive reform on our country, in 2017, George Soros transferred the bulk of his personal wealth, which is estimated to be approximately $18 billion, to his Open Society Foundation. This is now second only to the Bill and Melinda Gates Foundation in total US assets.

In addition, according to Judicial Watch, George Soros not only funds the noted anti-Christian groups, but his network is essentially funding the entire radical left-wing American progressive agenda. He has parlayed his immense wealth into becoming the biggest and most influential funder of far-left-wing causes in the United States and the world.

By his noted actions, it is quite obvious that George Soros is truly committed to converting America into a socialist state. It is now apparent that George Soros thinks the fastest and best path to achieving that goal is open our borders to unlimited immigration and to undermine our existing voting laws. He does not want just only American citizens voting in our elections but also illegal aliens that are present in our country. This was evidenced in the recent 2018 midterm elections. It was reported that in San Francisco, California, some local leaders were pushing for illegal immigrants to be allowed to vote in local elections. This would be the first step to allowing all illegal immigrants to vote in all elections.

With "open borders" and an increasing number of illegal aliens, this would greatly benefit the radical-left efforts in two distinct ways toward achieving their goal. The first way is that all the illegal immigrants will put an unsustainable strain on all aspects of our economy and financial institutions. As our country tries to accommodate the tremendous number of illegal immigrants, it actually supports Saul Alinsky's Rules for Radicals by increasing the number of people living in poverty. It also increases the country's spending on welfare, which in turn also increases our national debt. As these illegal immigrants become dependent on the government taking care of them, the second goal of the radical left can be achieved. That goal is that if these illegal immigrants are allowed to vote in our elections, the radical left knows that they will vote for them since they are the ones pushing for "open borders" and more and more welfare for them.

By achieving this goal, this in turn will establish a voting block for the radical far-left-wing Democrats that will ensure their total dominance of power essentially forever. The Republican Party will simply disappear from the political stage. It does not take a rocket scientist to figure out why the radical left is pushing so hard for "open borders" and essentially unlimited voting rights for all, not just citizens.

This was further in evidence in Florida during the recent 2018 midterm elections. There was a proposal presented to allow convicted felons to regain their voting rights added to local ballots.

This proposal was called the redemption proposal. The radical left had conducted a study and determined that a majority of felons would vote Democrat if allowed to vote. The proposal would allow felons to regain their voting rights if they had not committed another crime for five years and they had not been convicted of murder or a sexual-abuse crime. The scary thing is that Florida voters actually approved this proposed amendment to the Florida Constitution by a majority of nearly 65 percent.

This amendment was listed as Amendment 4 on the voter ballots for this election. This actually returned voting rights to more than a million people who had committed felonies (other than murder or sex offense) and who had served their time. This was the largest expansion of voter rights since the Voting Rights Act of 1965 and women's suffrage. The radical left is willing to do whatever it takes to gain voters in order to achieve power and then maintain it.

In addition to "open border," George Soros also supports amnesty for all illegal aliens and supports sanctuary cities, counties, and states. It is no coincidence that these hard-left-wing policies that are being implemented are currently in cities and states that have been governed by Democratic leaders and voted predominantly for President Obama and then for Hillary Clinton.

It is also very obvious that George Soros is behind much of the funding for the deep state and their efforts to "fundamentally change America." The time period when this occurred and when the deep state came out of the closet is also obvious when you compare what high-level Democrats such as Hillary Clinton, Barack Obama, and Chuck Schumer have said during an earlier time period and what they say now. With the funding by George Soros, the "deep state" felt they had a lock on power and that Hillary Clinton would be elected President in 2016. They firmly believed that there was no way Donald J. Trump could ever be elected President.

The following are examples of when the radical hard-left-wing arm of the Democratic Party took over the party and came out of the closet and revealed their true agenda for our country. This is when they totally changed their stance on illegal immigration and "open borders." On December 15, 2005, on C-Span, Senator Barack Obama stated the following about "open borders":

We all agree on the need to punish employers who choose to hire illegal immigrants. We are a generous and welcoming people here in the US. But those who enter our country illegally and those who employ them disrespect the "rule of law," and they are showing disregard for those who are following the law. We simply cannot allow people to pour into the US undetected, undocumented, unchecked, and circumvent the line of people who are waiting patiently, diligently, and lawfully.

He essentially repeated this stance on April 3, 2006, on C-Span 2, when he stated the following:

"Those who enter our country illegally and those who employ them disrespect the 'rule of law.' And because we live in an age where terrorists are challenging our borders, we cannot allow people to pour into the US undetected, undocumented, and unchecked."

On June 24, 2009, in Washington, DC, Chuck Schumer stated the following about illegal immigration: "People who enter the United States without our permission are illegal aliens, and illegal aliens should not be treated the same as people who enter the US legally." Even as late as November 9, 2015, when Hillary Clinton was running for president, during a speech in New Hampshire, she stated the following about a border wall: "I voted numerous times when I was a senator to spend money to build a barrier to try and prevent illegal immigrants from coming in."

The above statements are excellent examples of the hypocrisy of the radical, liberal, progressive, left-wing, socialistic-minded Democrats. They will say anything while running for office to get elected and then do what they really believe after they get elected. They then become and act like the true radical, liberal, progressive, far-left-wing individuals that they really are in pursuit of their true agenda. Just think about what these three individuals are saying now and observe just how hard they are fighting for their true agenda.

The real problem with illegal immigration is that we, the hardworking taxpayers of the country, have to pay for it. On

September 27, 2017, a report was released that depicted the impact as far as these costs to us taxpayers. This report was published by Mr. Matt O'Brien and Mr. Spencer Roley and was shown on the Sean Hannity TV program. This report stated the following: "At all of the federal, state, and local levels, taxpayers shell out approximately $134.9 billion to cover the costs incurred by the presence of more than 12.5 million illegal aliens and about 4.2 million citizen children of illegal aliens." If this is not proof of the implementation of Saul Alinsky's Rules for Radicals—which overstresses a system to the point of collapsing, after which you can replace it with whatever you want—I don't know what is!

With the election of President Trump in 2016, the deep state and the far-left-wing, radical, liberal, progressive Democrats were in trouble. They had essentially ignored the flyover portion of our country and all the hardworking middle-class citizens, which Hillary Clinton claimed were "deplorable and nonredeemable" voters. The deep state under the Obama administration felt so certain that Hillary Clinton was going to be elected that they did not even try to hide all of their corruption to ensure Hillary did get elected. When Donald Trump became president and the Republicans took over the House of Representatives and the Senate, the deep state was caught with their hand in the cookie jar.

The 2016 election put Republicans in charge. This was the worst thing that could have happened for the radical, liberal, progressive, socialist Democrats. The Republicans were now in power, and they were going to investigate the suspected corruption that had occurred that was evidenced by the investigation into Hillary Clinton's use of a private server for her e-mails. The deep state was now totally on the defensive, and now they had to protect themselves and at the same time reverse the horrendous mistake that the American population had made electing President Trump. They had to get President Trump out of office at all costs and by any means available. Let's now look at the deep state in action.

CHAPTER 14

The Deep State in Action

WE NOW KNOW THAT the deep state had been working in the closet for quite a while. This all changed, however, on June 16, 2015, when Donald J. Trump announced his plans to run for president. Initially, the radical left wing was pleased. Both the Clintons and the Obama administration felt that if Donald Trump were able, by some chance, to get the Republican nomination, Hillary Clinton would not have a problem defeating him in the 2016 presidential election. All they needed to do was to ensure that Hillary Clinton was elected. In their minds, it was a foregone conclusion that she would be elected. They could see the light at the end of the tunnel that they would be able to complete the "fundamental change in America" to socialism. This was the beginning of the largest abuse-of-power scandal in the history of the United States.

This is when the Obama administration began to weaponize the intelligence community, the Department of Justice (DOJ), and the Federal Bureau of Investigation (FBI) for political purposes. They also began to openly support a two-tiered justice system: one for conservatives and Republicans and one for the Clintons. This led to massive corruption on a grand scale.

Before we look at the web of corruption, conspiracy, and abuse of power by the deep state, we first need to consider some of the previous actions by the deep state. This is during the time period when they were working silently and quietly in the background. As with every upcoming election and especially presidential elections, the focus of many states always turns to preventing voter fraud. This is when many states focus on voter identification requirements and the cleansing of voter rolls. The goal is to remove deceased voters' names as well as anyone who had moved out of that jurisdiction. The purpose is to assure that only individuals who are authorized to vote actually vote. We hear a lot about states trying to pass regulations that require voters to have a photo identification (ID) in order to vote. Voter ID helps ensure that only qualified individuals actually vote. The radical left does not want any of these types of actions to occur. It is not hard to figure out why the radical left does not want these actions to be put in place. In fact, the Obama's Justice Department actually began mounting legal challenges against states that were attempting to protect the honesty of their elections such as requiring voter ID and the cleansing of voter rolls. This is when George Soros again entered the picture.

According to Judicial Watch, George Soros made national headlines in early 2016 when it was revealed that he was funding legal challenges across the country to block states that were attempting to protect the honesty of their elections. Legal challenges were initiated against commonsense measures like voter ID and regularly reviewing voter rolls in order to remove ineligible voters. Specifically, George Soros funded a legal team, headed by Marc Elias, to augment the legal challenges that the Obama Justice Department were pursuing against states that were trying to protect their elections. It should be noted that at that time, Marc Elias was legal counsel to Hillary Clinton's presidential campaign. We can now begin to see just how incestuous the corruption at the highest levels of our government was. We also can now see the connection between George Soros, the Obama Justice Department, and Hillary Clinton. This is the deep state at work.

You do not have to be a rocket scientist to see why the radical left is so opposed to voter ID and voter-roll-cleansing requirements. When one considers that Democrats have been in charge of Chicago for over eighty years, the only way this would be possible is if the Democratic Party machine in Chicago was able to control voting results. The same results for over eighty years defies the natural law of averages. This law states that in a fair and equal environment, there is a 50 percent chance that each of two parties should have an equal chance to win. This has been illustrated in the national presidential elections from 1933 to the present.

During this time period of eighty-six years, we have had fourteen presidents, seven of whom had been Republicans and seven who have been Democrats. So far in Chicago, the Democrats have been able to maintain control for approximately eighty years by winning 100 percent of the elections. This to me does not pass the logical-man concept. I feel that the only way this happens is if someone or some party is controlling the environment surrounding elections through voter fraud.

There is a common saying: "There are only two things that are for certain: death and taxes." For the Democrats to stay in power for over eighty years, it cannot just be a natural occurrence. Even Rudy Giuliani, a Republican, was able to be elected as mayor of New York. New York has always been a well-known Democratic stronghold. Chicago politics is a prime example of how voter manipulation can result in continuous power for Democrats when the voter environment is controlled.

There are other examples of obvious voter fraud in elections in other Democratic strongholds in our country. We all remember the "hanging chads" in the Florida counties of Broward and Palm Beach during the Bush/Gore presidential election of 2000. Both of these counties are known to be Democratic-controlled counties. The contested results of this election in these two counties had to go all the way to the Supreme Court to get final resolution for that election. Does anyone think it was unusual for a similar problem to occur with the voter results in Broward and Palm Beach counties during the 2018 midterm election? The integrity of the Florida vote was called into question when voting results from Broward and Palm Beach counties were continually changing.

On election night, Broward County election chief supervisor Brenda Snipes, a Democrat, reported a total of 634,000 votes had been cast. Then two days later, the total increased to 695,700; and then later the same day, it increased even further to 707,223 total votes. The election supervisor said they had found an additional

73,223 votes that had not been counted. It is also interesting to note that a number of bags of blank ballots were found in the back of a rental car at the Fort Lauderdale Airport by an Avis employee. Palm Beach County also had a similar occurrence. Two days after the election, their elections supervisor reportedly found an additional 15,000 votes that had not been reported on election night. Neither elections supervisor provided any explanation as to where these additional votes came from.

One had to wonder why sixty-five of the sixty-seven counties in Florida were able to get their votes counted on time, but the same two counties of Broward and Palm Beach had similar problems as during the 2000 presidential election with their ballots. The sixty-five counties that did get their votes counted on time included all the counties in the Florida Panhandle that had just experienced major Hurricane Michael just twenty-seven days earlier. They only thing that we know for certain is that the Democrats were in control of counting the votes during both elections.

When one considers the history of election misdeeds of the Broward County Elections Supervisor Brenda Snipes, one has to wonder just how much of this is actually fraud and an actual attempt to steal elections for Democrats in Florida. One thing it does do is answer the question as to why Democrats do not want voter ID or any other safeguards to ensure the integrity of elections.

When we look at some of the misdeeds of previous elections that have occurred in Broward County, the picture becomes much clearer. Mr. J. Christian Adams, a former Department of Justice (DOJ) official and now president of the Public Interest Legal Foundation, was on the Sean Hannity program on November 9, 2018. While at the DOJ, Mr. Adams prosecuted the Broward County election supervisor Brenda Snipes for election misdeeds. He indicated that during an interview with Ms. Snipes, he found out that she was responsible for the following actions/misdeeds:

- She had destroyed ballots during the 2016 primary race.

- She had more registered voters than citizens living in Broward County. She had doctored reports about cleansing voter rolls.

- She still had voters registered who were alive when Grover Cleveland was president and who had died in 1908.

- She had even lost the manual of instructions on how to remove deceased voter names.

In addition, an article in the Sun Sentinel on May 14, 2018, documented that a judge also had ruled that she had illegally destroyed ballots in the 2016 Wasserman Schultz primary race. No wonder the radical left does not want any commonsense regulations passed to improve the integrity of elections.

Even in the recent 2018 midterm election in California, the Democrats devised a new strategy that will allow them to steal every competitive district and swing state in the upcoming 2020 election. They tested the strategy for the first time in the California midterm elections. This strategy is documented by a mail out from the American Civil Rights Union Action Fund, Susan Carleson, chairman. The mail out described this new strategy, which is named *ballot harvesting*.

Ms. Carleson points out that on election night of November 6, 2018, as most folks went to bed, the election looked like a mixed verdict. It looked like the Democrats had won a couple dozen seats in the House, and the Republicans had actually increased seats in the Senate. Then over the next few days, races that looked like solid Republicans wins on election night were suddenly turning into Democratic wins as the absentee ballots were counted. It also appeared that almost all these contested races reversals were occurring in California. Even former House Speaker Paul Ryan commented to a reporter the following concern: "California just defies logic to me. We were only down twenty-six seats the night of the election, and three weeks later, we lost basically every California contested race." The question is, what is ballot harvesting?

Before the midterm elections, California Democrats passed a new law that permits a practice known as ballot harvesting. This is a two-step process: The first step is that the State of California sent mail-in ballots to every registered voter, whether they asked for one or not. The second step is that campaign operatives, union activists, and "community organizers" were allowed to go door to door to collect or harvest these mail-in ballots on behalf of voters. Under this new California law and ballot-harvesting scheme, anyone can walk into an election office and hand over truckloads of mail-in ballots, with no questions asked. The individual did not even need to provide any documentation or proof that the ballots they were turning in were legitimate.

The problem with this law is that there are no safeguards in place to prevent voter fraud. For example, what's to stop a campaign official from collecting or even buying blank ballots from voters and then filling them out themselves? Or what's to stop a community organizer from collecting thousands of ballots and then throwing out the votes for Republicans? In addition, what's to stop union activists from pressuring union members to hand in their ballots to prove that they voted for the "right" candidate? It is very possible that seats that had been held by Republicans for decades flip to the Democrats all because of this new strategy.

The bad news is that since the Democrats have secured control of the house, Nancy Pelosi outlined her blueprint for seizing control of our nation's elections and her new bill: HR 1. HR 1 is the designation that is normally given to the first bill introduced in a new Congress by the majority party. This is normally what the majority party considers to be their top priority. If HR 1 were to be implemented, it would be an unprecedented power grab and would mean the end of all free and fair elections and our country.

This would be accomplished by two provisions. The bill would require every state to adopt a vote-by-mail system. The second provision of this bill removes the authority to oversee elections away from the states and gives it to the federal government. This part of the bill is crucial for the Democrats because it ensures that Republican-run states would be powerless to stop *ballot harvesting*.

In addition, this HR 1 bill will implement a number of reckless policies that will trample on states' rights, disenfranchise voters, and make voter fraud all but inevitable. For example, this bill will implement the following policies:

- Restore voting right to millions of convicted felons, which has been a key Democratic demographic.
- Make it almost impossible for states to remove suspicious voter registrations from voter rolls.

- Force states to seek preapproval from the federal government for changes as small as modifying the hours of an election office or moving a voter location to a different part of town.

- Force states to adopt same-day registrations, which has been proven to increase voter fraud.

To me, this strategy sounds a lot like what also happened in Broward and Palm Beach Counties in Florida. Maybe California was not the only place they tried out a portion of this strategy.

What this strategy tells me is that the radical far left Democrats have developed a possible solution to the fact that in the past, they have not been able to obtain their radical goals at the ballot box. In the past, they have concentrated on obtaining their goals by placing activist judges on the Supreme Court. Since President Trump just named two originalist judges to the Supreme Court, these radical, far-left Democrats appear to be pursuing another option as they push their radical agenda.

We only have to think back to 2008 when Barack Obama was elected president. The Democrats also won control of both the House and Senate. This resulted in that passage of the Affordable Care Act (Obamacare) without a single Republican vote. If they can control our elections, they can ensure they get activist judges appointed to the Supreme Court. Then their goal to "fundamentally change America" can be achieved. The America we know will be gone forever.

The only good news is that the Republicans still control the Senate, and President Trump is president. Nancy Pelosi knows that HR1 would have no chance of passing the Senate or that President Trump would sign such a bill. Therefore, I am sure she will not bring the bill up for a vote in the House. We will not have to hear those famous words, "We have to pass this bill to see what is in it." If the Democrats ever get back in control of the presidency, the House, and Senate, our country will be lost. The 2020 election will be the most important election in our nation's history and will define the path that our nation will follow for the future.

With Judicial Watch exposing the evidence that George Soros and Marc Elias are significant actors in the actions of the deep state, let us now delve deeper into the connections between the Clintons, the Obama administration, and as well as other major players of the deep state. Some of these major players include John Brennan (former director of the Central Intelligence Agency), James Clapper (former director of the National Intelligence Agency), Loretta Lynch (former attorney general), all of whom were part of the Obama administration. In addition, other major players are James Comey (former director of the Federal Bureau of Investigation), Andrew McCabe, Peter Strzok, Lisa Page, and Bruce Ohr—all previous high-ranking officials in the FBI and/or the DOJ. Even Bruce Ohr's wife, Nellie Ohr, who worked for Fusion GPS, played a part in the deep state.

The web of corruption and abuse of power goes even deeper and was exhibited as early as 2001. This also is the time when a two-tiered justice system appears to have been put in place as far as the Clintons are concerned. A look at history reveals significant evidence that the deep state was at work. In 2001, after Bill and Hillary Clinton had left the White House, they decided to establish the Clinton Foundation. This was a charity to supposedly provide assistance to areas of the world that had suffered major natural disasters, like the earthquake in Haiti. However, when it became questionable where some of the funds that had been donated were going and to whom, an FBI investigation was launched into the foundation. There was even a grand jury impanelled for the investigation. This investigation was going on during the time period of 2001 to 2005, when George W. Bush was president. The deep state was still in the closet but definitely hard at work.

The investigation determined that many governments from around the world had donated to the Clinton Foundation. The problem was that from 2001 to 2003, none of these donations to the Clinton Foundation were ever declared to the Internal Revenue Service (IRS). It is interesting to note here that Lois Lerner was working at the IRS. At that time, she was in charge of the Tax Exemption Branch of the IRS. Lois Lerner was later promoted to the position of IRS director under President Obama. When Lois Lerner was interviewed about the Clinton Foundation investigation, she invoked her Fifth Amendment rights.

Another interesting fact to note is that the person that was running the Tax Division at the Department of Justice (DOJ) from

2001 to 2005 was none other than Rod Rosenstein. As we all know, Rod Rosenstein was later promoted to assistant attorney general under President Obama. In addition, another very interesting fact is that during this same time period of 2001 to 2005, Robert Mueller III was the director of the Federal Bureau of Investigation (FBI). Do you think that this was all just coincidence?

Just to add to the web of deep state questionable actions, another "coincidence" that occurred was that James Comey was also working for the FBI under Robert Mueller. Now guess who was assigned to take over the Clinton Foundation tax investigation in 2002. If you guessed James Comey, you just won a prize. All four of these individuals knew of and/or were investigators into the Clinton Foundation investigation. Do we even have to wonder why the grand jury was never utilized during this investigation? The two-tiered justice system for the Clintons was now in place.

The corruption plot thickens even further. After the 2008 presidential election when President Barack Obama was elected president, the Obamas and the Clintons joined forces. President Obama selected Hillary Clinton to be his secretary of state. This was done even though Hillary Clinton felt that Barack Obama had cheated her out of her right to become the first woman president. It is obvious that the goal to "fundamentally change America" was more important than their personal goals. The only problem for Hillary Clinton was that during her tenure as secretary of state, she displayed total mismanagement of the Benghazi tragedy and other scandals. The Benghazi tragedy cost the lives of Ambassador Christopher Stevens and three other Americans. Hillary Clinton, however, had to be protected by the deep state.

Enter Susan Rice, who was President Obama's national security advisor. She immediately came out and explained to the American people that this attack on the US Embassy was in response to an anti-Muslim video on YouTube. She claimed that it was not a terrorist attack at all. One has to ask, was this an attempt to cover up the incompetency of Hillary Clinton by the Obama administration?

Thanks again to Judicial Watch, the real story about how Hillary Clinton mishandled the situation was revealed. Judicial Watch was able to determine that the deceased ambassador had warned of a terrorist attack and had requested reinforcements months before the attack and even during the evening of the attack. All reinforcements were refused by the State Department, which resulted in the loss of four American lives. This all was eventually brought out into the open, but absolutely no repercussions were ever experienced by Hillary Clinton. Is this not another example of a two-tiered justice system for the Clintons?

It was during the investigation into the Benghazi tragedy that Judicial Watch, along with Congressman Trey Gowdy, who was the chairman of the select committee looking into the facts surrounding Benghazi, discovered that Hillary Clinton was using a private server while conducting State Department business. Further investigation into Hillary Clinton's use of this private server revealed that there was also an unlawful mishandling of classified information, and top-secret documents were found on her e-mails. Judicial Watch also was able to determine that it was Hillary Clinton's idea to use her own personal e-mail server to conduct State Department business. One has to ask why Hillary Clinton would want to do this. Further investigation into the situation provided strong evidence that this may have been done in order to hide a "pay to play" policy at the State Department under Hillary Clinton.

We all can remember the Uranium One issue during which the State Department under Secretary Clinton supported and approved the sale of 20 percent of the United States' uranium to a Russian company. For this to even happen does not pass the logical man concept. Why would we sell 20 percent of our critical supply of a material to a Russian company when it can be used to produce nuclear weapons? The United States does not even have enough uranium for our own use. Does a policy of "pay to play" come to mind? This is especially true when one considers the fact that the United States and the American people did not receive anything in return from the completion of this transaction. The only people and organization in the United States that did benefit from this transaction were the Clintons and the Clinton Foundation.

Prior to the sale approval, Bill Clinton was invited to Moscow to give a one-hour speech and then have a meeting with Vladimir Putin at his home. For this speech, Bill Clinton was paid $500,000.

Have you heard of anyone receiving that type of compensation for a one-hour speech, even if the individual is a past president?

The next evidence of a possible "pay to play" policy occurred after the sale was approved. The Clinton Foundation received approximately $145 million in donations from a number of entities directly connected to the Uranium One deal. Now I know that I am just a dumb fighter pilot and engineer, but even I am able to conclude that there seems to be a very high probability of a connection between all of the above occurrences to have even occurred.

Let us now look at what was happening at the FBI and DOJ when all of this was occurring. Would it surprise you to know that the FBI director at that time was none other than Robert Mueller? Would it also surprise you to learn that he even delivered a uranium sample to Moscow in 2009? In addition, during this time period at the DOJ, would it surprise you to know that the individual who was handling this case for the DOJ out of the US attorney's office in Maryland was none other than Rod Rosenstein? Why do these names sound so familiar today? Could it be due to the Russian collusion investigation?

What is even more interesting about the Uranium One deal is that the FBI actually had a mole inside the Russian organization who was providing information to the FBI on this highly questionable transaction. His name is William Campbell, and the Justice Department placed a gag order on him and threatened to lock him up if he spoke out about it. Does the term deep state come to mind? As far as I know, he has never been able to get his side of the story out to the public.

The question that has to be asked is, How does 20 percent of the most strategic material of the United States end up in Russian hands when the FBI has an informant mole providing inside information to the FBI about bribes and kickbacks that were occurring? Again, I may just be a dumb fighter pilot and engineer, but to me this reeks of a cover-up.

Another piece of very interesting information that needs to be considered during the time period that the $145 million worth of donations was being made to the Clinton Foundation is who was in charge at the IRS. If you guessed Lois Lerner, once again you would be correct. Lois Lerner was still at the Internal Revenue Services working for the Charitable Donations Division.

It is also interesting to note that after no action was taken against the Clinton Foundation as a result of the investigation conducted by James Comey, he left his government job to take a position with Lockheed Martin. During his tenure with Lockheed Martin, he was able to secure seventeen no-bid contracts for Lockheed Martin with the Hillary Clinton's State Department. One does have to wonder why Hillary Clinton decided to use her own personal server to conduct State Department business, or do we? Maybe we do not have to ask why Hillary Clinton deleted thirty-three thousand e-mails, acid-wash her hard drives, and actually destroy her Blackberry phones and SIM cards when Trey Gowdy subpoenaed these items? Does a two-tiered justice system again come to mind?

Let us now look again at James Comey's activities. From Lockheed Martin, James Comey actually returned to the government in 2012 when he was nominated to be the FBI director. On his departure from Lockheed Martin, they rewarded him with a $6 million thank-you bonus. Would this suggest that he was being rewarded for all of his efforts on securing no-bid contracts with the State Department? This, however, was not the end for James Comey and his contribution to the corruption by the deep state.

The level of corruption and abuse of power continued to build as the deep state continued to push their agenda. Now, as FBI director, James Comey was now in charge of the infamous Clinton e-mail investigation that Congressman Trey Gowdy had requested. Since this investigation also involved the Clinton Foundation, James Comey supposedly had the FBI investigate the IRS and Lois Lerner. It should not come as a surprise that the FBI exonerated Lois Lerner and the IRS. It is, however, interesting to note that as far as we know, the Clinton Foundation has never been audited in its twenty years plus of operations.

When one looks at all the facts, it is truly remarkable just how much of a tangled web of corruption has been weaved by the deep state in their efforts to protect Hillary Clinton. Additionally, would it surprise you to learn that James Comey's brother works for the law firm of DLA Piper, the law firm that does the Clinton Foundation taxes? The extent of the incestuous nature of the deep state is almost incomprehensible.

During the second term of Barack Obama as president, and being term-limited, it became the goal of the radical left-wing deep state to ensure that Hillary Clinton was elected president in the 2016 election. To the radical left-wing Democrats and the deep state, this was mandatory to ensure that the goal of "fundamentally changing America" into a socialist state was achieved. To ensure that this happened, the deep state decided they needed to do whatever was necessary to ensure that Hillary Clinton was elected.

This is when the deep state and Hillary Clinton essentially took over the Democratic National Committee (DNC) in order to ensure she received the Democratic nomination for the 2016 election. Their first obstacle was Bernie Sanders. This is sort of ironic because Bernie Sanders is a self-professed socialist. For the radical left, however, he evidently is not socialistic enough for them. Therefore, he had to be defeated in the primary election.

The problems for the DNC began to mount when, on June 12, 2016, Wikileaks founder Julian Assange announced plans to release e-mails related to Hillary Clinton that he had obtained reportedly from a Russian hacker. At that time, Debbie Wasserman Schultz was the head of the DNC. Bernie Sanders was running a very strong campaign against Hillary Clinton. The DNC had to take actions to stop Bernie Sanders from winning the Democratic primary nomination.

On July 22, 2016, Wikileaks did release twenty thousand of the e-mails that had been hacked from the DNC. With the information that was revealed by these hacked e-mails, it became obvious that the DNC was definitely biased against Bernie Sanders. Debbie Wasserman Schultz was forced to resign as chairman of the DNC. Donna Brazile was selected to replace her as chairman.

It now became Donna Brazile's responsibility to ensure Hillary Clinton received the Democratic nomination. Because of the actions of Debbie Wasserman-Schultz, it became obvious that the Democratic election nomination was "rigged" against Bernie Sanders. Donna Brazile even admitted that the Democratic primary nomination was "rigged" against Bernie Sanders while being interviewed by Sean Hannity on one of his TV shows in November of 2017. She later backpedaled to say that she did not mean that the fix was in for Hillary when she used that word. Donna Brazile, however, also had to resign the chairmanship of the DNC when it became known that she had given Hillary Clinton some of the questions prior to one of the debates between Hillary Clinton and Donald Trump. Once Hillary Clinton received the Democratic nomination, a full-court press was initiated by the deep state and Hillary Clinton to ensure she was elected president. Hillary Clinton's election had to be accomplished by any means necessary.

In the deep state members' minds, Donald Trump had less than a 2 percent chance of winning the election, which was being reported by the biased mainstream news media. Therefore, the corruption and abuse of power that was going on by the deep state did not have to be concealed any longer. With Hillary Clinton elected as president, their actions would never see the light of day. As such, they no longer needed to hide their actions and bias in their e-mails to one another, which was later revealed. Thankfully, Donald Trump did win the election, and all the corruption and abuse of power would come to light.

The bad news for the radical left-wing deep state was that not only did Donald Trump win the presidency, but the Republicans also won the House and Senate. Now it was time for the deep state to go into a full-court defensive course of action in order to protect themselves and continue to push their agenda. Unfortunately for them, the Republican House of Representatives initiated investigations into the deep-state actions. Judicial Watch also had a hand in securing a lot of information needed through the "Freedom of Information Act" requests for evidence of the corruption and abuse of power that had and was taking place.

Some of the first information that was secured from the deep state, FBI, and DOJ members were e-mails that had been sent between Peter Strzok and Lisa Page in March of 2016. These e-mails provided evidence of the extreme bias against Donald Trump immediately after he received the Republican nomination to run for president. It was very obvious that the deep state was going to do whatever was necessary to ensure Hillary Clinton was protected from any investigation that would hamper her chance of becoming president.

Additionally, these e-mails also provided evidence that the deep state had devised an "insurance policy" if by some chance the American people did make a horrible mistake and elect Donald Trump as president. This "insurance policy" would correct this huge mistake. These e-mails also revealed just how confident the deep state was that Hillary Clinton would be elected president. Their attitude was, they did not even have to be careful about what they said in their e-mails since they would never be made public.

To illustrate the extent of the corruption and abuse of power under the Obama administration, the FBI under James Comey opened an investigation into Hillary Clinton's mishandling of classified material on her personal e-mail server on July 10, 2015. FBI director James Comey assigned Peter Strzok as the lead investigator. Do you really think a full and complete investigation would occur?

It was also during this time period that it became evident that the corruption was at the highest levels of the Obama administration. In September 2015, Loretta Lynch, Obama's attorney general, instructed James Comey to refer to this investigation as a "matter" and not an investigation. This, however, was only the beginning of the problems for Hillary Clinton.

It was during the March–May 2016 time frame when Russian hackers were able to successfully hack into the e-mail account of Hillary Clinton's campaign chairman John Podesta. The hackers targeted over three hundred accounts at the Clinton campaign office, the Democratic National Committee (DNC) office, and the Democratic Congressional Campaign Committee office, obtaining a significant number of documents. This caused the deep state to became even more defensive and even more aggressive in their efforts to protect Hillary Clinton. Since some of the Russian hacking had occurred in May 2016, it became necessary to exonerate Hillary Clinton as soon as possible.

We now know that Peter Strzok actually drafted the exoneration letter for Hillary Clinton on May 2, 2016, which was before Hillary

Clinton was even interviewed as part of the investigation. We also know that this draft exoneration letter was changed to replace the words *grossly negligent* to *extreme carelessness* to describe Hillary Clinton's actions. This was done because "grossly negligent" is a crime while "extreme carelessness" is not.

Hillary Clinton was actually interviewed by Peter Strzok on July 2, 2016, as part of the investigation. This, of course, was after the draft letter of exoneration had already been written. In addition, for her interview, Hillary Clinton was not sworn in, and no documentation of the interview was kept. She also was allowed to have two other individuals present for the interview. The actual letter of exoneration was dated July 5, 2016. Does this sound like a two-tiered justice system?

On July 8, 2016, FBI director James Comey went on live television for a press conference and exonerated Hillary Clinton for any wrongdoing concerning her e-mail personal server. James Comey justified her exoneration by saying that no prosecutor would determine that there was sufficient evidence to pursue a criminal case against Hillary Clinton.

It should also be noted that Loretta Lynch had a meeting with Bill Clinton on June 27, 2016, in an airplane sitting on the tarmac at an airport in Arizona. This occurred just a few days before Comey's exoneration of Hillary Clinton. This meeting supposedly was just a "coincidental" meeting, and the discussion was supposedly about grandkids, but it lasted forty-five minutes.

It is also interesting to note that Loretta Lynch indicated that she was going to accept whatever conclusion James Comey came up with as far as the investigation into the "matter" was concerned. Do the words "the fix was in" come to mind when one considers how Hillary Clinton was exonerated? Normally, the attorney general would be the one holding the press conference, not the FBI director.

The next important date in the sequence of events was July 22, 2016, when Wikileaks released twenty thousand of the DNC e-mails that had been hacked. Then just eight days later, on July 30, 2016, the FBI director James Comey opened a "counterintelligence" investigation called Crossfire Hurricane into Russian efforts to influence our election. With both presidential campaigns going strong and the deep state having been successful in protecting Hillary Clinton's e-mail fiasco, it was time to develop an "insurance policy" just in case Donald Trump did win.

Since Donald Trump had mentioned that maybe the Russians had the thirty-three thousand e-mails that Hillary Clinton had deleted during a campaign rally, it would not be out of the realm of possibility to think that the deep state may be able to blame the Russian hacking of the DNC on the Donald Trump campaign. Even before Donald Trump was elected president, the deep state was at work creating an "insurance policy" based on possible collusion between the Russians and the Trump campaign. They felt that it would be easy for the deep state to sell this idea to the public since it was obvious it must have been the Trump campaign because the hacking occurred on the DNC and Hillary Clinton's campaign and not Trump's campaign. After all, Donald Trump had just been officially nominated as the GOP presidential candidate during the week of July 18–21, 2016.

When one considers that the Russian collusion investigation that was initiated on July 30, 2016, by none other than James Comey, it should not surprise you that the individual to head this investigation was Peter Strzok. Since the deep state had been able to successfully protect Hillary Clinton before the election with this combination of individuals, all they now needed to do is create a way to correct the terrible mistake if, by some chance, the American people did elect Donald Trump. The "insurance policy" had been put in place.

This "insurance policy" would be all that they needed to prove that Donald Trump's campaign had colluded with the Russians. This would be enough that the American people would call for Trump to step down, or if he did not, the Democrats would have enough evidence to impeach him. They knew that the mainstream news media would be able to convince the American people that Donald Trump had colluded with the Russians to win the election. We should also remember that some radical left-wing Democrats believe that the "truth is whatever you want it to be." All you have to do is repeat it enough, and it will become fact.

The FBI Russian "counterintelligence" investigation was ongoing for nine months between July 30, 2016, and May 9, 2017, under FBI director James Comey. It was during this time period between July 30, 2016, and up to the election in November 2016—it appears that the Obama administration weaponized the intelligence community for political purposes. Enter James Clapper and John Brennan, who were also important players of the deep state.

James Clapper was the director of the National Intelligence Agency (NIA), and John Brennan was the director of the Central Intelligence Agency (CIA) under President Obama. These organizations are responsible for surveillance of foreign entities as possible threats to the United States. Supposedly, if either the CIA or NIA identifies an American citizen during these surveillance activities, their names are not to be released. When these names are identified, it is called unmasking. During the last year of the Obama administration, which included the newly initiated FBI Russian investigation, the number of names of American citizens that were unmasked increased by 350 percent.

What is also unusual is just who some of these administration officials were that were requesting the unmaskings. They were not all FBI or DOJ personnel. For example, it was reported that Samantha Powers, President Obama's United Nations Ambassador, requested more than three hundred unmaskings of individuals. I have to wonder why the UN ambassador would need to unmask so many individuals. I also wonder how she fitted into the Russian investigation about Russian collusion. Once identified and unmasked, these individuals were then identified for possible further investigation. This can be a very powerful weapon if used for political purpose.

As was discussed earlier concerning the 1963 communist goal of capturing one or both of the US political parties, there is evidence that there has been some success in the Republican Party. This was evidenced by information uncovered by Judicial Watch. In late 2015, some anti-Trump Republicans allegedly hired a research firm called Fusion GPS to conduct "opposition research" on Donald Trump. This type of activity is not unusual during election campaigns. What is unusual is that a party would do this on one of their own potential candidates. This is when the plot of corruption and abuse of power really thickens.

The research that was being conducted by Fusion GPS consisted of "opposition research" by a former MI-6 British Intelligence Officer named Christopher Steele. Christopher Steele was working for Fusion GPS as well as the FBI. His assignment was to get any dirt on Donald Trump in order to prove collusion with the Russians. His efforts resulted in the creation of the Steele dossier on Donald Trump. Supposedly, the dossier contained dirt on Donald Trump that he had obtained from Russian sources. The only problem with the dossier was that information was not and could not be verified. Even Christopher Steele could not verify the information contained in the dossier. This, however, did not deter the deep state from using the dossier. We should remember many of the deep states believe "truth is whatever you want it to be."

Once it became apparent that Donald Trump was going to be the Republican nominee, Fusion GPS decided to sell its services to Hillary Clinton's campaign and the Democratic National Committee (DNC). However, it was necessary for Hillary Clinton's campaign and the DNC to cover up efforts in this regard. Here is where Marc Elias, who had teamed with George Soros as discussed earlier, again enters the picture.

Marc Elias had been a longtime legal counsel for Hillary Clinton. At this time, he was the general counsel for her campaign. Marc Elias, who worked for Perkins Core, became the go-between the Clinton campaign, the DNC, and Fusion GPS. To hide just who actually paid Fusion GPS for the dossier, Perkins Core was paid more than $12 million by the Clinton campaign. They, in turn, paid Fusion GPS.

The goal of the deep state" now was to get the information contained in the Steele dossier out to the public. It should also be noted that on July 30, 2016, when James Comey initiated the "Crossfire Hurricane" investigation into the Russian collusion probe, Bruce Ohr of the Department of Justice (DOJ) met with Christopher Steele. Bruce Ohr's wife, Nellie Ohr, who worked for Fusion GPS, had set up this meeting. The purpose of this meeting was to discuss the Steele dossier. In addition, Fusion GPS was trying to get the mainstream news media to publicize the contents of this dossier. The only problem was that the dossier was so outrageous with scandalous allegations that could not be verified even the anti-Trump news media outlets would not print the dossier. This, however, did not stop James Clapper and John Brennan from trying to get the information out.

This was accomplished by leaking the information to news sources for use. They would leak information from the dossier to their news sources, who in turn would print news stories using the information. In this way, the deep state was able to get the dossier information out without identifying just where the information came from. This is called *circular reporting*.

The information contained in the Steele dossier was so outrageous and scandalous that even Christopher Steele would not verify the accuracy of the information. During an interrogative interview in England while under oath, Christopher Steele could only say that maybe there was a possible fifty-fifty chance that some of the information was true. The Steele dossier was a document that even the author could not verify to be true.

Even though the Steele dossier was known to be extremely questionable, this did not stop the deep-state members located at the highest echelons of the DOJ and FBI from going after Donald Trump. This is when the corruption and abuse of power was on total display by members of the DOJ and FBI.

With all the unmasking of individuals by members of the Obama administration, the FBI found a way to spy on the Trump campaign in their efforts to prove collusion between the Trump campaign and the Russians. This was done by executing a fraud on the Foreign Intelligence Surveillance Act (FISA) court system.

Since the news media would not print the dossier, what they would print was the leaked information by members of the deep state to selected members of the media who would write stories describing the leaked information. The DOJ and FBI then used these stories as justification and evidence to obtain FISA warrants to spy on members of the Trump campaign. The fact that the information that was being used as justification came from the

Steele dossier, which was paid for by the Hillary Clinton campaign, was not revealed directly to the FISA court.

The deep state felt that they could prove a case of collusion between the Russians and the Trump campaign if they were able to spy on members of the Trump campaign by getting them to turn on Donald Trump. Carter Page was the first individual that the deep state began to spy on. He had been unmasked and had just left the Trump campaign. The problem was that the Steele dossier was not and could not be verified but was still used to obtain the FISA warrant to spy on Carter Page. Since this was not made clear to the FISA court judges, it became a fraud on the court. The reason is that a high-ranking member of the DOJ or FBI has to sign off on the warrant request, which signifies that the information being provided is true and verifiable. If this is not true, then this becomes a criminal offense against the FISA court.

On October 22, 2016, James Comey as FBI director signed the first request to get a FISA warrant to spy on Carter Page. This was the first of four requests for FISA warrants obtained. It would have been very easy for James Comey to verify the Steele dossier. Christopher Steele was working for the FBI. All he would have to do is determine when the last time Christopher Steele had been in Russia. Later review of his passport indicated that Christopher Steele had not been in Russia for at least seven years. Just how current could the dossier be if it was based on Russian sources as claimed by Christopher Steele?

We now know that James Comey also signed the second and third warrant requests. The fourth FISA request was reported to have been signed by Rod Rosenstein, the deputy attorney general. In addition, while still at the FBI, Andrew McCabe, the deputy FBI director, later stated that without the dossier, there would be no FISA warrant. The false and fallacious Steele dossier justified all these requests. It is, however, interesting to note that after the first FISA warrant request signed by James Comey on October 22, 2016, the FBI fired Steele on November 1, 2016, for lying and leaking information.

If President Trump had not been elected, it is quite possible that all of this corruption and abuse of power by members of the deep state probably would not have come to light. It did, however, come to light based on the efforts of Judicial Watch and their "Freedom of Information" requests. After significant stonewalling and delays, e-mails between Lisa Page and Peter Strzok were released.

The information that was revealed was very significant. This is where the information was obtained about the existence of an "insurance policy" was revealed. When Lisa Page e-mailed Peter Strzok about her fear that Donald Trump may be elected president, Peter Strzok responded with, "We won't let that happen." In another e-mail, he indicated that even if he did get elected, they had an "insurance policy" to address the Trump presidency. This insurance policy would either force President Trump to step down, or he would be impeached.

After Donald Trump won the election on November 8, 2016, the deep state was in deep trouble. The newly elected Republicans in the House and Senate began to investigate Hillary Clinton's exoneration and other aspects of the assault on President Trump. There just seemed to be too much evidence of corruption at the highest levels of our government.

The deep state fell back into a defensive posture of protection of itself by using the tactics of delay, delay, and delay"This is why it took so long for the information to be released to answer Judicial Watch's "Freedom of Information" requests as well as requests for information from both the House and Senate Oversight Committees. Their goal was to delay as long as possible and at least until the 2018 midterm elections. Their hope was that the Democrats would regain control of the House and hopefully the Senate.

The deep state saga of corruption continued on after the election. James Comey remained on as the FBI director. When a FBI director is appointed, it is for a term of ten years. President Obama had appointed James Comey. The president can, however, fire the FBI director for any reason or no reason at all. President Trump allowed James Comey to remain on as FBI director even though he was not happy with the way Comey had handled the Hillary Clinton e-mail investigation.

In January of 2017, President Trump requested James Comey to brief him on the Russian investigation that he had initiated back on July 30, 2016. During this briefing, the subject of the Steele dossier came up. James Comey briefed President Trump that the Steele dossier was fallacious and was unverifiable. The question is, Did James Comey lie to the president, or did he lie on October 22, 2016, when he signed the first FISA warrant request? His signature on the request was his certification that all the information used as justification for the warrant request was true and had been verified. Even a dumb fighter pilot and engineer like me can figure out that he had to be lying on one of these occasions. What we know now is that he lied on the FISA request.

As more and more evidence of corruption at the highest levels of our government was revealed and as additional information was released to the House and Senate Oversight Committees, the members of the deep state began to turn against one another. When the evidence surfaced that the Steele dossier may have been used as the justification for the FISA warrants, this became a problem for many of the deep state members. Judicial Watch efforts had a significant impact on getting this information out.

When it became apparent that James Comey was becoming a liability to the deep state, Rob Rosenstein wrote a memo to President Trump recommending that James Comey be fired for the way the Hillary Clinton investigation had been handled. President Trump agreed and fired James Comey on May 9, 2017.

With the firing of James Comey, the deep state had to protect itself from the ongoing investigation. Supposedly, as a way to protect himself, James Comey had created written memos documenting his meetings with President Trump. Comey then gave copies of these memos to one of his professor friends at Columbia University to be leaked to the news media at the New York Times. James Comey even admitted that he had done this on June 8, 2017, when he was testifying before the House Intelligence Oversight Committee. He testified that he had done this to force a Special Counsel to be appointed to take over the Russian collusion investigation. He was successful, and on May 17, 2017, Rob Rosenstein, the deputy attorney general, appointed Robert Mueller III to be the Special Counsel to investigate any Russian collusion during the 2016 election and the Trump campaign.

The appointment statement instructed Robert Mueller to investigate "any links and/or coordination between the Russian Government and individuals associated with the campaign of President Trump, and matters that arose or may arise directly from the investigation." To me, the wording of this statement exhibits a total political bias in that it limited the investigation of Russian collusion to only the Trump campaign. It did not include any mention of investigating for any possible Russian collusion and the Hillary Clinton campaign. Do you think that just maybe they already knew that there was no collusion between the Trump campaign and the Russians? I have noticed in the past that when Democrats accuse someone of doing something shady, it is because they are doing it themselves.

It is also interesting to note that usually when a Special Counsel is appointed, it is known that a crime had been committed. The investigation that is then conducted determines just who committed the crime. In this case, only one of the two campaigns was investigated in order to determine who had committed the crime of collusion. It would appear that the deep state wanted to investigate Donald Trump as an attempt to prove that he had committed the crime of collusion in order to get him removed as president. Does this sound like an "insurance policy" to correct what they saw as a terrible mistake that the American people had made?

This started a twenty-two-month-long investigation of the Trump campaign for any possible evidence of Russian collusion. This was essentially the first two years of President Trump's four-year term. This also provided a subject for the bias mainstream news media to continually report negatively about President Trump essentially twenty-four hours a day. This was meant to convince the American people that they had made a serious mistake when they elected President Trump.

A very interesting chain of events occurred at this point. Rob Rosenstein, the deputy attorney general, had been running the DOJ because President Trump had not yet appointed a new attorney general. President Trump had been interviewing candidates to become the attorney general. One of the last individuals to be interviewed for the position was no other than Robert Mueller III.

Robert Mueller had previously been the director of the FBI, and James Comey had worked for him. Robert Mueller was interviewed the day before President Trump selected Jeff Sessions to become the attorney general.

This had to have been seen as a huge problem for the deep state. As the deputy attorney general, Rob Rosenstein was running the DOJ and was also in control of the Russian investigation. If Jeff Sessions, however, became the attorney general, the deep state would lose control over the Russian investigation. For the deep state—something had to be done.

With the confirmation of Jeff Sessions as attorney general, efforts by the deep state were initiated to convince Jeff Session that he should recuse himself from the Russian investigation The rationale used was that since the investigation was into the Trump campaign and Jeff Sessions had been part of the campaign, he could not be in charge of an investigation into a campaign that he had been a part of. It worked, and Jeff Sessions recused himself from the investigation. The deep state was still in charge of the investigation, and the insurance policy was still intact. They still had a path to either indict President Trump or at least get enough dirt on President Trump to allow the Democrats to impeach him if they could win back control of Congress during the 2016 midterm elections.

With the appointment of Robert Mueller as Special Counsel, it is interesting to note just what was the composition of the team he put together to conduct this investigation. Of the nineteen prosecutors selected by Robert Mueller, fourteen were registered Democrats. Of those fourteen individuals, twelve had donated over $77,500 to Democratic campaigns at both the federal and state levels. In addition, at least one (Jeannie Rhee) had represented Hillary Clinton and the Clinton Foundation as a lawyer in two court case proceedings in 2015. Robert Mueller also appointed Andrew Weissmann as his lead investigator. Andrew Weissmann was at Hillary Clinton's election party on election night until it was cancelled. Do you think that there was any bias against Donald Trump on this team of investigators?

Robert Mueller's investigation went on for twenty-two months and cost the US taxpayers something north of $25 million. It consisted of 2,800 subpoenas, 500 search warrants, 230 court orders, and approximately 500 interviews of individuals. So what were the results that were obtained from this twenty-two-month investigation? The following are the results of this investigation.

A total of thirty-four indictments were issued, of which twenty-five were issued for Russian individuals. Twelve of the Russians were intelligence agents for Russia's GRU. These GRU agents were charged with conspiracy to commit computer crimes, identity theft, and money laundering. The remaining thirteen Russians were business individuals or affiliated companies and were also charged with the above crimes. Since none of these individuals or companies live in the US, they will never come back to the US for trial.

The following is the list of nine Americans associated with the Trump campaign that were indicted. Included are the charges filed and the current status of the charges.

- Roger Stone, a longtime friend and advisor to Donald Trump, was charged with lying to Congress, witness tampering, and obstruction. He pleaded not guilty in federal court on January 29, 2019.

- Michael Cohen, former Trump personal attorney, was charged with tax evasion, bank fraud, campaign finance violations, and lying to Congress. He pleaded guilty August 21 and November 29, 2018, and was sentenced to three years in prison.

- Paul Manafort, a former Trump campaign chairman, was charged with tax and bank fraud, conspiracy, and witness tampering. He was convicted on August 21, 2018, on eight counts after he pleaded guilty and was sentenced to seven and a half years in prison.

- George Papadopoulos, a former Trump campaign aide, was charged with lying to the FBI. He pleaded guilty on October 5, 2017, and served fourteen days in prison.

- General Michael Flynn, President Trump's former national security advisor, was charged with lying to the FBI. He pleaded guilty on December 1, 2017, and has not yet been sentenced.

- Rick Gates, a former Trump campaign aide, was charged with conspiracy against the US and lying to the FBI and the Special Counsel's office. He pleaded guilty on February 23, 2018.

- Alex van der Zwaan, an attorney, was charged with lying to the FBI. He pleaded guilty on February 20, 2018, and was sentenced to thirty days in prison.

- Richard Pinedo, a data broker, was charged with identity fraud. He pleaded guilty on February 12, 2018, and was sentenced to six months in prison.

- Konstantin Kilimnik, an associate of Paul Manafort, was charged with obstruction of justice and conspiracy to obstruct justice. He too resides outside of the US, which presents many legal challenges to prosecuting the case against him.

What is interesting to note is that there were no indictments of Russian collusion of neither President Trump nor any individuals associated with the Trump campaign. Most of the indictments were for lying to Congress, the FBI, or Special Counsel. Other indictments consist of tax evasion, bank fraud, conspiracy, and witness tampering.

Let us now look at what other facts have come to light during the time of the Special Counsel's investigation. This was accomplished even with all the delays and stonewalling done by the DOJ and the FBI. Judicial Watch and the Oversight Committees in Congress have been somewhat successful in obtaining some information that illustrates just how deep the corruption and abuse of power has been by the deep state.

It was Judicial Watch's efforts that obtained the evidence that Hillary's campaign and the DNC actually paid for the Steele dossier and were trying to cover this fact up. This evidence came to light when Hillary Clinton's campaign chairman, John Podesta, was testifying before the Senate Intelligence Committee in early 2018. Mr. Podesta claimed that he did not know that Perkins Core was working with Fusion GPS and Christopher Steele. The only problem with the claim was that sitting right next to him at the time was Marc Elias, a Perkins Core partner and Hillary Clinton's campaign general counsel. It is extremely hard for me to believe that Hillary Clinton's campaign chairman did not know that the source of the $12 million that paid for the Steele dossier was her campaign.

Other evidence that came to light resulted when some of the e-mails between Peter Strzok and Lisa Page were released. It became obvious that the insurance policy was the plan to get an investigation into the so-called Russian collusion by President Trump started. This was true even though they knew that there was no evidence of collusion. This was revealed when additional information came to light that even after the nine-month antiterrorism investigation into Donald Trump's campaign that James Comey had initiated after he had cleared Hillary Clinton on her e-mail "matter," one of the released Strzok—Page e-mails stated, "There is no there, there." In addition, it was reported that both James Comey and Peter Strzok both did not think that General Flynn had lied to the FBI as indicated in a report to the House of Representatives.

The above evidence would suggest that there was not sufficient evidence that a crime had been committed to even appoint a Special Counsel to conduct a Russian collusion investigation of the Trump campaign. What does seem plausible, however, is that the deep state did have a plan, an "insurance policy," to investigate individuals until they could establish by any manner possible that a crime must have been committed in order for Donald Trump to have been elected president.

With all the unmasking of individuals associated with the Trump campaign, who then became targets who could be investigated, just maybe someone could be persuaded to provide information about Donald Trump that would establish Russian collusion. If this could be established, then the Democrats would have grounds to impeach Donald Trump and correct the terrible mistake the American people had made.

It appears that one of the major tactics that was being used by the Mueller team during this investigation was to interview an individual and actually set up a perjury trap. They would then threaten to charge these individuals with lying or anything else that they could to intimidate the individual or their families in order to get them to either "compose" information about Donald Trump or plead guilty to a lesser crime. All they had to do would be provide information about Donald Trump that fit their scenario that he had committed collusion with the Russians.

This was the case with Roger Stone, a Republican strategist, and Dr. Jerome R. Corsi. Dr. Corsi is a well-known conservative author who has written over twenty books. Mueller's team was questioning both of these individuals about Wikileaks's e-mail releases. Dr. Corsi told them he would not confess to a lie in order to satisfy Mueller's team in their quest to destroy Donald Trump. In fact, Dr. Corsi has even filed a lawsuit against the Mueller investigation.

Just recently, some of the congressional closed-door testimonies of a number of officials, such as Lisa Page and Peter Strzok, have been released. During Lisa Page's testimony, she confirmed that President Obama told them to lay off Hillary Clinton when they were investigating her e-mail "matter." Both Lisa Page and Peter Strzok confirmed that Loretta Lynch was making the decisions on the investigation into Hillary Clinton's e-mail "matter." They also confirmed that President Obama wanted to be kept informed about the investigation. It is obvious that Hillary Clinton was exonerated for political purposes, and the "fix" was in.

In addition, the closed-door transcript of James Baker, who was the FBI's lead attorney under James Comey, states that he thought Hillary Clinton should have been indicted under the Espionage Act. He felt that there was sufficient evidence that she had violated 18 USC 793 (F)(D) and (E) of the Espionage Act. These sections address the "gross negligence" and intentionally mishandling classified documents. James Baker's statement does not track with James Comey's TV exoneration of Hillary Clinton when he stated that no competent lawyer would proceed with a criminal case against Hillary Clinton. I guess James Comey did not feel that his lead attorney for the FBI was competent.

Do we have to wonder why Hillary Clinton would delete thirty-three thousand e-mails, BleachBit-wash her hard drives, and actually destroy devices and SIM cards? Would it be to destroy evidence? It is not hard to conclude that the Hillary Clinton e-mail investigation into the "matter" was "fixed" in order to protect her. Does a two-tier justice system seem to be in place?

Other information that was revealed is that the original investigation that James Comey initiated on July 30, 2016, was based on evidence provided by the fallacious Steele dossier. With all the unmaskings during the last year of the Obama administration, it is very obvious that the intelligence community of our government had been weaponized for political purposes.

On April 10, 2019, Congressman Jim Jordan from Ohio was on the Sean Hannity TV show. He reminded everyone what Chuck Schumer had said two years and three months earlier when President-elect Trump called the Russian collusion investigation a "witch hunt." Chuck Schumer warned President-elect Trump that "if you mess with the intelligence community, they have six ways from Sunday at getting back at you." I guess we now know how they do it.

Robert Mueller's investigation was completed in March 2019. A minor redacted copy of his 448-page report was released on Thursday, April 17, 2019. Robert Mueller's conclusion concerning any Russian collusion by the Trump campaign was the following: "The investigation did not establish that members of the Trump campaign conspired or coordinated with the Russian government in its election interference activities." This essentially states that there was no collusion, and no conspiracy was found to be present by the Trump campaign. This was a pretty clear-cut conclusion on this issue.

We must still remember, however, that Robert Mueller is part of the deep state. The second part of the investigation had to do with any possible obstruction by President Trump. When addressing the possibility of obstruction by President Trump, Robert Mueller stated the following: "Based on the facts and the applicable legal standards, we are unable to reach this judgment. Accordingly, while this report does not conclude that President Trump committed a crime, it does not exonerate him."

What he did do instead was to cite ten cases of possible obstruction. The following are those ten examples he cited:

- President Trump putting pressure on James Comey to end the probe of General Michael Flynn

- The president's reaction to the continuing of the Russian investigation

- The firing of James Comey and the aftermath

- The appointment of the Special Counsel and efforts to remove him

- Further efforts to curtail the Special Counsel's investigation

- Efforts to prevent public disclosure of evidence

- Additional efforts to have Jeff Sessions, the attorney general, take control of the investigation

- President Trump ordering White House counsel to deny that he tried to fire Robert Mueller

- President Trump's actions toward Michael Flynn, Paul Manafort, and other possible witnesses

- President Trump's actions toward Michael Cohen

I am not a lawyer, but to me the above cases cited seem to be largely void of any specifics. They seem like talking points to me.

Mueller's report was essentially written in two major segments. Section 1 addressed the collusion and/or conspiracy concepts. Since there was no collusion on the part of President Trump nor members of his campaign, there was no evidence to be found. This was known after the first nine-month investigation by James Comey when Peter Strzok stated in his e-mail to Lisa Page that "there is no there, there." This did not stop the deep state from pursuing the appointment of a Special Counsel, using possible collusion as the basis for the appointment.

The second major segment of the report appears to have been written totally for political purposes. The above noted ten cases of possible obstruction are mostly statements about how President

Trump reacted publicly to the news media as they tried to pursue the idea that he must have colluded with the Russians in order to win the election. The mainstream news media continually pushed Russia, Russia, Russia in the majority of the negative reporting on President Trump. This 92 percent of negative reporting on President Trump day after day would cause any normal person to become frustrated and angry about the "hoax" that was being played out on him. The president still does have a right of freedom of speech, just like anyone else does, and a right to defend himself.

One does not have to wonder why President Trump referred to the mainstream news media as "fake news." This was especially true for CNN and MSNBC cable news channels. For two years in their daily drumbeat, they hammered daily about Russian collusion, Russian collusion, Russian collusion. The first section of the Mueller Report proved President Trump was correct about the mainstream news media being fake news.

With the release of his report and the conclusion of no Russian collusion or conspiracy by President Trump in the first segment of his report, Robert Mueller used the second part of his report to provide the "red meat" for the radical left deep state politicians to switch from Russian collusion to obstruction. Of course, the mainstream media was totally willing to seize upon the idea of pursuing the obstruction angle to destroy President Trump. Their mantra switched from Russian collusion to obstruction, obstruction, obstruction without any apology for being wrong for two years about collusion.

In my opinion, it would appear that Robert Mueller and his team worded the second part of his report in such a manner as to allow the radical left politicians to still be able to use it as "sufficient" evidence from a political perspective to impeach the president. This way, the Democrats could still achieve the goal of impeachment. This is further evidenced by the fact that even Robert Mueller stated that the evidence cited did not rise to the level of obstruction in the legal sense. This to me is why he indicated that Congress should decide if they think obstruction occurred. This sounds totally political and not based on legal grounds.

Additionally, if we look at both of the concluding statements, we can definitely see the difference. In his first statement of conclusion about collusion and conspiracy, he was very clear and straightforward in a legal sense. He clearly stated that there was no evidence to establish either collusion or conspiracy had occurred. In his second concluding statement about obstruction, however, the wording is more oriented toward a political perspective. The wording of this statement that "he was not able to reach a judgment that no obstruction occurred, but that it still does not exonerate him" sounds like a political response, not a legal one.

Since the report was prepared for the current attorney general William Barr, he did conclude that no obstruction occurred by President Trump. There was no evidence that President Trump tried to conceal any information from the Special Counsel. He freely provided over 1.4 million documents that the Special Counsel had requested. He did not preclude any member of his administration from being interviewed by the Special Counsel through the use of "executive privilege." This is totally different from the investigation that Independent Counsels or Special Counsels conducted into Presidents Nixon and Clinton. Both Presidents Nixon and Clinton made extensive use of executive privilege during these two investigations. The major difference between Nixon, Clinton, and President Trump is that Nixon and Clinton were guilty while President Trump was innocent.

The radical left-wing Democrats could not wait until the Mueller report was released since they had succeeded in regaining control of the House of Representatives during the 2018 midterm election. They just knew that the Mueller report would provide all the evidence that they needed to impeach President Trump. They would be able to impeach President Trump and then get on with their agenda to "fundamentally change America."

With the release of the Mueller Report to Attorney General William Barr, the radical left-wing Democrats soon found out that they had a problem. When Attorney General Barr publicly stated that the report found no collusion, no conspiracy, and no obstruction, the radical left-wing Democrats just could not believe that these were the results of the Mueller Report. They just could not accept the fact that the deep state's "insurance policy" had not been successful. They did, however, still have a possible way to use the Mueller report to their advantage.

With the way the Mueller report had worded the second half of the report about obstruction, the radical left-wing Democrats in the House of Representatives felt that they could use obstruction as their path to impeachment. Congressman Jerry Nadler, the new chairman of the House Judiciary Committee of the now Democratic House of Representatives, immediately subpoenaed an unredacted copy of the Mueller report. Their goal now was to use this as the way to impeach President Trump. Of course, the mainstream news media was more than willing to help. As an example, Bill D'agostino of News Buster reported that within the first twenty-four hours after release of the Mueller report, the mainstream news media used the term *impeachment* 309 times. There is no doubt in my mind what the next two years will be like for President Trump and America.

The deep state was able to cause all the now documented turmoil for President Trump during the first two years of his presidency when the Republicans had control of all three branches of our government. Just think of what they can do after the 2018 midterm election in which they actually regained control of the House of Representatives.

Another example of the extent the radical left-wing Democrats will go to get enough evidence of obstruction against President Trump occurred in July of 2018. Since they could not accept Attorney General Barr's assessment that there was no obstruction and with the "political" wording of the second part of the Mueller report, the Democrats decided to subpoena Robert Mueller to testify before the House Judicial and Intelligence Oversight Committees. They felt that Robert Mueller would be able to provide the information that they wanted for them to pursue their goal of impeachment. The only problem with this tactic was that the Republican members of these committees could also ask questions.

Prior to actually testifying before these committees, Robert Mueller made it perfectly clear that he did not want to testify before either committee. He even called a press conference that lasted a little over nine minutes where he stated that the report stated his position on the investigation. He indicated that he would only testify to information that was contained with the four corners of the report.

Robert Mueller did testify on July 24, 2019. This turned out to be a complete disaster for the Democrats. It soon became very clear why Robert Mueller did not want to testify. It became obvious that Robert Mueller was not even that familiar as to what actually was in the report. When he was asked questions about different aspects of his report, he seemed confused and had significant pauses before answering. He would stutter or stammer during his answers, or he would ask what his report said. When the individual asking the question would read the information from his report to him, he would then state that the information was correct. He also was continually referring to his report in an attempt to locate the subject matter that was being addressed. It appeared that he was not very familiar with the report's content. In addition, Robert Mueller deflected or refused to answer questions more than two hundred times, many times stating that the question was beyond the purview of his investigation.

Probably the most crucial error on his part was when he was asked about Fusion GPS. It became apparent that he did not know what or who Fusion GPS was. When asked how he decided on the members chosen for his team, he seemed a little taken back when it was pointed out to him that fourteen of the nineteen prosecutors were registered Democrats. He also did not seem to know that Jeannie Rhee had represented Hillary Clinton and the Clinton Foundation in the past. In addition, with his answer to the question about how many interviews of the approximately five hundred interviews conducted by his team did he sit in on, he indicated that it was very few.

As a result of Republicans asking questions, it became apparent that Robert Mueller was just a figurehead for this investigation. It became apparent that Andrew Weissmann, his deputy lead attorney, most likely had chosen the team members and had most likely written the report. Andrew Weissmann also most likely wrote the statement that Robert Mueller read at his nine-minute press conference, after which he did not take questions. No wonder Robert Mueller did not want to testify before Congress.

It was almost sad to watch him struggle through both of these hearing on July 24, 2019. With his apparent lack of knowledge of what was in his report, this did more damage to the Democrats' case than provided any additional support to help them advance their goal of gaining more information to impeach President Trump. The Republicans did a tremendous job exposing the fallacies of the second half of the Mueller report and exposing the deep state's "insurance policy." Robert Mueller came across as a senior-age individual who really needed to retire and enjoy his golden years.

After the Mueller report had been released and before he was subpoenaed to testify before Congress, I was totally surprised by Gary Abernathy of the *Washington Post*. In an opinion piece published on April 15, 2019, Mr. Abernathy admitted that Fox News had been right all along. In his opinion piece, he stated the following:

> Fox News hosts such as Tucker Carlson, Laura Ingraham, and especially Sean Hannity have been slammed for spending nearly two years clamoring for an investigation of the investigators. It would behoove serious journalists to put aside their political biases and delve into a story that might actually be worthy of Watergate comparisons—even if it includes the painful admission that Fox News had been right all along.

So what does the future look like for the United States for the next few years and beyond? I do have some optimism that just maybe, in the short term, with the Republicans still in control of the presidency and the Senate and with Attorney General William Barr, hopefully the idea of equal justice for all can be restored. If not, our country is in trouble. My small amount of optimism comes from the recent revelations of the corruption and abuse of power, which appears to have occurred during the Obama administration and the reprehensible actions by members of the deep state coming to light. Hopefully, all the actors in this disgusting plot will be identified and punished. I do think William Barr is a good and honorable man and will bring justice by doing the right thing for our country.

For the long-term, however, I still am not very optimistic about the future of the United States. I firmly believe that the 2020 election will determine if we can save our country as the America we know or will the radical, liberal, progressive, left-wing, socialistic-minded Democrats win and be able to "fundamentally change America." I also firmly believe the deep state is not dead yet, and with $18 billion being provided by George Soros, the battle for the soul of the United States is still in jeopardy. The one thing we can be sure of is that God will be watching.

CHAPTER 15

The Future

A S THE NEXT TO last chapter in this book, I think it is important to go into more detail as to what I think the short-term and long-term future holds for our country. I consider the short term to be defined as being from August 2019 to November 2020 and the 2020 presidential election. I define the long term as being from January 2021 forward when whoever is elected in the 2020 election takes office. The 2020 election will define America's future.

Even with all the deep state's efforts to conceal their actions of corruption and the abuse of power, the deep state's "insurance policy" to destroy Donald Trump is beginning to see the light of day. Their hypocrisy and the double standard of a two-tiered justice system are also coming to light. From what I have observed since the 2018 midterm elections, when the Democrats regained control of the House of Representatives, there is no doubt in my mind that the radical left-wing Democrats plan to continue their efforts to get President Trump out of office one way or another.

The left-wing-biased mainstream news media are more than willing to continue to push a negative narrative about how bad President Trump is to the American people. Now that they have lost the Russia, Russia, Russia collusion topic, they have moved on to obstruction, obstruction, obstruction. Since this is beginning to fail, as more and more details about the deep state's actions are coming to light, they appear now to be moving on to racism, racism, racism. In addition, we can expect as we get closer and closer to the 2020 election, their mantra will include recession, recession, recession. It almost seems like these radical left-wing Democrats are hoping for a recession. That shows us what they think about the American people.

The small amount of optimism that I have is based on the Republicans being able and willing to continue looking into all the corrupt dealing that were going on behind the scenes by the actions of the deep state. Hopefully, justice will finally be served and the truth revealed for all of America to see.

President Trump's newly appointed Attorney General William Barr had stated that he is going to continue looking into how all of this Russian-collusion business occurred. He even testified in front of Congress that he did think spying had been done on the Trump campaign. He also said that if there was corruption and the abuse of power by members of the upper echelon leadership of the DOJ, FBI, and even the previous administration, they will be held accountable. In other words, the deep state members will be held accountable if crimes were committed.

Congressman Jim Jordan from Ohio did remind us on April 10, 2019, on the Sean Hannity show, that twenty-five people from the DOJ and FBI have already either been demoted, fired, or have resigned. We do know that Attorney General Barr is looking into the unmasking of American citizens, the Steele dossier, and the possible FISA abuse. If I was a member of the deep state, I would be worried, and I would get a lawyer.

The good news is there are still a number of investigations ongoing and reports to be out soon. These investigations into the investigators are all efforts to hold the deep state accountable for their actions. Some of these investigations and potential releases of the information include the following:

- Additional Judicial Watch releases of information obtained from "Freedom of Information" requests.
- Any possible results of the fourteen additional indictments filed from the Mueller investigation that are still pending.

- Inspector General (IG) Michael Horowitz is conducting an IG investigation into possible FISA warrant abuses by FBI and DOJ members, which should be released soon.

- An investigation into the illegal leaking of information is being conducted out of the Utah Office of the attorney general by a prosecutor named Huber. He was tasked to do this by Jeff Sessions before he resigned as attorney general. This report should also be out soon.

- There are still over fifty closed-door testimonies that could possibly be released similar to those of Peter Strzok, Lisa Page, and James Baker by Congressman Doug Collins.

- President Trump had stated that he would declassify the FISA warrant applications and the FBI 302 reports of interviews that the FBI conducted during specific investigations.

- There also is potential evidence of Ukrainian collusion into our 2016 presidential election. In fact, Ukrainian investigators have asked US prosecutors, "Why don't they want their evidence on Democratic collusion during the 2016 election?"

These are all excellent sources of information that would be extremely useful in getting to the bottom of just how all the abuse of power and corruption did occur and just who was responsible. You notice that you do not hear any Democrats requesting the release of this information.

What really is sad about this whole situation is that there was Russian collusion, but not by the Republicans. The information that has come to light so far suggests that Russian collusion did occur, but with the Clinton campaign and the Clinton Foundation. I can only hope that a second Special Counsel be appointed by Attorney General Barr to look into Democratic collusion, obstruction of justice, and that the Hillary Clinton e-mail "matter" be reopened. I do hope that he considers this if he does not feel comfortable doing the investigation in house.

I definitely feel that if he does, the house of cards created by the deep state will collapse in on them. They will then be held accountable, and equal justice for all will be restored. We should know that this should all be accomplished between now and the 2020 election for the good of the American people.

One thing we can be assured of, however, is that in the meantime, the Democrats in the House of Representatives will continue to try and find a way to use section two of the Mueller report on obstruction to impeach President Trump. In addition, the deep state will continue to push their agenda until the truth does come out. They will continue to try and block any attempt by Attorney General Barr to get to the truth.

As previously noted, I define the long-term as being from January 2021 forward to the end days. The 2020 election will determine the future of America, good or bad. This, of course, will depend on if the radical left-wing Democrats win the presidency; then they will continue full speed with their agenda to "fundamentally change America"—most likely to the point that the America as we know will not be able to be recovered.

As I consider all the information that I have been able to research and learn from the Bible and the prophecies that are predicted in the Bible, I do not have a lot of optimism about the future of the United States. This lack of optimism is based on what has been happening in our country since the 1960s, and especially since the turn of the century. It seems that a war on Christianity and God has been declared.

Our nation was formed on Judeo-Christian principles in 1776. God blessed our nation through the 1950s. In the 1960s and beyond, it appears to me that Satan has been very active in his war against God. And now the radical, liberal, progressive, left-wing segment of the Democratic Party have been able to secure enough power to establish what I consider to be an evil structure in our political system.

Since the year 2000, the radical left has been extremely hard at work to destroy our nation's belief in God. With the Clintons and the Obama administrations, it became very evident that their true goal was to "fundamentally change America." Their goal has been to replace our system of capitalism with socialism. They have been following Saul Alinsky's Rules for Radicals and have been very successful in their pursuit of these rules.

At the center of their pursuit is their attempt to remove God and anything associated with God from our society. They have been trying to do this through money and the power that money can provide. The Bible warns us that money is the root of all evil. In 1 Timothy 6:10 (NIV), it states, "For the love of money is a root of all kinds of evil, Some people, eager for money, have wandered from the faith and pierced themselves with many griefs."

Money provides the opportunity to essentially buy power and influence. Once power is gained, Satan takes advantage of the situation to tempt individuals who he senses are susceptible to corruption. When these individuals do gain power, the old saying that "power corrupts and absolute power corrupts absolutely" comes into play and appears to be very true. Take George Soros for example and all of his efforts along with his $18 billion.

As described earlier, the radical, liberal, progressive, left-wing Democrats and the deep state have done extremely well in implementing Saul Alinsky's Rules for Radicals as well as adopting many of the 1963 communist goals. The communists always said that the best way to defeat the United States is from within. From what I have been able to ascertain, the radical, liberal, progressive, left-wing of the Democratic Party is now well on their way to achieving their goal. My lack of optimism is based on the actions of the deep state and the radical, liberal, progressive, left-wing segment of the Democratic Party.

As a Christian, it saddens me greatly to see our country being systematically destroyed: first by the removal of God from our society and then by their attempt to replace capitalism with socialism. Even though socialism sounds good in theory, it only brings misery and despair to the majority of the people that have to live under it. This had been evidenced throughout the world wherever it has been utilized as the government system employed. It is great for the ruling elite leaders of the system, but only misery and despair for the masses.

A current example of this is being played out currently in Venezuela. Venezuela was once a thriving democracy. The country has abundant natural resources such as oil and gas and had a thriving economy. Then strongman Nicolás Maduro gained power and began to impose socialism on this wealthy country. During the most recent election, Maduro was challenged for the presidency by a newcomer, Juan Guaidó, who wanted to restore democracy to Venezuela. When it appeared that Guaidó had won the election, Maduro refused to concede and used the military to stop the challenger from assuming the presidency. Protests and chaos began to disrupt the entire country. Inflation soared, and the economy simply fell apart. This resulted in nothing but misery and despair for the people of Venezuela. Strongman Maduro began to act as a dictator and used the military to stay in power. Maduro even used the military to block humanitarian aid at the border that had been sent from other countries to provide aid and relief to the people of Venezuela.

In chapter 9, we learned from a Scottish history professor at the University of Edinburgh, Alexander Tyler, from his studies, that democracies are always temporary in nature. He stated,

> A democracy will continue to exist up until the time that voters discover that they can vote themselves generous gifts from the public treasury. From that moment on, the majority always votes for the candidates who promise the most benefits from the public treasury, with result that every democracy will finally collapse over loose fiscal policy, (which is) always followed by a dictatorship.

Maduro actually implemented socialism on the people of Venezuela. When the people began to see what was happening, they tried to stop the progression to socialism. Maduro was then forced to resort to a dictatorship in order to stay in power. Professor Tyler did outline eight sequential steps that democracies go though. The last three steps are as follows:

6. From complacency to apathy
7. From apathy to dependence
8. From dependence back to bondage

Venezuela was at step 8 when Maduro imposed his dictatorship on the people of Venezuela.

It was during August 2019, that the U.S was fully engaged in the political "war game" of determining who will run for president against Donald Trump in the 2020 election. When we consider the agenda of the ten remaining radical, liberal, progressive, left-wing, socialistic-minded Democratic presidential candidates that are seeking the Democratic presidential nomination for the 2020 election, we have to wonder if the United States is at step 6 of Professor Tyler's path to another failed democracy. Their agenda of Medicare for all including illegal aliens, free college tuition for all, forgiveness of all college debt, a minimum income payment for all, and the "New Green Deal" appears to me to be oriented at those individuals who will vote for whoever promises the most benefits from the public treasury. This to me suggests that the radical left wing of the Democratic Party thinks the United States is at step 6 of Professor Tyler's path to a failed democracy and now is the time for them to push their socialistic agenda. If they succeed in winning the presidency in 2020, then the United States will progress through to step 7 to dependency, just like Venezuela did. From this political state, it is only short time period until step 8 is enacted, and a dictatorship is established. The United States will then suffer just like Venezuela did, and our country will progress into bondage and complete step 8 of Professor Tyler's path to failure. I do not know of any society where socialism has been utilized that has actually raised the standard of living of the masses.

The seeds of failure of socialism are actually contained in the basic concept of socialism. As the definition of socialism explains, it is a theory of a social organization that advocates the means of production, distribution, exchange, and it should be owned and regulated by the community as a whole and not by individuals. In other words, a few elites of the society have control over all the resources and assets of that society and essentially dictates to the masses who produces what items and how they are distributed to the remainder of the society. The individuals in the society are paid or provided for based on the worth that the elites establish that each individual actually contributes to the production of these items. These items are then distributed for the good of the society, which is the exchange function of the economy. It is a government-controlled economy by the elites who ensure themselves are well taken care of while the masses suffer in the environment that results from government control over their lives. Essentially, the masses have to give up their liberty and independence for the supposed good of the society. As the old saying goes, "Socialism works just fine until you run out of everyone else's money."

Socialism concentrates on the society as a whole and not on the individual. As such, there is no incentive for individuals to try to develop new items or advance technology in order to better themselves. Under socialism, technology does not progress with individual research as individuals attempt to better themselves. Under capitalism, there is always an opportunity for any individual to succeed based on his or her own talents in their pursuit of happiness. Socialism only allows for progression of the society as a whole. Socialism only works well for the elites at the expense of the masses in general.

I think an excellent example of this was the Soviet Union. Communist socialism seemed to be working until the world environment that the Soviet Union was part of changed. When President Ronald Reagan decided to do the Star Wars defense system that would be able to defeat the Soviet Union's intercontinental ballistic missiles, it put the Soviet Union at a distinct disadvantage. In a socialist-planned economy, it assumes that as far as technology is concerned, they knew all that they needed to know. Therefore, production of the products and goods for the society needs can be planned for with the limited resources and assets that are available. The problem occurs when the world environment changes due to advances in new technology that occurs and was not planned for under a socialism-planned and regulated system. A planned economy is not able to rapidly adapt or adjust to the unforeseen change. It then becomes difficult to keep up with the unforeseen change because the resources and assets have already been allocated to the planned production of the society. Any reallocation of resources has a dramatic impact on the economy of the controlled and regulated society.

This is exactly what happened to the Soviet Union. When President Reagan declared he was going to build "Star Wars," the

Soviet Union essentially bankrupted their economy trying to adjust resources and assets that had already been allocated. When the Soviets could not sustain their economy while trying to counter Star Wars, the Soviet Union's communistic socialism government system failed after seventy-two years. Currently, Russia's economy has kind of a hybrid economy based primarily on socialism but with a system of oligarchs actually planning and producing items for the government. This is somewhat like a small opening to capitalism, but controlled by the government.

A government system based on capitalism rewards individuals for the advancement of technology. This results in the creation of new products or items that enhance all the lives of the people living under capitalism. Capitalism is not based on the assumption that we know all that we are going to know or need to know for our society. Every individual has the incentive and opportunity to develop or create new items and/or technology that results in benefit to the whole society. This has been known at the *American dream* since 1776.

From my perspective, it seems that when governments or a nation are swayed to accept socialism, or if a political party of a nation is able to impose socialism on a society, then that nation's economy begins to degrade as the rest of the world advances. This has been shown to be true by evidence of some of the recent problems with some of the economies in Europe, such as Greece. The European style of socialism has not produced very strong economies in many of the European nations.

One may ask, what about China? China is a communist, socialist nation like Russia with a planned and government-regulated economy. The question is, why has China been able to compete in the world economy structure as technology has advanced? China realized that for them to be successful, they had to be able to obtain the newest technology in order to compete with the United States. So how did they do it?

When President Nixon made it a point to open up China to the world, China used this opportunity to advance their knowledge by obtaining new technology from other countries. They have been able to take advantage of the United States by insisting that for any agreed trade policies with China, United States companies and companies from other countries have to provide technology to them in order to do business in their country.

In the 1970s, it was estimated that China was fifteen to twenty years behind the United States from a technological perspective. At that time, Russia was the United States' largest competitor for world influence. The problem for the United States was that since China was also a communist country, it would not bode well for the United States if China decided to team with Russia to compete against the United States. Thankfully, the communists in China did not really like the communists in Russia.

After President Nixon opened China's economy to the world, the United States essentially adopted an informal trade policy with China that encouraged United States' companies to transfer technology to China. According to Victor Davis Hanson, a senior fellow at the Hoover Institution, it was later during the Jimmy Carter administration (1977–1981) that President Carter issued a formal trade policy and guidelines on how United States companies would aid China in advancing their technology to assist them in improving their economy. The problem with this trade policy is that China was able to take an unfair advantage of the United States and was essentially stealing new technology from American companies doing business in China. Since then, China has been able to make up the fifteen to twenty years that they were behind us, and now they have essentially become the United States' equal as far as technology goes.

Later when President Reagan (1981–1989) won the Cold War with Russia in the 1980s, this trade policy with China was not as important to the United States as it had been when Russia was more of a threat. No one since then, however, has taken any action to stop this transfer of technology to China until President Trump.

The presidential administrations after President Reagan really did not want to challenge China about their obvious theft of American technology. When our trade deficit with China swelled to $500 billion under President Obama, and with the loss of so many jobs to China, President Trump decided that he would take action to correct this enormous trade deficit unbalance with China.

This is why President Trump has imposed tariffs against China in order to get China to negotiate new and fair trade agreements that do not take unfair transfer advantage of America's technology advances. It is not too difficult to understand why China is reluctant to agree.

In addition, in the past, China has also been able to purchase advanced technology outright by purchasing new technology from others. I witnessed this firsthand while I was in the Air Force. In 1988, I was stationed at Kelly Air Force Base at the San Antonio Air Logistics Center (ALC). At that time, Kelly AFB was one of seven Air Force logistics center for logistic support of all the Air Force weapons systems. I was assigned to the Materiel Management (MM) directorate and was responsible for $5 billion worth of budget authority to procure spare parts for a number of aircraft weapon systems and aircraft engines. One of the engine systems that Kelly AFB, ALC supported was the F-100 engine, utilized in the F-16 aircraft fleet. I was responsible for procuring all the engine turbine blades for repairs for this engine. The manufacture of these blades utilized a new cutting-edge technology that involved a single crystal growth pattern for each blade. This was totally new technology for engine blade production at that time.

In 1988, I had a real problem when the United States government agreed to sell F-16 aircraft to China. Being a fighter pilot myself and having been flying the F-111 for the previous seven years, I had been trained to consider that communist governments were my potential enemy. In order to support the sale of the F-16 aircraft, a group of Chinese military officers had to come to Kelly AFB in order to establish a supply channel to support the engines for their F-16 aircraft. I found myself sitting in a conference room across the table from three communist Chinese officers in their military uniforms. This was extremely hard for me to do as I sat across the table from these three individuals with red stars on their caps. The last time I had seen this red star was on a tail of a MiG fighter during dissimilar aircraft training while flying the F-111. I just could not understand why the United States would be selling our most advanced technological aircraft to a country that I had been trained to consider to be a potential enemy. It took everything I had to remain silent. In addition, to this day, I still do not like Macy's red star logo when I pass by a Macy's store due to my military training.

As I thought about why would the United States sell F-16 aircraft to China, I only had to think back to the Vietnam War. I remembered how politics played a major role in that war. Politics, especially Democratic politics, was a significant problem for our fighter pilots flying over North Vietnam. This was evidenced with my disbelief and resulting distrust of Democratic policies when I learned just what the Democrats were providing to North Vietnam from the televised CBS documentary program titled *Vietnam: The Ten Thousand Day War.*

Peter Arnett was interviewing Secretary of State Dean Rusk, and he asked Secretary Rusk if it was true that the United States was providing the North Vietnamese with our next day's bombing targets. Secretary Rusk's answer of yes was totally unbelievable and incomprehensible. To think that our leaders would even consider such a thing, let alone do it, was unthinkable. He tried to justify it on humanitarian grounds. No wonder F-105 pilots flying over the North had approximately 40 percent to 50 percent probability of being shot down—and the Democrats wonder why the military does not trust them! I wonder just how many of my friends were either killed or became POWs as a result of actions like this by our leaders.

When I think about our government selling F-16s to China, I just attributed it to politics. This was just another example of politics in action. When our military troops left South Vietnam in 1973, there still was a South Vietnam. When our government cut off all funding to South Vietnam in February 1975, that is when the politicians lost the Vietnam War. It was not long after that that North Vietnam initiated another offensive similar to the one in 1972 to take over the South. This time, they were successful, and the country fell on April 30, 1975.

As part of my research and as previously noted, I have referenced Dr. Hindson's 1996 book Final Signs. He predicted that during the "end days," there will be a one-world government, a world economy, and a world pseudo-religion. I do agree with him that there will probably be a world economy based on the Bible prophecies and what is currently happening with the advancement of financial activities now occurring with the internet and computer activities. I do not, however, necessarily agree with him about the establishment of a one-world government.

There have been previous attempts to structure a one-world order. After World War I, the League of Nations was formed. This effort failed to stop World War II. The United Nations was formed as an attempt to settle disagreements between nations after World War II. The success of the United Nations has been dubious at best. I feel that the problem with this type of organization is the fact that there are so many different perspectives from all these nations. It seems to me that it would be impossible to mesh all these nations together in a unified agreement structure.

I just feel that the reality of the nature of mankind's greed, arrogance, pride, and egotistic tendencies would preclude any hope of obtaining a sufficient level of agreement between all the nations and different culture groups of people across the world. It would seem to me that this could only occur if the United States, Russia, and China could agree. Even if socialism is imposed across the world, I do not see the elites in all these nations being able to agree on who would lead the world. In addition, since Satan is at work in our world, I think he would be very active in promoting his evil that would result in wars between nations. The Bible does says that there will be a wars and rumor of wars until the end of days.

In all fairness to Dr. Hindson, it should be noted that the world has significantly changed since 1996, especially the United States. Computer technology has expanded exponentially since 1996 to a level I am sure Dr. Hindson, as well as the majority of us, could not have even imagined. In addition, the Democratic Party has also changed significantly since 1996.

This significant change in the Democratic Party occurred during the first presidential term of Bill Clinton. Prior to the Clintons, there were liberal Democrats as well as moderate Democrats. Hillary Clinton was the first Democrat that I know of to say that she would prefer to be called a progressive Democrat as opposed to a liberal Democrat. This to me meant that she was acknowledging that she was further left than what a liberal stood for.

At that time, if you called a liberal a socialist, they were offended. Since that time period, a progressive does not seem to be offended anymore when called a socialist. In fact, they seem to be proud of the socialist title. This is when I feel the deep state was gaining in strength as the far-left-wing radical side of the Democratic Party. I have to wonder what Dr. Hindson would think now about the difference between a liberal and a progressive today. I also have to wonder what Dr. Hindson would think about the all-out war against Christians and all the left's efforts to remove God from our society.

The Bible predicts that a false prophet will come forth and lead ten Middle East nations against Israel, which will result in the Great Tribulation. This will be during the time of the Antichrist, who will be backed by Satan. I feel that the Antichrist will be a world system that is based on an economic order based on the computer internet system along with a world political system based either on socialism or Islam.

As far as a world religious system, I am sure it will most certainly not be based in a belief in God. I feel it will be a false religion created by nonbelievers to appease themselves for nonbelief in God and/or a belief in a political system that replaces God. I think it is interesting to note that when an atheist says that he or she does not believe in God, it is almost an admission on their part that there is a God.

As we have witnessed just how the radical, liberal, progressive, left-wing, socialistic-minded Democrats and deep state individuals have been working so hard to "fundamentally change America" since President Obama was elected, I just do not have much optimism for the future of the United States. I feel that they have been able to set up and implement a very formidable network and structure from which there is a very high probability that they will be able to achieve their goal.

This does not mean that I am completely pessimistic about the future of the United States. As a Christian, I know that all things are possible with God. I know that our future can be changed. It is like the old saying that asks, is the glass half empty or is it hall full? I would prefer to think about the glass as being able to be refilled. I also believe, however, that the only way for this to occur is for our country to return to God. If this occurs and our nation does return to its Judeo-Christian roots and with a firm belief in God by our leaders, our future can be changed, and the end days can be extended into the future. Since we do not know when God will return, we as Christians must just live each day as if it is our last.

What I do know is that socialism is not the way to go. A governing system based on socialism, which requires a nonbelief in God, always results in sorrow and hardship for the masses. The elites in that type of system want it because they flourish under socialism and live well with power and control. The masses just suffer as they struggle just to survive.

I think an excellent example of how radical, liberal, progressive left-wing policies result in the lowering of the standard of living of the people living under socialism is to compare the economic results of the last twenty-one months of President Obama's administration to the first twenty-one months of President Trump's administration. An excellent comparison was provided by an op-ed by Andy Puzder, published in the *Wall Street Journal* on November 27, 2018, which stated the following:

- During President Obama's final six full quarters while he was in office, the GDP growth of our economy struggled along at 1.5 percent.

- During President Trump's first six full quarters in office, the GDP growth rate doubled to 3.0 percent. During the last twenty-one months that President Obama was in office, job openings increased at a meager average rate of nine hundred openings per month. During the first twenty-one months under President Trump, job openings increased to an average rate of seventy-five thousand openings per month.

- And finally, during the last twenty-one months of President Obama's term, the number of Americans finding jobs was at an average rate of 157,000 per month. During President Trump's first twenty-one months, Americans finding jobs increased to an average of 214,000 per month. This is an increase of 36 percent.

I think this op-ed is an excellent comparison of the results that are achieved under policies based on socialism versus results that are achieved under policies based on capitalism.

Is there any question why President Obama caused our national debt to increase by $9 trillion during his two terms as president? As previously noted, this is more than the total added to the national debt by all the previous presidents combined! Also, as previously noted, socialism is great until you run out of everyone else's money; but by then, it is too late.

During the Christmas season of 2018, two of the most ridiculous examples of the radical, liberal, progressive, left-wing war against God were noted. The first example was a principal in a school in Elcorn, Nebraska, that banned candy canes form her school. She felt that since the candy cane is shaped like a J, this could represent Jesus. Therefore, in her mind, it must be banned. The second and probably the most ridiculous comment I heard, which to me is a total affront to God, was uttered by an associate psychology professor at Minnesota State University, Mankato. This professor accused God of being a sexual predator because he impregnated the Virgin Mary without her consent. Can you imagine what God thought about this comment from this professor? I know I would hate to be him when he stands before God during the final judgment on mankind after the battle of Armageddon.

I feel that we are definitely at a turning point in our history. If the atheists win in 2020 and the country is "fundamentally changed" to socialism, then our future is doomed. However, if we turn back to God, he will once again bless the United States. Our future can be bright and fruitful into the future once again. As the battle for the soul of our country continues, I can only provide a warning to the atheists. That warning is—God does exist! We also should all remember the words of President Ronald Reagan: "Freedom is never more than one generation away from extinction. We didn't pass it to our children in the bloodstream. It must be fought for, protected, and handed on for them to do the same."

CHAPTER 16

Update 2020 to 2025

T HE 2020 ELECTION PUT President Trump against Joe Biden. The deep state had worked extremely hard against President Trump throughout his first term as President. They impeached him and tried everything they could come up with ways to slow down his agenda. It was a very close race. In fact, at 10:00 p.m. on the night of the election there were many races that had not been called. In some of the Congressional races, when it looked, like Republicans were going to win, the next morning these races were called for the Democrats. I think what happen was that there was a lot of voter fraud going on by the deep state.

I think that the deep state just kept counting votes until they won if the race was close. The deep state knew what states and areas that would result in a win for them and all they had to do was keep counting ballets until they had enough. This was done through "ballet harvesting." I remember when Kayleigh McEnaney, the President's Press Secretary, had been keeping track of voter fraud and had a three ring one-inch binder full of signed affidavits of fraud voting activities. During one of her press briefings, she displayed one of these signed affidavits by a truck driver from New York that certified that he had driven a semi-truck filled with 26 pallets that were loaded with filled in ballets from New Your to

Philadelphia. He arrived at 2:00 a.m.in the morning and was told to just leave the trailer in the parking lot of the voting location and that he could return to New York. In addition, she also had another signed affidavit that a number of blank ballots were found in the back seat of a taxi. None of these affdavits were allowed in the lawsuits because they were told that they did not have standing.

The results of that election were that Joe Biden did win and became the 46th President. The radical far left-wing progressive Democrats had won. This was why I was not very optimistic about the future of the United States. It soon became evident that President Joe Biden was going to proceed with President Obama's pledge to "fundamentally change America." Many individuals from President's administration were place in President's Biden administration. The deep state was still intact, and it was becoming even more radical. People like Nancy Pelosi, Chuck Schumer, Bernie Sanders, Alexandria Ocasio-Cortez (AOC) became leaders of the Democratic Party. They along with the behind the scenes backing of Barack Obama and the funding by George Soros, the radical far left-wing Democrats began to implement their radical policies like open boarders, the war on fossil fuels, and the "Green New Deal."

One of the very first thing President did was to cancel the Keystone Pipeline. This was one of president Trump's big projects to make America energy independent. Over the next four years, President Biden continued to wage war on fossil fuels by closing many of the areas that President Trump had opened up for exploration. Beyond this he also began pushing the mandate for conversion to electric cars.

The next thing President Biden was to open up the boarder to the point that at least 12 million illegal alien immigrates have been allowed into our country and were set free to go any where they wanted and were never screened. We don't know how many got-aways have also entered during that time period. These millions of people from all over the world were allowed in with no vetting of their backgrounds or no idea of their intentions. This resulted in many criminals and gang members like MS-13, to enter and begin to commit crimes like murder, rape and the trafficking of women and children. This has resulted in over 350,000 children to become lost in our country. Crimes rates for murder and rape began to increase and our country became less safe. The Department of Homeland Security (DHS) Secretary, Alejandro Mayorkas, continually stated that the boarder was closed as did President Biden and Vice President Kamala Harris. president Biden had made Vice President Harris the Boarder Czar as her responsibility. As far as I know, she only went to the boarder once and I am not sure if she ever left the El Paso, Texas airport.

The next thing that President Biden did was to orchestrate the most tremendously disastrous withdrawal from Afghanistan ever seen by the world from any location. This resulted in the deaths of 13 of our military men and women. If a person needed an example on how not to do a withdrawal from a location, just review this event. I am sure our enemies were very impressed. As a retired military officer, I could not believe just how incompetent this event was completed. It was a complete disaster, and it showed the world that the United States no longer needed to be feared as a superpower.

Then at home, the radical, progressive far left-wing administration began to push and implement their socialist polices such as Critical Race Theory (CRT) in our schools and learning intuitions. The Woke policy of Diversity, Equality, and Inclusion (DEI) was pushed as mandatory in just about everything including our military. Sanctuary cities and states became more plentiful and policies that supported the criminal individuals of the illegal alien immigrants were now being implemented in blue cities and states. Many of these illegals immigrates were committing more crimes which caused the crime rate to increase across the country. Our country was becoming less safe due to the radical, progressive far left-wing Democratic polices.

The "Green New Deal" was also being pushed by the Biden administration which began to affect our economy and resulted in increased prices and inflation. All the while, the cognitive decline of Joe Biden was being covered up by the administration and the bias left-wing news media. The deep state politicians would repeat over and over that Joe Biden was just as sharp as ever and people were having a hard time keeping up with him.

But what was really happening was that his handlers were not allowing him to answer questions from the news media. They were also putting caps on his daily schedule sometimes as early as 10:00 a.m. in the morning but usually at 2:00 or 4;00 p.m. in the afternoon. He would get lost while exiting the stage when he was allowed to speak but did not answer any questions. If he was allowed to answer questions, he would have a card with the names of those he should call on for questions. It was obvious that these questions were pre-planned so his decline in cognitive abilities would not be as evident.

Meanwhile, Merrick Garland, who President Biden had made him his Attorney General and in charge of the Department of Justice (DOJ) was weaponizing the DOJ to go after President Trump. Yes, this is the same Merrick Garland That President Obama had wanted to nominate for the Supreme Court when that vacancy occurred just before the 2016 election. If Hillary Clinton had won the 2016 election, this would not have been a problem for the deep state. But president Trump won, and he filled this slot along with two other vacancies that occurred during his term. This was a huge problem for the deep state because President Trump had been allowed to nominate three Supreme Court Justices. Do you think that Merrick Garland was reluctant to go after President Trump, since he was the one that had kept him from becoming a Supreme Court Justice.

Also, during the 2016 election, George Soros was also at work. He contributed 45 million dollars to the campaigns of 75 radical candidates that were running for their cities and state Attorney General positions. Many of them won and with their hatred for President Trump these Attorney Generals became the instruments of how the deep State was going to destroy President Trump from ever running again for President. They brought four different lawsuits against President Trump to try to ruin his reputation and tried to destroy his business and even tried to bankrupt him. In addition, Merrick Garland even appointed a Special Counsel (Jack Smith) to investigate President Trump. His nomination was not even legal but was done anyway because of Jack Smith's hatred for President Trump.

As Special Counsel, Jack Smith was tasked to investigate President Trump for the January 6, 2021, so called "insurrection" of the US Capital Building. He was also asked to investigate the improper storage of government documents at President Trump's home at Mar-a-Lago in Florida. Even with all these efforts to destroy president Trump, he was still able to run for president in 2024.

During the election campaign of 2024, the debate between President Trump and president Biden resulted in a complete disaster for president Biden. His lack of cognitive abilities became totally evident to the public. This was a complete disaster for the Biden Campaign. The deep state could no longer hide Biden's cognitive decline from the public. That is when Obama, Pelosi, and Schumer knew that the Democrats were in trouble. The popularity for Present Trump was continually growing. They decided to force Joe Biden out of the election. That was about a hundred days before the election, and they decided to go with Kamala Harris as their candidate.

President Trump's popularity was continually growing because of the radical hard left-wing progressive policies of open boarders, CRT, DEI, and Wokeness were still in place. VP Kamala Harris said she was not going to change any of President Biden's policies. The American people were no longer buying these polices as good and were switching support to president Trump. The weaponization of the DOJ also was not working as the public began to see just what was going on and they were rejecting these efforts. The two-tiered legal system for the Democrats versus Republicans was becoming evident. Such as the handling of Hillary Clinton's e-mail problem and Joe Biden's classified documents problem and how the legal system was being used against President Trump only increased his support. The American public was refuting the left's deep state efforts to convince then that capitalism was bad, and socialism is good. The efforts by the deep state and the radical left policies were failing. This only increased their distain and hatred for President Trump.

For me, the turning point on my negative optimism for our country occurred on July 13, 2024, and the assassination attempt on President Trump's life at Butler, Pennsylvania rally. When President Trump turned his head to look at a chart that he had been using in most if his rally's, the assassin's bullet struck his ear instead of his head. This to me was Devine intervention by God to save President Trump's life. When president Trump stood back up with fist raised saying FIGHT! FIGHT! FIGHT! I knew that God had decided not to give up on the United States. President Trump said later that he normally used this chart later in the rally, but he had moved it up closer to the beginning of the rally. This to me is the empirical evidence that God has decide to give the United States a second chance. He caused President Trump to turn his head towards the chart at precisely the exact moment for the assassin's bullet to miss. God saved President Trump's life.

President Trump then went on to win the 2024 election in a landslide with a strong mandate from the American people. He won the popular vote 77,302,580 to 75,017,613. He also won all seven swing states and the Electoral College by 312 to 226. The progressive, far left-wing, liberal, socialists Democrats had failed in their attempt to "fundamentally change America.," at least for now. The win was so big it was too large to just keep counting until they won. God is giving our country a second chance to return to our Judeo-Christian principals.

So far, in his first 100 days, President Trump has been able to close the boarder and has begun deporting many criminal illegal alien immigrates. His Administration has also now begun fighting to remove CRT, DEI, and Wokeness from our society wherever it exists. There is starting to be some efforts by a few states to return God to our schools. The fight will be hard, but God never said life would be easy.

The deep state is still fighting very hard to stop President Trump at every Executive Order he does. Since the radical far left-wing progressive socialists Democrats were not able to pack the Supreme Court, they did find a way on the legal side using some of the US Federal District Courts activist judges to resist President Trumps efforts. During that last year or so during the Biden Administration Chuck Schumer was bragging about the fact that they had been able to approve the appointment of 235 activist judges to the US Federal Court System. What is happening now is the Democrats are filling injunctions to stop or pause President Trump from completing the actions in some of these activists' courts that he is allowed to do under the duties of the President in the Constitution, The effect is that these activist judges can stop action across the Nation that only the Supreme Court can do. This makes these judges stronger than the entire Supreme Court itself. I am sure that the Supreme Court will rule on the side of the Administration on appeal. In addition, since these courts were established by Congress and not the Constitution, I think Congress will limit the power of these judges to only the districts that they were appointed to.

However, as long as these liberal, progressive far left-wing socialists Democrats keep fighting for their toxic socialist policies like allowing transgender males to compete in women's sports and supporting illegal criminals like MS-13 gang members who have been deported, the American people will continue to elect Republicans. I hope they do because they have not learned that the majority of the American population do not agree with their socialist policies. The majority of the American people do not want America to be "fundamentally changed." We want true Democracy that our founders established with our Constitution. If Trump is allowed to put our country back on the right course, then we will not have to write the United States obituary of "Born in 1776 — Died in 2020."

AFTERWORD

As I COMPLETED WRITING this manuscript, it occurred to me that over my lifetime, I noticed a similar, particular pattern of behavior exhibited by a number of individuals that I had dealt with during my military career and during the time that I was running my own business, which is also present in the actions of a number of the current radical, liberal, progressive, left-wing Democrats. As such, I am providing this afterword as food for thought. This particular pattern of behavior was present in a number of senior military officers that I served under and also with power brokers in the civilian world. Many of these individuals displayed similar personality characteristics that I now see are extremely prevalent in many of the current radical, liberal, progressive, left-wing Democrats and Hollywood elites.

Some of these characteristics include a very high sense of self-importance and the need for power. They tend to feel that they are always correct, and they feel that they are special and deserve to be in power. In addition, they tend to be arrogant and impatient with those who do not agree with them. They also tend to socialize with like-minded individuals and are very intolerant of other individuals that do not agree with them. When you try to negotiate with these type of individuals or even try to just have a discussion, their idea of negotiation is when you agree with them. They also tend to need admiration from others and are always trying to achieve higher and higher status in relationships since they believe that they deserve it.

They tend to think that they are better than everyone else and tend to have disdain for those of a lower social class.

Before my wife switched her college field of study to English, she wanted to major in psychology. Being an engineer and a dumb fighter pilot, I did not always understand why some of the individuals that I had to deal with seem to act differently from many others that I had to deal with when they were displaying many of the above characteristics. During discussions with my wife about these individuals, she mentioned that these characteristics are typical of a "narcissistic personality disorder." Not knowing what this meant, I decided to look it up in her Diagnostic and Statistical Manual of Mental Disorders (DSM-5). The following is what this manual had to say about the subject.

The DSM-5 described a "narcissistic personality disorder" as an enduring pattern of grandiosity, a need for admiration, and a lack of empathy. The DSM-5 went on to describe this by the following six characteristics:

A. An enduring pattern of inner experience and behavior that deviates markedly from the expectations of the individual's culture. The pattern is manifested in two or more of the following areas:

    1. Cognition (i.e. ways of perceiving and interpreting self, other people, and events)

    2. Affectivity (i.e. the range, intensity, liability and appropriateness of emotional response.)

    3. Interpersonal functioning

    4. Impulse Control

B. The enduring pattern is inflexible and pervasive across a broad range and personal and social situations.

C. The enduring pattern leads to clinically significant distress or impairment in social, occupational, or other important areas of functioning.

D. The pattern is stable and of long duration, and its onset can be traced back at least to adolescence or early adulthood.

E. The enduring pattern is not better explained as a manifestation or consequence of another mental disorder.

F. The enduring pattern is not attributed to the physiological effects of a substance (e.g. drug abuse, a mediation) or another medical condition (e.g. head trauma).

The DSM-5 goes on to provide the following as the "diagnostic criteria" for "Narcissistic Personality Disorder":

A pervasive pattern of grandiosity need for admiration and lack of empathy, beginning by early adulthood and present in a variety of context as indicated by five (or more) of the following:

1. Has a grandiose sense of self-importance (e.g. exaggerates achievements and talents, expects to be recognized as superior without commensurate achievements).

2. Is preoccupied with fantasies of unlimited success, power, brilliance, beauty, or ideal love.

3. Believes that he or she is "special" and unique and can only be understood by, or should associate with other special or high-status people (or institutions).

4. Requires excessive admiration.

5. Has a sense of entitlement (i.e. unreasonable expectations of especially favorable treatment or automatic compliance with his or her expectations).

6. Is interpersonally exploitative (i.e. takes advantage of others to achieve his or her own ends).

7. Lacks empathy: is unwilling to recognize or identity with the feelings or needs of others.

8. Is often envious of others or believes that others are envious of him or her.

9. Shows arrogant, haughty behaviors or attitudes.

I really noticed these characteristics while observing the current radical, liberal, progressive, left-wing Democrats. Individuals like

Bill and Hillary Clinton, Barack Obama, and many members of the deep state. Members like James Comey, James Clapper, John Brennan, Robert Mueller, Peter Strzok, Lisa Page, Andrew McCabe, Loretta Lynch, Bruce and Nellie Ohr, and Rod Rosenstein. All of these individuals seem to believe that "truth is whatever you want it to be." They also seem to feel that they know what is best for our country; therefore, they must do whatever it takes to ensure that their political agenda is achieved. And now individuals like Alexandria Ocasio Cortez, Bernie Sanders, Nancy Polisi, Chuck Schumer, Gaven Newson, and Barack Obama, who are trying to lead the Democratic Party.

Since I do not personally know any of these political individuals that I have named, I can only observe their public comments and actions upon which to base my conclusion. I am also not saying that all Democratic politicians are "narcissistic," but what I am saying is that I think a lot of the current extreme radical, liberal, progressive, left-wing, socialistic-minded Democrats do display many of these "narcissistic" characteristics. I am also not saying that only Democrats display these characteristics. I am sure that there are Republicans that also display these characteristics. I think it may be part of the political culture.

I am basing my conclusion totally on just observing the public actions of these individuals, which have been on public display since 1993 and with the election of Bill Clinton as president. Bill Clinton was the first baby-boomer president and the other individuals I mentioned also are those that grew up under the environment of Mutually Assured Destruction (MAD) and the possibility of a nuclear war. Many of these individuals were young adults during the late 1960s and the early 1970s. As the DSM-5 stated, this pattern of characteristics usually begins during early adulthood. As I discussed in chapter 10 and 11, the environment during MAD had a significant impact on shaping the attitudes and behavior of these individuals.

As I mentioned, I have provided this afterword as food for thought. I think that if you do consider the actions of these individuals with an open mind and compare their actions and behaviors to the information from the DSM-5, you may come to the same conclusion that I have. If you are like me, I do have difficulty when having a conversation with individuals who seem to believe that "truth is whatever you want it to be." Also, just think back—how many times have you even seen a radical, liberal, progressive, left-wing Democrat actually change his or her mind and agree with Republicans on policies that are actually for the betterment of the country and not just for the advancement of their power authority?

I finish this book with the thought that each of us has to decide what is right or wrong for ourselves. What I do know is that without God, our nation, as well as each of us individually, is doomed. To me there is enough empirical evidence that God does exist! Unfortunately, I also feed that many atheists will not be swayed by the evidence, especially if they also have a narcissistic personality disorder.

LIST OF ACRONYMS

AB Air Base

ACLU American Civil Liberties Union

ACSC Air Command and Staff College

A.D. After the Death of Jesus

AFB Air Force Base

AFIT Air Force Institute of Technology

AFLC Air Force Logistics Command

ALC Air Logistics Center

ATGSB Advanced Test for Graduate Studies in Business

B.C. Before the Birth of Christ

CIA Central Intelligence Agency

CPCF Congressional Prayer Caucus

Foundation DMZ Demilitarized Zone

DNC Democratic National Committee

DOD Department of Defense

DOJ Department of Justice

DSM-5 Diagnostic and Statistical Manual of Mental Disorders 5

DU The University of Denver

DVD Digital Video Disk

EEC The Europeans Economic Community

EPA Environmental Protection Agency

EUB Evangelical United Brethren Church

FAC Forward Air Controller

FBI Federal Bureau of Investigation

FDR Franklin Delano Roosevelt

FIP Flight Instruction Program

FISA Foreign Intelligence Surveillance Act

FOL Forward Operating Locations

GAAP Generally Accepted Accounting Principles

GDP Gross Domestic Product

IAF Industrial Areas Foundation

ID Identification

IFR Instrument Flight Rules

IG Inspector General

INS Inertial Navigation System

IP Instructor Pilot

IRS Internal Revenue Service

ISU Iowa State University

IWSO Instructor Weapons Systems Officer

DU The University of Denver

DVD Digital Video Disk

EEC The Europeans Economic Community

EPA Environmental Protection Agency

EUB Evangelical United Brethren Church

FAC Forward Air Controller

FBI Federal Bureau of Investigation

FDR Franklin Delano Roosevelt FIP Flight Instruction Program

FISA Foreign Intelligence Surveillance Act

FOL Forward Operating Locations

GAAP Generally Accepted Accounting Principles

GDP Gross Domestic Product

IAF Industrial Areas Foundation

ID Identification

IFR Instrument Flight Rules

IG Inspector General

INS Inertial Navigation System

IP Instructor Pilot

IRS Internal Revenue Service

ISU Iowa State University

IWSO Instructor Weapons Systems Officer

JFK John Fitzgerald Kennedy

KIA Killed in Action

KJV King James Version of the Bible

MAC Military Airlift Command

MACV Military Assistance Command Vietnam

MAD Mutually Assured Destruction

MBA Master's Degree in Business Administration

MM Materiel Management

MMM Material Management Resources

MMS Materiel Management for Small Aircraft

MR Military Regions MS Masters of Science

MTBF Mean Time between Failure

NIA National Intelligence Agency

NIV New International Version of the Bible

OCS Officer Candidate School

ORI Operations Readiness Inspection

PE Professional Engineer

PIT Pilot Instructor Training

P&L Profit and Loss

POW Prisoner of War

PR Purchase Request

RIF Reduction in Force

RINO Republican in Name Only

ROTC Reserve Officer Training Corp

RSU Runway Supervisor Unit

RTU Replacement Training Unit

SAT Scholastic Aptitude Test

SPO System Program Office

SWL Southwestern Laboratories Inc.

TAC Tactical Air Command

TASG Tactical Air Support Group

TASS Tactical Air Support Squadron

TFS Tactical Fighter Squadron

TFW Tactical Fighter Wing

UPT Undergraduate Pilot Training

UST Underground Storage Tank

WRM War Reserve Materials

WRSK War Reserve Spare Parts Kits

WSO Weapons Systems Officer

WTO World Trade Organization

www.ingramcontent.com/pod-product-compliance
Lightning Source LLC
Chambersburg PA
CBHW070910120626
46546CB00001B/205